WOMEN OF JEME

Lives in a Coptic Town
in Late Antique Egypt

T. G. Wilfong

Ann Arbor
The University of Michigan Press

Copyright © by the University of Michigan 2002
All rights reserved
Published in the United States of America by
The University of Michigan Press
Manufactured in the United States of America
⊗ Printed on acid-free paper

2005 2004 2003 2002   4 3 2 1

A CIP catalog record for this book is available from the British Library.

Library of Congress Cataloging-in-Publication Data

Wilfong, Terry G.
    Women of Jeme : lives in a Coptic town in late antique Egypt / T. G. Wilfong.
        p. cm. — (New texts from ancient cultures)
    Includes bibliographical references and index.
    ISBN 0-472-09612-5 (cloth : alk. paper) — ISBN 0-472-06612-9 (pbk. : alk. paper)
        1. Women—Egypt—Jeme (Extinct city) 2. Jeme (Extinct city)—Social life and
customs. 3. Copts—Egypt—Jeme (Extinct city) I. Title. II. Series.

    HQ1137.E3 W55 2003
    305.42'0932—dc21
                                                                    2002075738

Bequame sinnen, onder correctie reene
Ic mij stelle; mach wijsheyt in mij vermeert sijn,
In consten kenne ic mijn perfectie kleene,
Noch leerkint; dus meesters moeten geeert sijn.
Seer geerne wil ic van constenaers geleert sijn.
—Anna Bijns, Refereynen (1528)

CONTENTS

ILLUSTRATIONS

PREFACE

This book you are reading is the result of a course of study that I began in 1987. The project was initially an attempt to survey the economy and society of the town of Jeme[1] in the last two hundred years of its existence. Situated opposite modern Luxor in southern Egypt, Jeme was a settlement that had its roots back in the time of the Pharaohs, continuing to develop as Egypt fell under Ptolemaic, then Roman, then Byzantine, and finally Arab Muslim control. In its final phases, Jeme was home to a Christian population in the first centuries of Muslim rule, a population that communicated and recorded their words and deeds mostly in Coptic, the latest phase of the indigenous Egyptian language. Jeme was not a particularly important or large town and, even in its heyday, was little known outside its immediate area. Abandoned before the year 800, Jeme became a ghost town, largely forgotten. Its abandonment may account for the preservation of its remains: when scholars and travelers of the early nineteenth century began to take an interest in Jeme, much of the town was still standing.

Although the ruins of Jeme were looted and partly destroyed in the nineteenth and early twentieth century, University of Chicago excavations at the site in the 1920s and 1930s recovered and recorded a massive amount of evidence. The remains of more than a hundred houses, four churches, and other buildings survived, amidst the debris of hundreds of other structures. There the excavators found an impressive array of artifacts that attest to the material culture of Jeme. Among these artifacts were thousands of texts, mostly legal documents, tax receipts, letters, lists, and accounts—in short, valuable witnesses to the activities and transactions of everyday life at Jeme. Taken in conjunction with texts and other artifacts removed from the site before the excavation, the Jeme material provides an almost unparalleled wealth of evidence for life in an Egyptian town from about 600 to 800 CE.

Jeme was interesting to me for a number of reasons. As a University

[1] Pronounced something like JAY-muh.

of Chicago student, I was certainly influenced by the fact that much of the material from the excavation of Jeme was conveniently located in the Oriental Institute building, where I worked. As an Egyptologist-in-training, I saw Jeme as a rare opportunity to study an ancient Egyptian town, documented by both Egyptian language evidence and archaeological remains. To an aspiring economic and social historian, the Jeme material appeared to be a treasure trove for the investigation of how an ancient population lived. As an archaeologist manqué, I couldn't help but be excited by the discovery of texts in a documented archaeological context, with the potential to bridge the great divide that seemed to exist between archaeologists and textual specialists. An added benefit was that, although the Jeme texts and the archaeology of the site were relatively well published, and there were some substantial studies of nearby sites and the law as represented in the Jeme texts, little further analysis and synthesis of the Jeme material had been attempted. A social and economic history of Jeme would, it seemed at the time, allow me to satisfy a wide range of interests and make a contribution to scholarship.

The first result of my study of the Jeme material was a bibliographical essay on Jeme and environs (Wilfong 1989) that taught me, above all, how large the subject was, as well as how much primary and secondary literature on the subject remained to be mastered. But a test case that used both textual and archaeological evidence to reconstruct a family archive (published as Wilfong 1990 and now part of chapter 5 of the present volume) gave me an idea of the results that I could obtain. My research was greatly assisted by two important "hands-on" experiences. In 1990, I guest-curated an exhibition of the Jeme material in Chicago at the Oriental Institute Museum.[2] This work on "Another Egypt: Coptic Christians at Thebes (7th–8th Centuries AD)" gave me a much better appreciation for the material culture of Jeme (as well as a taste for museum work that persists to this day). My participation in the Oriental Institute's Bir Umm Fawakhir Survey in January 1992 got me to Egypt and enabled me to visit the site of Jeme itself. This trip gave me a crucial appreciation of the archaeology of the site, as well as the physical realities described in the texts.[3] Before this visit, I had written blithely

---

[2] This exhibition was made possible through the efforts of Lorelei Corcoran, Emily Teeter, Ray Tindel, and Karen Wilson, whom I thank for this opportunity.

[3] The hospitality of the Oriental Institute's Bir Umm Fawakhir expedition and the Epigraphic Survey at Chicago House in Luxor enabled me to see the remains of

of the interaction between the people of Jeme and the inmates of the various monasteries in the area (in Wilfong 1989). Experiencing the true distances (and differences in terrain) between Jeme, the local monasteries, and the lairs of the solitary monks in the west Theban hills gave me an appreciation of the efforts involved in these seemingly simple interactions that no amount of map-measuring could convey.

Thankfully, I ultimately became distracted from grand ideas of a monumental study of Jeme by what was, to me back then, a curious and unexpected trend in the sources. Women seemed to occupy a strikingly visible and active position in the Jeme documentation, in contrast to the admittedly rather vague notions I had of women's status in Egypt after the coming of Christianity. Anyone reading the standard religious authors of the time could be forgiven for thinking that women were largely restricted to home, family, and obedience to their husbands, in contrast to the more active and visible roles for women seen in the Pharaonic period. But this impression (hardly accurate, I would readily admit now, but reinforced by much of the scholarship then available) was directly at odds with the documentary evidence I was seeing—the letters, accounts, and legal documents of everyday life that showed what women were actually doing, as opposed to what they were being told to do.

And so my project shifted to focus specifically on the women of Jeme—their roles, their status, and their activities as seen in the textual and archaeological sources. Although a few brief but significant discussions of women in connection with the monasteries around Jeme had been previously published,[4] the women of Jeme themselves remained largely unstudied and a highly promising area for research. By treating all the available material from Jeme—textual, archaeological, iconographic—as a great "archive" in the Foucauldian sense,[5] I felt that I could generalize from this evidence to form certain conclusions about the roles, status, and condition of women at Jeme. By including nontextual material in the Jeme "archive," I hoped to be able to get

---

Jeme in its western Theban setting, and I would like to thank Peter Dorman, Ray Johnson, Carol Meyer, Lisa Heidorn, and Henry Cowherd for facilitating this trip.

[4] See, in particular, Winlock and Crum 1926, 131–133, and Krause 1956, 61–62 and 151–175. Note also the scattered, relevant remarks in Till 1954 and Steinwenter 1955.

[5] Foucault first developed this definition of the "archive" in his *Archaeology of Knowledge* (Foucault 1971, 126–140); a somewhat more concise discussion of Foucault's "archives" can be found in the interview in Foucault 1989, 58–59.

closer to the lived experiences of the women of Jeme by situating the texts in the material culture in which they were produced and of which they were a part. From analysis of the Jeme material, I felt that I could go on to make wider statements about Late Antique Egypt in general.

I was especially fortunate in the timing of my research: scholarship on Egypt in Late Antiquity was burgeoning in the time I was working on my study. Indeed, the late 1980s and early 1990s was a time in which the study of Late Antique Egypt can be said to have come into its own. Although much of the major early work on this topic came in articles, a few books were of special importance to me: Alan K. Bowman's masterful overview for Graeco-Roman and Late Antique Egypt, *Egypt after the Pharaohs*,[6] Leslie S. B. MacCoull's study of the Late Antique Egyptian poet Dioscorus and his world (MacCoull 1988), and the catalogue of an important exhibition of Late Antique Egyptian art and artifacts at the Rhode Island School of Design Museum, "Beyond the Pharaohs" (Friedman 1989). The appearance of Roger Bagnall's *Egypt in Late Antiquity* in 1993 was a major event for the study of Late Antique Egypt—although concentrating on a slightly earlier period than the Jeme material, this book is crucial for anyone attempting to make sense of the Jeme texts. Indeed, the dog-eared state of my own copy of the book is some testimony to its ongoing importance to my work. Rather than cite it on nearly every page of the dissertation or the present revision, as would quite easily have been possible, I have limited my citation of it to discussion on certain specific points, but the reader should be aware that it has informed my overall viewpoint and is an indispensable reference for anyone interested in Late Antique Egypt.

I was aided in my work on the women of Jeme by a general increase in interest in women in the ancient world. The treatment of this topic had, by the time I began my work, gone from the relative neglect of what one author has described as "the 'obligatory' last chapter on hairstyles and dress" (Setälä 1989, 61) to a full-fledged scholarly endeavor, influenced to some extent by larger trends in feminist history and theory but centered firmly on the evidence and its interpretation. The work of Egyptologists such as Janet Johnson, Barbara Lesko, Lana Troy, and Gay Robins was especially significant for my study; they have done much to rectify the relative neglect accorded women in the Egyptological

---

[6] Now available with updated bibliography as Bowman 1996.

scholarship of the past. Gay Robins's 1993 book, *Women in Ancient Egypt*, in particular remains an indispensable resource and a landmark of scholarship on the subject. For women in the Greek papyri of post-Pharaonic Egypt, the early studies of Deborah Hobson (1983) and Sarah Pomeroy (1984, 1988), and work such as Edgar Kutzner's 1989 study of the women of Roman Oxyrhynchus, have been followed by a torrent of articles and monographs on the subject. Finally, important work on women in Late Antiquity such as the books by Gillian Clark (1993) and Susanna Elm (1994), along with Joëlle Beaucamp's monumental study of women under Byzantine law (1990, 1992), were especially important in helping me situate the material in its legal, historical, and spiritual contexts. These studies brought together for me the different traditions that helped shape the lives of the women of Jeme.

Beyond this specific work on women in the ancient world, I also wanted to take into account the general developments in women's history. By the time I had begun my study, the very category of "women" had undergone serious questioning by scholars. No longer could we take for granted the existence of "women" as a constant, unchanging entity across time; instead we had to distinguish carefully between making assumptions based on biological sex and arriving at a more complex and nuanced understanding of socially constructed gender. The classic formulation of this situation is, of course, the famous article "Gender: A Useful Category of Historical Analysis" by Joan Scott (1986), and I found this, along with Scott's later work (e.g., Scott 1991, 1992) to be invaluable in thinking about the construction of gender at Jeme. Since much of the material that I was using was textual, I became especially interested in the discourse of gender in the sources, how ancient understandings of gender were related to the means and modes of expression available in Late Antique Egypt, and how we could arrive at generalizations on the basis of this evidence.

And so my initial work on the women of Jeme became my 1994 doctoral dissertation in Egyptology at the University of Chicago: "'The Woman of Jeme': Women's Roles in a Coptic Town in Late Antique Egypt." In this study, I approached the women of Jeme from what I saw as the major spheres of action in which they were involved: private life, public life, religious life, and economic life. This was preceded by a chapter on the discourse of gender at Jeme: my attempt to arrive at the ways in which gender was socially constructed in the Jeme material and how this had an impact on the lives of women (and men) in the town. On many levels I was still finding my way with the material through attempting to make generalizations about the status and roles of women based on the admittedly fragmentary and incomplete evidence. Indeed, my major source of dissatisfaction with the dissertation was that much of it read like an apology for the evidence that was lacking rather than a celebration of what had survived.

Once the dissertation was finished, I had the good fortune to come to the University of Michigan, where I began to think about how to revise my work for publication. I was also fortunate in soon having my dissertation solicited for the new University of Michigan Press series "New Texts from Ancient Cultures." As a result of the refereeing process, I received much valuable input as to specific points, as well as more general conceptual and structural issues that needed to be considered to turn this dissertation into a book. In particular, one of the referees called for a major restructuring of the original dissertation to refocus the discussion on some individual women of Jeme. Although at the time I had no idea how long this would take, this proposed reorganization coincided with my own desire to highlight the particular strengths of the material, and I gladly accepted the recommendation. This new direction for my study was in line with more general trends in social history and archaeology, where some scholars were beginning to move away from concentrated study on "women" and even "gender" as general categories and instead focus on individuals in the context of a variety of factors. Gender and biological sex are certainly important to understanding individuals in ancient cultures, but so are age, class, ethnicity, and other factors.[7] The importance of looking for individuals in the Egyptian evidence was emphasized to me by the work of two colleagues—Dominic Montserrat and Lynn Meskell. I read and commented with great interest on drafts of what would become *Sex and Society in Graeco-Roman Egypt* (Montserrat 1996b) and *Archaeologies of Social Life* (Meskell 1999), in part because I found them so inspirational for my own work and my own thinking. Given the extensive but fragmentary nature of the Jeme evidence, this approach of finding individuals in the sources and using them to try to understand what

[7] For a useful survey of the kinds of work being done on individuals and the theoretical background of this approach, see Meskell 1999, 9–52, also 53–106, which places this endeavor in the context of feminist theory.

was going on in the culture seemed a much more productive way to approach my material. Although my study remained tied specifically to the women of Jeme (in order to take advantage of the work I had done before), I shifted the work to focus intensive scrutiny on a few well-documented individuals, supplementing it with evidence of other individuals but always keeping in mind the factors in these individuals' lives beyond their varied experiences of being a "woman" in Jeme society.

The time that I was at work on my revision was a very lively period in terms of scholarship on Late Antique Egypt. Indeed the first volume in the series my book was to appear in—*Settling a Dispute* (Gagos and van Minnen 1994)—was an important influence, if only for its example of how to focus on individual texts in order to get at broader trends in ancient society. This same approach is found in James Keenan's chapter on Egypt from 425 to 600 CE for the *Cambridge Ancient History* (Keenan 2001), early drafts of which I found to be very inspirational. Antti Arjava's *Women and Law in Late Antiquity* (1996) was a most useful survey of a difficult subject. And again the work of Roger Bagnall, this time his *Reading Papyri, Writing Ancient History* (1995a), has proven enormously valuable, with its emphasis on the use of ancient texts in conjunction with a wide variety of methodologies from other disciplines to write history.[8] Other research projects of my own (on menstruation in ancient Egypt, Coptic literary texts relating to Constantine the Great and constructions of the body, the discourse of lesbian activity in Late Antique Egypt, for example) as well as contributions to work on Medinet Habu excavation material (pottery, seals, and other small finds) and my newer research on the University of Michigan excavations at Karanis, Soknopaiou Nesos, and Terenouthis, were all ongoing influences on my thinking about the women of Jeme.

My ideas on how to present the women of Jeme were further shaped by involvement in two projects. In 1997, the newly formed Institute for Research on Women and Gender at the University of Michigan sponsored an exhibition at the Kelsey Museum of Archaeology and a related speaker series on "Women and Gender in Ancient Egypt: From Prehistory to Late Antiquity." Although this project did not directly

---

[8] It also has the distinction (for me, at least) of being nearly the first book in human history to sport a photograph of a Coptic ostracon on its cover; as far as I know, only Monika Hasitzka's edition of an archive of Vienna ostraca (Hasitzka 1995) had done so before.

concern the women of Jeme, work with students on our exhibition catalogue[9] helped me think of ways to reapproach my topic, while discussions with the speakers in our series (Lana Troy, Lynn Meskell, Janet Richards, Brenda Baker, Dominic Montserrat, Ann Ellis Hanson, and Jennifer Sheridan) proved very inspirational to me in my revisions. In the meantime, I had been involved in the International Workshop on Papyrology and Social History's project to prepare a sourcebook of texts relating to women in the papyri. My work on the translations of various Jeme texts for the project[10] and interaction with the other contributors to the book were valuable to me in terms of contemplating how to bring my Jeme book to print.

And thus the book has attained its present form, with less of an emphasis on generalizations about women at Jeme and more of a focus on specific individuals and the wide grid of factors that helped shape their experiences. Because of the relative unfamiliarity of the Jeme material, I begin with an introduction to this substantial body of evidence. The first chapter sets the stage for what is to follow, with a survey of the ideals set up for women's lives at Jeme by local religious authorities. I've done this as much to put the reader near the position that I was in before looking at the Jeme material itself as to show the ancient "theoretical" framework in which the Jeme women's lives were operating. Then, in chapter 2, I introduce two Jeme women, Elizabeth and her niece Abigaia, through the lens of the evidence that they left behind. We see their sometimes contentious interactions with each other and family members as they attempt to divide a family inheritance. Chapter 3 takes off from Elizabeth and Abigaia to examine how these two women, and many others, existed within the structures of family and community. Religion was an integral part of the lives of the women of Jeme, and in chapter 4 we see how they participated in the religious life of their town and their region. We encounter another Elizabeth, this time an elite woman who donated murals for the decoration of a church where she had herself commemorated. We also see three women who made the painful decision to give up their children to a local monastery. In chapter 5, we explore the texts and archaeological evidence relating to Koloje, a woman moneylender from a family of moneylenders, and through her examine how the women of Jeme fit into the town's economy. Finally, in an

[9] Published as Wilfong 1997.
[10] Published as Rowlandson 1998.

epilogue we trace the rediscovery of Jeme by modern scholars through the recovery of its remains and conclude with an encounter between a nineteenth-century feminist author and the ruins of Jeme.

As I came close to finishing this book, a number of new publications of Coptic documentary texts, including those from Jeme, and other topics relating to the book began to appear.[11] Although none of these volumes directly addresses the subject of the present book, I regret not having been able to make greater use of their insights in general. In most cases I have been able to incorporate at least general citations of these books where appropriate and have gladly made more extensive reference to them when possible. Clearly we are on the verge of a veritable explosion of new work relating to the areas covered by the present volume, and I look forward to seeing what will appear next.

The inclusion of this volume in the series "New Texts from Ancient Cultures" may seem to require some comment. It is true that this book contains no editions of unpublished texts, which were the initial emphasis of the series. But Coptic documentary texts on the whole have not been used much outside the field of Coptic Studies, and it is likely that at least some of the texts discussed in this volume will be "new" to most readers. For those already familiar with the texts in question, I do provide a substantial number of new readings and new interpretations that will hopefully encourage these readers to look on the corpus from a different perspective. Further, one could argue that the corpus of documentary texts from Jeme and environs as a whole, especially taken in conjunction with the archaeological remains, forms a rich "text" (in the postmodern sense of the word) that is certainly new. This "text" is just waiting for interpreters from different disciplines, and I would venture to offer the present volume as a guide, at the least, to what the "text" has to offer. I would also note the precedent of the first volume in the series (Gagos and van Minnen 1994): although this publication did present the edition of an unpublished text, it is the innovative approach of the book and its use of a single text as an entryway into the legal anthropology of Late Antique Egypt that are the truly "new" contributions it has made. In any case, given the interest and intent of the editors of the series, I have no doubt that future volumes will redefine the notion of "new texts" even further.

[11] Including Beidenkopf-Ziehner 2000 and 2001, Clackson 2000, Krawiec 2002, and O'Brien 1999.

Finally, some remarks on the title of the book may be in order. Most scholarly book titles represent a compromise of some sort between explicitness and concision to avoid the overly cumbersome: how to sum up a complex subject in a single line? In the case of the present volume, the use of the terms "Coptic" and "Late Antique" in the title seem to call for further explanation. "Coptic" has many meanings in different situations—it is used to refer to modern Egyptian Christians, various aspects of Christianity in Egypt in the past, and, in the usage commonly favored by scholars, the latest phase of the indigenous language used by these Egyptian Christians. To call Jeme a "Coptic town" has a precedent in Uvo Hölscher's excavation report of the site (Hölscher 1954), in which he refers to the ruins of Jeme as the "Coptic" town to distinguish them from the earlier remains. But few scholars today would be entirely comfortable with such a use of the term as a chronological designation. Certainly, Jeme is a town characterized by Coptic texts: only a tiny fraction of the textual material from the period under discussion is in another language, and Coptic was certainly the main language of written and spoken communication in Jeme. So one might accurately characterize Jeme as a "Coptic" town in terms of language, and this is indeed the main reason that I have done so.

I must confess, though, to using "Coptic" also in a less precise way to invoke the nature of the population of Jeme as predominantly Christian, even though most of the material covered in the book comes from after the Muslim conquest of Egypt in 639-642. The chronological situation of this "Coptic" town might have just as easily been described as "Early Islamic" rather than "Late Antique" Egypt in the title: certainly this would be a better fit in terms of political history. This book is not, however, a work of political history and the designation of its period as "Early Islamic" seems not entirely appropriate. Although Jeme's ultimate rulers for much of the period covered by this book were indeed the Umayyad and Abbasid caliphs and the governors and officials they appointed, socially and culturally Jeme (and much of Egypt at this time) remained part of the very end of Late Antiquity, carrying on from developments of the Graeco-Roman and Byzantine periods, and indeed bringing vestiges of the earlier Pharaonic period as well.[12] The classic

---

[12] Already in his defining work on Late Antiquity in 1971, Peter Brown noted the frequent overlap between the early years of Muslim rule and the final stages of Late Antique culture (Brown 1971, 194-203).

formulation of Late Antiquity as ending around 750 is roughly paralleled by the Jeme evidence, which probably cuts off by 785. So although the Jeme material comes mostly from what is often called the Early Islamic period in Egyptian history, it remained to the end resolutely Late Antique in terms of culture and society.

Thus, in spite of the alternatives, I am hopeful that the reader will agree that *Women of Jeme: lives in a town of almost entirely Christian and Coptic-speaking population, in Egypt in the early Islamic period (at least politically, but still largely Late Antique in terms of culture)*, although perhaps more explicit and accurate, would strain the patience of even the most dedicated subtitle aficionado, and that *Women of Jeme: Lives in a Coptic Town in Late Antique Egypt* will suffice.

ACKNOWLEDGMENTS

Faculty and friends at the University of Chicago and elsewhere were instrumental in the completion of my original dissertation, and for this revision I would again like to single out Janet Johnson, Edward Wente, and Fred Donner (the members of my dissertation committee), as well as Robert Ritner (who first introduced me to the study of the Coptic ostraca that ultimately led to this project) for their ongoing contributions and support. The Oriental Institute Museum, which generously supplied photographs for this book, has been an essential resource for me, and I would especially like to thank Emily Teeter for her help with the Medinet Habu material and John Larson for help with archival material and photographs. Jaromir Malek generously allowed me access to the papers of Walter E. Crum in his keeping at the Griffith Institute in Oxford, and I greatly appreciate the help and facilities he and his staff provided. The Research Archives of the Oriental Institute in Chicago and expertise of its archivist Charles E. Jones were crucial to my work, as they are to anyone writing a dissertation at the Oriental Institute. Dissertation-related research was funded by the University of Chicago Edward L. Ryerson Travel Fellowship, and completion of the dissertation was generously supported by a Mrs. Giles M. Whiting Dissertation Fellowship.

For the revision of my dissertation into the present book, I had the benefit of detailed comments from three anonymous referees and the series editors, and I thank all of these for their input and interest. I also greatly appreciate the valuable input of Sarah Clackson, Ann Ellis Hanson, and James G. Keenan on the manuscript at various stages, as well as the more general support and suggestions I have received from Leslie MacCoull, Lynn Meskell, Jenni Sheridan Moss, Thelma K. Thomas, and my colleagues in the Department of Near Eastern Studies, the Kelsey Museum of Archaeology, and the Institute for Research on Women and Gender at the University of Michigan.

I began this revision under the editorship of Ellen Bauerle and completed it under Collin Ganio: I thank both for their interest, enthusiasm, and, above all, patience. The final copyediting and camera-ready copy for this book was carried out by Peg Lourie, to whom I am deeply indebted, and was supported by a grant from the University of Michigan's College for Literature, Science and the Arts, International Institute, and Department of Near Eastern Studies, for which I am very grateful.

I would like to thank my friends, family, colleagues, and students for their encouragement and support in the long process of revision. Special thanks go to Miriam Reitz Baer and Remko Jas for their encouragement and their hospitality on various research trips over the years and also to Carl Nyman for his support and sense of humor. Traianos Gagos initially solicited my dissertation for the series and has been a constant source of enthusiasm, kindness, and good cheer. Janet Richards was instrumental in getting me through this revision process, not only with her sound criticism and suggestions through many drafts but also with her unfailing help and encouragement over the years. This book simply would not have been possible without Dominic Montserrat, Chuck Jones, and especially Greg Madden, who have been there for me from the very beginning of this project and whose friendship I value more than I can say.

I dedicate this book to the memory of Klaus Baer, my first teacher in Egyptology.

All dates in this book, unless otherwise indicated, are in the Common Era (CE/AD).

All examples of Coptic words and phrases are transliterated to give a conventional phonetic rendering of the Coptic, using the following alphabet: a b g d e z ê th i k l m n o p ks r s t u ph kh ps ô sh f h j c ti. (Greek words are transliterated in the same way, excepting, of course, the final six letters exclusive to Coptic.) For readers unfamiliar with Coptic, it may be helpful to note the frequency of consonantal clusters used in the language and that final *-e* in Coptic is usually not silent. The conventional pronunciation of one important Coptic word in this book, *shime*, "woman," may appear ambiguous in transliteration: it would have been more like suh-HEEM-ah than SHEEM. The Coptic words and phrases cited in this volume are mostly in the Sahidic dialect of Coptic, although with influences from other dialects; the best general reference for the Coptic language is now Layton 2000.

In transliterations and translations, the following conventions are observed:

Square brackets [ ] indicate a break in the original text, with restorations supplied within the brackets when possible.

Parentheses ( ) indicate something added to the original text, usually to clarify an ambiguity in the original.

Terms in and/or derived from Coptic or Greek are generally in italics, e.g., *shime*, *cor*, *skhat*, etc.

All translations of texts from the Coptic in this book are by the author, taking into account earlier translations when available.

The spellings of names of people and places often feature minor variations in the original Coptic (e.g., the name of the woman whose archive forms the centerpiece of chapter 5 is variously spelled Koloje, Kolôje, Kôlôje, Koulôje, Kelôje, etc., while the name of the town of Jeme itself is found as Jeme, Jême, Jêma, etc.). I have normalized these spellings, mostly without indication of long vowels, for the ease of the reader, unless the variant spellings seem to be relevant to the discussion. For both personal names and place names, I have tended to use the form by which they are most commonly known (thus Epiphanius rather than Epiphanios, Pisentius rather than Pesynthios or Pisentios, Deir el-Bahri rather than Dayr al-Bahri) but have tended not to use modern equivalents for biblical names applied to individuals in documents (thus Maria or Mariam rather than Mary, Petros rather than Peter, Johannes rather than John).

Denominations of money have also been standardized in both the translations and discussions of texts. Thus the highest denomination gold coin in the Jeme texts is variously known as the nomisma, the holokottinos, and the solidus (plural solidi): I have used solidus/solidi exclusively. Similarly, for a low denomination coin, the carat, kerat, keration, I have used carat. The relative values of the denominations cited are, more or less, 1 solidus/nomisma/holokottinos = 3 tremisses = 24 carats = 240–288 *she* = 960 *cor* (there is some variation in value, for which see references cited in individual occurrences of the relevant denomination). Fractions of the solidus and tremis are also common in these texts.

The Town of Jeme
in the Seventh and Eighth Centuries CE

Around noon on the third of March in the year 601, a scribe observed a solar eclipse in southern Egypt. This anonymous scribe recorded the event in ink on a flake of limestone and further noted that this eclipse occurred in the year in which Petros, son of Paulos, was the magistrate of the town of Jeme.[1] This record is one of the earliest dated texts from nearly two centuries' worth of Coptic textual evidence for the inhabitants of Jeme. The Jeme texts represent an extensive and rich body of documentation that is complemented by literary sources and the relatively well-preserved archaeological remains of the town itself. Taken together, the evidence from Jeme documenting the lives and activities of its inhabitants is an extremely valuable corpus for the social and economic history of Egypt from around 600 to 800 and provides a unique set of evidence for women's lives in this period.[2]

Jeme was built on and around the remains of a Pharaonic temple on the western side of the Nile River in southern Egypt (see fig. 1). Situated in the low desert plain, Jeme was out of the reach of the Nile's annual flood but close enough to house people who worked the fertile agricultural land in the river's floodplain. Further to the east, across the river, lay the city of Apé, ancient city of Thebes and site of the modern city of Luxor, a major political and religious center through much of Egypt's history. To the north and south of Jeme on the western Theban plain were the remains of the ancient mortuary temples, on and around which were built settlements and monasteries. To the west of Jeme was the high desert, heralded by a group of low mountains and cliffs dominated by the peak known as "the Holy Mountain of Jeme" (now known as the Sheikh Abd el-Qurna). These western mountains held the burial grounds of earlier centuries (including the well-known

---

[1] Stern 1878, no. 1; see also Allen 1947; for the dating, see Till 1962, 172; for another early Coptic text from a nearby site, see Worp 1990.

[2] For general bibliography and references on Jeme and environs, see Wilfong 1989, and note the comments thereupon in Krause 1993, 1:86–89. Note especially Hölscher 1954, Otto 1975, Krause 1982, Godlewski 1986, and Timm 3:1012–1035.

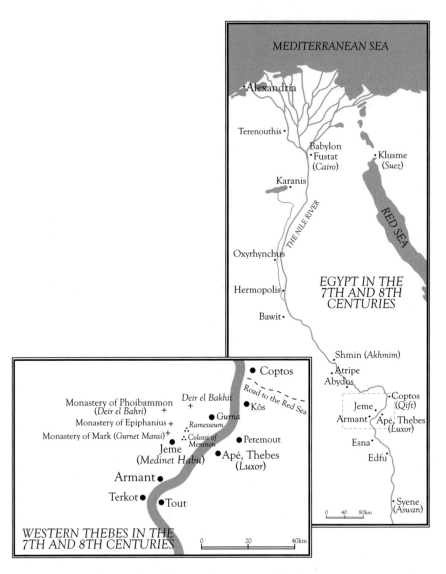

Fig. 1. Map: Egypt and the western Theban area
in the seventh and eighth centuries CE

Valley of the Kings) and formed a natural enclosure for Jeme and its neighbors, a group of settlements and monasteries that are generally referred to as the western Theban area. In this primarily rural area of agricultural land, monastic institutions, and freelance ascetic practitioners, Jeme was the nearest substantial town.

By the time of the eclipse in 601, the town of Jeme had been in existence in some form for more than 1,500 years. Jeme began as an administrative settlement near the Pharaonic mortuary temple of Ramesses III (now known as Medinet Habu), itself built near and around earlier temples and completed sometime around 1150 BCE. The cult at the Ramesses III temple seems to have continued well past the death of the king, and the walled precinct of the temple eventually came to be used for the administration of the extensive royal burial grounds to the west. Residential structures in the temple precinct are first attested at the beginning of the Twenty-first Dynasty (around 1069 BCE).[3] It was in the grounds of the temple precinct that the rewrapping of the plundered royal mummies took place before their reburial in mass tombs.[4] Building activity, often centering on priestly tombs and mortuary chapels for the divine votaresses of Amun, took place in the temple precinct throughout the Third Intermediate Period (1069–664 BCE) and into the Saite Period (664–525 BCE) and led to further settlement, by which time the town had acquired the name Jeme. Habitation seems to have slacked off during the Late Period (525–332 BCE) and Ptolemaic Period (332–30 BCE), as Egypt fell to various foreign powers, although there was much building activity at the structure known as the Small Temple and written records from the period are not lacking. Stamped Rhodian amphora handles of the third and second centuries BCE from the site[5] attest to the importation of foreign products during this period (and coincide with the presence of a Greek-literate population). Settlement at Jeme picks up again after the Roman conquest of Egypt in 30 BCE, perhaps due to the protection afforded by the ruined temple precinct wall, and the town nearly came to fill the temple precinct by the third century CE.[6] In addition to the

---

[3] For the early history of Jeme that follows, see in general Hölscher 1954, 1–35.

[4] See Hölscher 1954, 5 and Reeves and Wilkinson 1996, 106.

[5] Now *SB* XX 14320–14324; see Wilfong 1992, 85–87 and now Wilfong 2002b.

[6] See Vandorpe 1999, 222–227 for the town of Jeme in Graeco-Roman times; also, in general, note Bataille 1952 and the essays in Vleeming 1999.

existing temple structures and new mud-brick houses, Jeme in the Roman period also had such amenities as new wells, lime kilns, and a bath house. By this time, Greek was long the standard language of administration in Egypt, and hundreds of Greek texts (mostly unpublished material from the University of Chicago Medinet Habu excavations) of the first few centuries CE attest to this. The Egyptian language continued on as a language of daily life for many of Jeme's inhabitants, as attested by the many Roman period documents in Demotic (the cursive Egyptian script derived ultimately from hieroglyphs) found at Jeme.[7] In this period, the town and the surrounding regions (including the ancient cemeteries to the west) were often referred to as "the Memnoneia," presumably after the nearby colossi of Memnon—a pair of enormous statues of Amenhotep III (1390–1352 BCE) that became popular tourist attractions in the Graeco-Roman period, when they were identified with Memnon and his mother Aurora.[8] The size of Jeme dramatically increased in the later Roman period, as is well attested in the archaeological record.[9] Mummy labels from a Jeme cemetery of the late third and early fourth centuries CE attest to something of the makeup of the inhabitants of the town in the Roman period—a population probably of mostly Egyptian ancestry (but with both Greek and Egyptian names), who reflected in general the population trends observed elsewhere in Roman Egypt.[10]

Beyond Jeme, the later Roman period saw the shift in control of Egypt to the Eastern Roman (later Byzantine) emperor in Constantinople and, just as significantly, the first substantial evidence of Christianity in the area. By the fifth and sixth centuries, most, if not all, of the population of Jeme and the west Theban area were Christians, and many of the Pharaonic temples in the area (along with other

[7] Lichtheim 1957 and Parker 1940 for the published texts; see O'Brien 1999 for a detailed study of women in the Demotic texts from Jeme and the Theban area in general.

[8] See Bataille 1952, 1–27. Both "Jeme" and "the Memnoneia" are used frequently, although usage of "Jeme" in Coptic texts usually seems to be in some reference to the town at the Ramesses III temple (as in "the Holy Mount of Jeme," referring to the mountain peak visible from the town), whereas "the Memnoneia" seems less tied to the settlement and more universally applicable within western Thebes. See also the use of the names "Kastron Memnoneia" and "Kastron Jeme" discussed below.

[9] Hölscher 1954, 36–44.

[10] Published Wilfong 1995, with information on context, and now republished as *SB* XXII 15391–15451. See discussion of this corpus in Scheidel 2001, 10–16.

structures) had been converted into churches and monasteries. Magical texts[11] and Gnostic books like Bruce Codex[12] in Coptic from the west Theban area in this period, however, attest to the complexity of the conversion process. (Of course, the varieties of Christianity throughout Egypt were often considered nonstandard and even heretical elsewhere in the Christian world.) Jeme in the fifth and sixth centuries was a growing town; having filled the Ramesses III temple precinct, the structures of Jeme began to spread outside its enclosure wall. Substantial documentary evidence for Jeme in the fifth and sixth centuries is meager in any language, but this situation changed at the opening of the seventh. The record of the eclipse in 601 marks the beginning of nearly two centuries of extensive textual evidence from Jeme, mostly in Coptic— the latest phase of the indigenous Egyptian language written in a predominantly Greek alphabet.

The time from 600 to just before 800 was a high point for Jeme; the archaeological and textual sources attest to the relative prosperity of the town and the activities of its inhabitants. The first fifty years of this period played out against an especially dramatic political background.[13] As the century began, the Byzantine rulers of Egypt were actively persecuting many of the inhabitants of Egypt because of the particular nature of their beliefs: the majority of Egyptians by this time were Monophysite Christians, whose doctrines conflicted with those of the official variety. The Sassanian Persians seem to have taken advantage of this dissension to facilitate their conquest of Egypt in 616; numerous refugees from this invasion fled south to Jeme and environs, where conditions seem to have remained relatively safe. The Sassanian rule of Egypt lasted little more than a decade, as the Byzantine ruler Heraclius was able to retake Egypt in 627. The persecution of Egyptian Christians resumed and even intensified after the Byzantine reconquest, and the Muslim conquest of Egypt in 639–642 seems to

---

[11] Magical texts with good western Theban context are *O.Medin.Habu.Copt.* 4 (discussion in Brashear 1983) and Papyrus Carnarvon from Deir el Bakhit (translated, with references, in Meyer and Smith 1994, 270–273); others may also derive from the area.

[12] Said to come from Medinet Habu, although not obtained through controlled excavation: Schmidt and MacDermott 1978, ix.

[13] For this and what follows, see the recent surveys in Ritner 1998 and Kaegi 1998; for the general background of Egypt in the centuries preceding 600, note also Keenan 2001.

have come as almost a relief to the beleaguered Egyptians. Egyptian Christians were not systematically persecuted in the first few centuries of Muslim rule (although they were subject to special taxes and occasional, nearly random, repression), but the Muslim conquest did have the effect of cutting the Egyptian Christian population off from the remaining parts of the Byzantine empire.[14] Through these tumultuous years, Jeme and its inhabitants seem to have passed relatively unscathed; if anything the Sassanian and Muslim conquests seem to have increased the town's population and prosperity. Habitation at Jeme and environs is particularly well documented from the Muslim conquest to the end of the eighth century.

In its own immediate neighborhood, Jeme had considerable significance as the central town. Its nearest neighbors included institutions like the Monastery of Phoibammon, built in and around the mortuary temple of Hatshepsut at Deir el-Bahri,[15] and the Monastery of St. Mark at Gurnet Marai near the Pharaonic workers' village at Deir el-Medina,[16] as well as smaller and less formal monasteries such as the Monastery of Epiphanius,[17] founded in and around a Pharaonic tomb, and the so-called Monastery of Cyriacus.[18] There seems to have been some sort of settlement, probably a monastery, at the nearby Ramesseum,[19] while remains survive for a pottery works at Gurna,[20] possibly with an attached settlement, monastic communities at Dra Abu el Naga and Deir el Bakhit,[21] and a second, smaller Monastery of Phoibammon to the west.[22] There were various other monasteries in

[14] For the Christian population in the postconquest period in Egypt in general, see Wilfong 1998b and references there.

[15] See Krause 1981 and 1985, Godlewski 1986 and 1991, and note the recent translation of the foundation document for this monastery in MacCoull 2000. Also note the useful study in Beidenkopf-Ziehner 2000, 2:155–245.

[16] See Martin, Coquin, and Castel 1991.

[17] See the essential publication Winlock and Crum 1926, as well as the texts from the site in Crum and Evelyn White 1926, and note also Peel 1991.

[18] See now Bács 2000.

[19] Discussed below in chapter 4 and the epilogue; see also Wilfong forthcoming.

[20] Although the archaeology of the site has not been fully published yet, see the publication of pottery and small finds in Mysliwiec 1987.

[21] References in Wilfong 1989, 125–126, and Coquin, Martin, and Grossman 1991, respectively.

[22] This was actually the original Monastery of Phoibammon in the region, but its remoteness led to the foundation of the larger institution at Deir el-Bahri, closer to

the region, known from either archaeological remains or textual witnesses, and many solitary monks living in the ancient and abandoned tombs in the mountains to the west of Jeme. Indeed, monasticism could be considered one of the most important "industries" of the region, second only to agriculture; the many monasteries in the western Theban area had a major impact on the regional economy.[23] The economic and social interaction between the inhabitants of the monastic communities and those of the town of Jeme shows them to have been interconnected to such an extent as to form a general west Theban community. Jeme also had administrative connections to its near neighbors. The magistrates of Jeme (known by the title *lashane*,[24] an office usually occupied by two men at once) and the primary judicial/arbitrational body at Jeme (known as the "Great men,"[25] Coptic *noc nrôme*) had a certain degree of control or, at least, influence over the nearby monasteries. So Jeme provided local administration, goods, raw materials, food, and money, while the monasteries contributed human resources, handicrafts, and spiritual guidance. Because of this interconnectedness, evidence from the outlying monastic communities can be used to help supply information lacking from the Jeme corpus. To some extent self-sufficient, Jeme and the western Theban community had extensive interaction among themselves but considerably less contact with the rest of Egypt.

In the wider context of Egypt in the seventh and eighth centuries, however, Jeme was not a particularly prominent town. Administratively, Jeme was under the control of the pagarch or district administrator[26]

Jeme. See Bachatly 1961, 1965, and 1981, Boutros Ghali 1991, and Krause 1981, 1985, the latter two articles essential in distinguishing the relationship between the two Phoibammon monasteries.

[23] Note the discussion in Godlewski 1986, 79–88.

[24] See the standard reference in Steinwenter 1920, 38–60 and the listing of known *lashanes* in Till 1962, 234–235.

[25] Again, see Steinwenter 1920, 22–23, 43–44; note the brief discussion of this body in a monastic context in Kahle 1954, I:33.

[26] Known in the Coptic sources sometimes by the Arabic title Amir; see Steinwenter 1920, 6–18 for this office. The pagarchs at Armant mostly had Arabic names (see the list in Till 1962, 234–235); they were seconded by an official known as the *dioiketes*—occupants of this office had Coptic names of Egyptian and Greek origin (Steinwenter 1920, 19–25 and again the list in Till 1962, 234–235). Note the official letter to a local monastery in Bell 1925, 266–275 for an example of the style of communication adopted by these officials.

in Armant,[27] to the south, and it no doubt suffered from comparison to the much larger town across the river—Apé, ancient Thebes, modern Luxor.[28] In spite of sometimes being known as the Kastron Memnoneia (Fort of the Memnoneia) or the Kastron Jeme,[29] Jeme had no military installation; the name seems to have come about at least in part because of the ancient enclosure wall surrounding the town. The nearest actual fort (probably abandoned by 630) was the Roman *castrum* across the river built in and around the ancient temple at Luxor.[30] Although the many monasteries in the western Theban area were important as homes, training grounds, and pilgrimage attractions for monks, ecclesiastical power in the region centered instead at the bishoprics in Coptos to the north and Armant to the south. The economic importance of Jeme was certainly considerable in the western Theban area but does not seem to have extended too far beyond this. Jemeans regularly transacted business with individuals as far south as Terkot and as far north as Coptos, and some Jemeans had connections as far away as Syene (modern Aswan), Fustat (now in modern Cairo), and Alexandria, but the people of Jeme generally tended to interact mostly with individuals in nearby towns and monasteries. Jemeans did contribute further to the overall economy through the payment of taxes and other fees and tributes, but the amounts involved were not exceptional. If not exactly isolated, Jeme was not well known beyond the Theban area and is rarely mentioned in outside documentation. Language may have contributed to this relative obscurity; the evidence suggests that the usual medium of communication was not the Late Antique *lingua franca* of Greek, nor the later standard language of Arabic, but was almost exclusively the indigenous Coptic. Lacking most of the cultural and political amenities of the larger cities in Egypt, Jeme was, at best, a "provincial" country town.

The town of Jeme that can be reconstructed from its physical remains was substantial but not particularly large by the standards of the time. Jeme covered an area of at least 11 hectares (or 27 acres) at its

---

[27] Timm 1:152–182.

[28] Timm 1:133–136, 6:2904–2919; note also the references in Coptic texts to this town under its ancient Egyptian name of Nê (Timm 4:1762–1762).

[29] In some documents, Jeme inhabitants simply refer to their town as "the Kastron": for examples of how these terms were used, see the legal documents translated at the beginning of chapter 2.

[30] See the publication in el-Saghir [and others] 1986.

height in the seventh and eighth centuries.[31] The earlier stone structures of the Ramesses III temple complex and the massive mud-brick wall that enclosed the temple precinct provided a framework around which the town had been built (see fig. 2). Ultimately, the town grew outside the boundaries of the ancient enclosure wall: considerable building occurred to the west of the wall and also to the north, into the ruined precinct of the Eighteenth Dynasty mortuary temple of pharaohs Ay and Horemheb. The great majority of structures in the town were multistory houses made of mud brick, of which more than a hundred examples survived into the early twentieth century (see pls. 1 and 3). These houses seem to have originally been laid out in an orderly plan of large blocks, but the gradual addition of more and more houses into the available space meant that, by the end of the eighth century, much of the town was a jumble of houses jammed together along increasingly narrow streets. In particular, the houses built on top of the enclosure wall were crowded, often precariously, into a relatively small space. Given the height of the houses, these streets likely would have been shadowed and relatively dark. Rather unusually for the time, many of the streets in Jeme were named,[32] perhaps due to the complexity of the town's layout, and neighborhoods or outlying areas of the town sometimes appear to have had names.[33] Parts of the Ramesses III temple were reused for housing;[34] builders converted the complex of storerooms at the western end of the temple into dwellings by constructing multistory mud-brick structures within the ancient storerooms. A number of these houses in the temple storerooms had their doorways cut through the ancient stone walls; separate entrances to upper and lower levels in these structures attest to the division of such multistory houses into separate, condominiumlike units.

[31] Compare this to 16 hectares for the Roman period town at Syene, around 24 hectares each for the Graeco-Roman Fayum towns of Soknopaiou Nesos and Philadelphia, nearly 100 hectares for the city Hermopolis, and the approximately 750 hectares allotted for the capital at Alexandria (Bard 1999, 153, 309, 311, 147, and 130, respectively).

[32] See Timm 3:1018–1019.

[33] Thus one quarter is known as Roma in Jeme, and other quarters are identified as Ouai, Pbasik, Tmnc, and Tmoh (see Timm 3:1030); these may be specific neighborhoods, quarters, or outlying adjuncts of Jeme. Since the Byzantine-trained scribes and administrators in Egypt at this time are sometimes referred to, anachronistically, in Coptic texts as Romans, it is possible that this Roma is the part of Jeme occupied by officials and Greek-literate scribes.

[34] As in Hölscher 1954, plate 44.

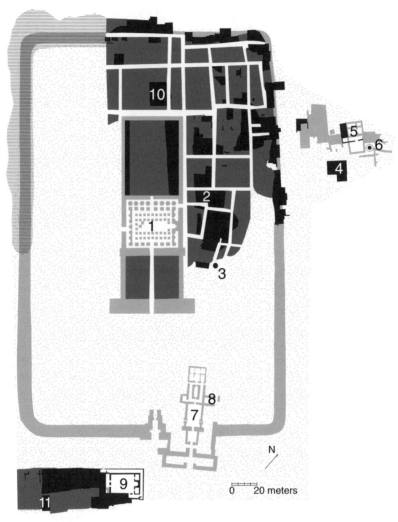

1. The Holy Church of Jeme;
2. Location of House 34 (see chap. 5);
3. Ancient Well Reused by Jeme Inhabitants; 4. Storehouse;
5. Church; 6. Well; 7. Church in Ptolemaic Temple; 8. Location of Elizabeth Mural (see chap. 4); 9. Small Church (site of Roman period bath house); 10. Storehouse; 11. Lime Kiln

▪ Buildings excavated and published

▤ Buildings still standing at site, unpublished

▪ Debris of Jeme buildings, cleared by excavators

▪ Earlier structures reused by Jeme inhabitants

☐ Probable extent of Jeme

Fig. 2. Plan of the remains of Jeme
(after Hölscher 1934, plates 32 and 34, and other observations)

Most of the houses at Jeme consisted of two or three stories based on a simple plan: a central staircase and rooms on both sides of the stairs at each level, frequently with a cellar below the ground floor (see fig. 4 for a composite of typical houses). The houses often featured barrel-vaulted ceilings on the ground floor, and at least one room in most houses contained wall niches for storage as well as a special niche or stand for water jars. Unbaked mud brick was used for most construction, although baked mud brick and stone were frequently used for important structural elements (lintels and sills, for example, as well as consoles and holders for water jars),[35] and wood was used for smaller and more portable elements, such as doors and window shutters. Rough pottery pipes and tubes were used to promote ventilation and perhaps for disposal of waste.[36] Plaster was sometimes used on the walls inside houses; in a number of cases the plaster was decorated with incised inscriptions or painting,[37] while textile wall-hangings may have been used for decoration and warmth in other cases. Windows tended to be small and relatively high up in the walls, the idea being to allow a certain amount of light and air circulation but at the same time guard against outside heat or cold as much as possible. Doorways would have been fitted with wooden doors that pivoted in sockets found in the sills; doorway lintels were sometimes made of stone and decorated with crosses, doves, and other religious symbols. Keys found at the site suggest that at least some of the doors were once fitted with locks.[38]

Crowded in among the houses of Jeme were other structures, mostly storehouses and workshops, that served the specialized needs of the town's economy.[39] In many cases, however, it seems that private houses were used for businesses. The main activity of Jemeans—agriculture— has left little trace on the physical remains of the town itself, although the textual evidence repeatedly refers to its products and to the private grain storage areas that were a part of larger houses. The preserved remains of the town do not show the large granaries common in Roman

[35] Hölscher 1954, 58–61 and plates 36–37.

[36] See Winlock and Crum 1926, 92; the examples of pipes from Jeme cited there are now in the Oriental Institute Museum (numbers 27629–27631).

[37] Examples in Hölscher 1954, 47, figure 54.

[38] Hölscher 1954, 66 and plate 38; the smaller keys were probably not for house doors.

[39] Note structures 76 and b (Hölscher 1954, 50–51), most likely storerooms: location of these is shown at numbers 10 and 4, respectively, in the plan of Jeme above, figure 2.

period Egyptian towns such as Karanis.[40] Governmental or administrative structures have left no traces, and the only public building known from the Roman period—a late Roman bathhouse—was no longer in use. The inhabitants of Jeme used public wells for their water, including a large and elaborate well dating back to the original building of the Ramesses III temple (3 in the map of Jeme in fig. 2).[41] Finally, at least one lime kiln on the outskirts of the town surviving from the Roman period may have continued to serve the inhabitants of Jeme through the seventh and eighth centuries (11 in the map of Jeme in fig. 2).[42] Lime remained important in the making of plaster, mortar, pottery, and glass—all materials known from Jeme and nearby sites.

The focal point of Jeme, on many levels, was the church built in the second courtyard of the Ramesses III temple, known as the Holy Church of Jeme in Coptic documents (number 1 on the map of Jeme in fig. 2). Builders adapted many of the existing structural elements of the temple courtyard to the design of this church, adding more (and smaller) columns, an apse, a well, and a baptismal font, as well as a wooden roof in approximation of contemporary Byzantine church architecture.[43] The Holy Church of Jeme was at the physical center of the town, and its wooden roof would have been visible from most points in the town. The Holy Church of Jeme was the center of town religious life and also a focus of legal and economic activity, where legal documents were witnessed and oaths were sworn regarding financial transactions. The church may also have served as the seat of the town's administration as well. The church itself would have controlled a certain amount of resources, as witnessed by the donations to churches found in the documents.[44] At least three other churches are known in Jeme. One church, built in the remains of the small temple that was the focus of so much activity in the Ptolemaic period (7 in the map of Jeme in fig. 2), contained an elaborate series of murals about the life of St. Menas—murals that seem to have been financed by a woman named Elizabeth and are discussed in detail below in chapter 4. Another church,

---

[40] See Husselman 1952 and the structures published in Husselman 1979.

[41] See Hölscher 1954, 40–41.

[42] See Hölscher 1954, 40.

[43] See Hölscher 1954, 50–54 and plate 45. The presence and design of the now-lost roof is reconstructed from the beam-holes made into the surviving stone structure.

[44] See chapter 4. For the economic resources and activities of churches in Late Antique Egypt as seen through the Greek evidence, see Wipszycka 1972 and 1992.

the so-called Small Church, was built on the foundations of the earlier bathhouse and decorated with stone carvings (9 in the map of Jeme in fig. 2). An even smaller church was built in the northern part of the town, among the Roman period structures in the ruins of the Ay and Horemheb mortuary temple (5 in the map of Jeme in fig. 2). Other churches may have once existed in the town, and the textual evidence suggests this,[45] but no physical remains of these have survived.

Together the churches of Jeme served the needs of a town population that was probably between 1,000 and 2,000 people at any given time[46]—not so large even by ancient standards but substantial nonetheless. What we know of the demographics of this population must be inferred from textual and archaeological evidence that is, for the most part, indirect. The physical remains of the inhabitants of Jeme in the seventh and eighth centuries that could furnish much information on the numbers and physical state of the population have not survived or, perhaps more accurately, have not been recognized or recorded by archaeologists. Bodies from nearby monasteries have been subject to more investigation but have yet to yield much information.[47] Statistical evidence for the population of Jeme is almost completely absent—there is certainly nothing like the census records of the Roman period or even the collection of mummy labels with records of age at death that survive from Jeme in the third and fourth centuries. Although conditions may have changed slightly from the few centuries preceding,[48] it is unlikely that these changes had a substantial demographic impact. So we can reasonably assume from the earlier evidence some basic trends among the population of Jeme that are further supported by anecdotal

[45] See Timm 3:1019–1023.

[46] Badawy 1978, 29 estimates that Jeme had 18,860 inhabitants, but this is far too high in light of both what is known of populations in other Late Antique towns in Egypt and generally accepted methods for estimating population from archaeological sites. See Meyer 2001 for a handy guide to such methods; some can obviously not be applied to Jeme because the necessary data are lacking (e.g., total covered floor space). But the simple formula of 125 people per hectare seems to fit with what can be determined from other evidence: Jeme covered a total of about 11 hectares, and this would be consistent with a population of about 1,375, which seems realistic given the textual evidence.

[47] Note Castel 1979, Bachatly 1981, 28 and plates 113–115, and see the photographs of human remains in Bács 2000.

[48] See the groundbreaking study Bagnall and Frier 1994, along with the publications that have followed, notably Scheidel 2001.

evidence among the Jeme texts. Infant and child mortality was probably high, as is true of most premodern cultures. Likewise, the childbearing years were dangerous for women. For those who survived such perils, however, ages in the fifties and sixties would not have been uncommon, and some few may well have survived as long as the woman Senplenis from the late third century, who died at the age of eighty and was buried near Jeme.[49]

Although perhaps not so well suited for understanding the demography of the population of Jeme, the surviving evidence provides much information for the conditions in which the people of Jeme lived. The archaeological evidence from Jeme not only shows the physical environment of the town, with its multistory mud-brick houses, storerooms, workshops, and churches, but also vividly illustrates the material culture of the town,[50] particularly when considered in connection with the textual sources and the artifactual remains from the nearby monasteries, especially the Monastery of Epiphanius and Monastery of Phoibammon. Our understanding of the material culture of Jeme may well be, perhaps inevitably, skewed in favor of the more elite levels of the population, but, given the state of research on the evidence, there is little one can do about this bias at present, except to be aware of it.

First and foremost, the activities and lives of the inhabitants of Jeme are witnessed by the extensive remains of pottery from the site.[51] The pottery from Jeme is typical for its time: rough storage and cooking vessels, the large, ribbed, two-handled amphorae for storing wine, a wide variety of finer and more delicate ceramics, including the characteristic plates and bowls (sometimes with stamped decoration) of Egyptian Red Slip Ware. The people of Jeme stored food, wine, and water in these vessels, cooked with them, ate and drank from them, mended them as needed, and ultimately, when they had broken beyond repair, wrote on their fragments. A broad range of pottery lamps, again typical of those found elsewhere, were used to illuminate the relatively dark and close Jeme houses, fueled by vegetable oils or animal greases.[52]

[49] Mummy label of Senplenis, published in Wilfong 1995, 175, now *SB* XXII 15426.
[50] As published in Hölscher 1954, Wilfong 2002b, and Teeter forthcoming.
[51] Hölscher 1954, 74–78 and plate 48, and from there some pieces republished in Hayes 1972, 387–392.
[52] Hölscher 1954, 67–71 and plate 40.

Less immediately practical artifacts of pottery also survive from Jeme, in particular a wide variety of ceramic figurines of humans and animals, both mold-made and handmade, some elaborately decorated with paint and some left entirely plain.[53] The varying levels of artistry that went into their making are probably matched by their varying uses as votive figures, children's toys, or interior decoration. Clay and even mud were used for sealings—of jars, doors, and documents—and many such seal impressions have survived, along with the stamps of pottery and stone that produced them.[54] Manufacture of ceramics is not attested at Jeme itself, not surprising given the amount of smoke and pollution a pottery works would have generated. There was, however, a complex of kilns at nearby Gurna; fragments of broken pottery in and around the kilns at the site[55] show wares and forms very similar to those of Jeme and other west Theban sites, and it is very likely that the Gurna pottery works was at least one major source of ceramics for the area.

Many types of metal artifacts survive from Jeme, of varying levels of practicality and craft.[56] Metal vessels from the site include bowls, kettles with lids, bottles and goblets of bronze, as well as ladles of bronze and iron, some with elaborate adjustable handles. Metal tools such as axes, chisels, knives, hammers, and saws attest to crafts and building work and simpler chores, while needles and awls indicate varying kinds of sewing and leather work. Fishhooks and harpoons point to the common activity of fishing, done both as a primary occupation at Jeme (several individuals were identified in texts by the occupation "fisherman"), as well as a casual activity to supplement household food supplies. Metal bridles attest to the use of animals at Jeme for more than food and further support the implications of the many ceramic horses, donkeys, and camels from Jeme that these animals were often used for transportation and the carrying of goods. More specialized metal tools such as apothecary scales, thorn-removers, tweezers, and spatulas suggest professional activities relating to medicine as well as personal hygiene and adornment. More explicit evidence of adornment

[53] To be catalogued in Teeter forthcoming. A few examples can be seen in Hölscher 1954, 58 and plate 44:D–F, and on plate 2a–b of the present work.

[54] Hölscher 1954, 61–62, now fully published in Wilfong 2002b.

[55] Published in Mysliwiec 1987.

[56] See Hölscher 1954, 63–67 and plates 38–39; some of the pieces alluded to below are unpublished but will be described in Wilfong forthcoming. For metalworking in Late Antique Egypt in general, see Bénazeth 1992.

is found in the jewelry from the site: pendant crosses of lead, bronze, and mother of pearl, earrings, pendants, and rings of bronze, chains and beads of various materials, and even elaborate inlaid silver bracelets (not surprisingly, though, none of the gold necklaces attested in the textual sources has survived). Relatively few coins were found at Jeme,[57] but the textual evidence makes it clear that a range of denominations of coins in bronze and gold circulated at and around Jeme. A small lock for a box and related small keys may well attest to means of safekeeping of coins and precious jewelry. The churches of Jeme and the nearby monasteries have also yielded a number of metal artifacts of high quality, including lamps that mimic the forms of pottery lamps, as well as much more elaborate examples of a lamp hung from chains in the form of a dove, an openwork incense burner in the form of an orb surmounted by a cross, and a complex censer showing a lion atop a ram from the Monastery of Epiphanius.[58] Molds for tiny pendant crosses are the only direct evidence of the metalworking industry at Jeme,[59] and many of the metal items from Jeme may have come from elsewhere.[60]

Objects of certain materials have not survived from Jeme, but their presence can either be confirmed through textual references or inferred from parallels at other sites. Aside from a few glass beads on a chain and small vessels (all likely to be Roman in date),[61] glass was not found (or noted) at Jeme and may not have been common there to begin with. Textiles are well known from Egypt throughout the Late Antique and Early Islamic periods, but these tend to be the elaborately decorated articles of clothing often found in burials. The presence of such textiles at Jeme can be inferred from the wall-paintings in one of the churches, where the people represented wear clothing with the typical decorations, possibly also from certain decorated ceramic figures of women praying, the well-known "orant" figures, both discussed below in chapter 4.

[57] Note the hoard of small-denomination bronze coins of the fourth to sixth centuries found in House 21 and the early seventh-century gold solidus of Heraclius found in House 77 (Hölscher 1954, 37, 50).

[58] Respectively, Hölscher 1954, 64 and plate 38:4; 63 and plate 38:3; Winlock and Crum 1926, 95 and plate 35.

[59] Unpublished (Oriental Institute Museum numbers 14807–14809); see Wilfong forthcoming.

[60] For a useful discussion of the nature and extent of metalworking in Late Antique Egypt from the Greek documentation, see Bagnall 1993, 84.

[61] The beads are unpublished; see Hölscher 1954, 71 and plate 40:32–33 for the vessels.

Clothing figures prominently in Jeme texts, and certain objects known from the archaeological record may have functioned as buttons for clothing.[62] One suspects that the usual items of clothing at Jeme were more often the undecorated tunics, robes, and leggings of the kind known from late Roman townsites.[63] Textiles used for bedding and wall-hangings must have also existed at Jeme but have left no traces. Some textiles were probably made at Jeme, while others may have come in from trade with local monasteries, where fragments of looms have survived.[64] Belts, aprons, and shoes made of leather and sandals made of basketry survive from nearby monasteries as well as from other townsites,[65] and these presumably approximate at least the simpler kinds of leather apparel and accessories worn at Jeme. Small bits of wood survive from Jeme—furniture pieces mostly—hinting at the beds, chairs, small tables, and reading stands known from other sites,[66] while nearby monasteries have yielded agricultural equipment and other items made of wood likely to have been owned by Jeme inhabitants as well.[67] Baskets, brooms, brushes, sieves, sleeping mats, and fishnets made of various plant fibers are attested from the Monastery of Epiphanius[68] and were doubtless also part of the equipment owned by Jeme inhabitants. West Theban monastic sites also preserve an important set of evidence either lacking or unnoticed at Jeme: plant and animal remains attesting to the range of foods eaten. Taken with the textual evidence, we find that the following were commonly eaten at the Theban monasteries: bread made from wheat, lentils and other beans, greens, dates, figs, grapes and olives, various kinds of oil, butter, milk, cheese and eggs, honey, fresh and dried fish, salt for seasoning, and with water and wine to drink.[69] Jeme's inhabitants ate the same kinds of things, probably along with various kinds of meat, such as beef, lamb, goat, fowl, and pigeons,

[62] Unpublished; one example is mentioned in the discussion of the contents of Jeme House 34 below in chapter 5.

[63] See Thomas 2001.

[64] Discussed in Winlock and Crum 1926, 68–71.

[65] Winlock and Crum 1926, 72–78; Castel 1979.

[66] Unpublished; similar examples were found at the Monastery of Phoibammon, for which see Godlewski 1986, 118–122.

[67] See Winlock and Crum 1926, 57–66 and plates 16–17.

[68] Winlock and Crum 1926, 71–75 and plates 22–25.

[69] Winlock and Crum 1926, 144–150 and Bachatly 1961; the latter also notes the presence of gourds, melon seeds, safflower, sycamore figs, carob pods, lupines, juniper berries, and citron.

that were excluded from the monastic diet.[70] Plants used for animal fodder and flax used for the manufacture of linen are especially common in the Jeme textual sources, if not in the archaeological record.

The Jeme texts are, in fact, the sources of much of our specific information about the inhabitants of Jeme and their activities. The texts themselves, of course, are archaeological artifacts as much as the pottery, metalwork, and such but have not usually been treated as such. Many of the Jeme texts were taken or looted from the site or nearby monasteries, with no record being kept of their archaeological context. Many, however, do have recorded context, and this has often proven of great use in determining relations between texts, or relations between texts and other artifactual material.[71] The physical nature of the texts themselves and the materials on which they were written can also provide useful information—there is often a connection between material and the nature of a particular text. Various kinds of objects contain what might be referred to as incidental inscriptions: notes on pottery jars as to content or ownership, short pious inscriptions on bronze lamps or ceramic basins,[72] and the brief inscriptions scratched into the plaster walls of houses referred to above. Graffiti can be found scratched or painted on stone, especially in the mountains and ancient tombs to the west of Jeme, recording names, prayers, and pious wishes.[73] More formal inscriptions on stone and wood can record information similar to graffiti, often in a more elaborate and formulaic way; such inscriptions are sometimes also used to commemorate deaths, sometimes giving information about the deceased and the date of death.[74] Pieces of broken pottery and flakes of limestone, both conventionally known as ostraca (singular: ostracon), were perhaps the commonest writing material at Jeme, normally written with an ink made of lampblack. The material often suggests the origin of an ostracon: pottery ostraca tend to come from the town, while stone ostraca frequently come from monastic sites in the mountainous hills to the west.[75] Although often containing ephemeral information, ostraca were also quite durable and could equally well be used for more permanent records: notes, memoranda,

[70] Winlock and Crum 1926, 149.
[71] See, e.g., Wilfong 1990 and chapter 5 below.
[72] Wilfong 1992, 88 (lamp, now *SB* XX 14325) and 87–89 (double basins).
[73] Note especially the texts in *Gr.Mon.Epiph.* and *Gr.Mont.Theb.*
[74] Note the tombstone from the Jeme excavations in Hölscher 1954, 59.
[75] See the brief discussion in Wilfong 1989, 104.

and lists, as well as more formal letters, legal documents, and even literary texts.[76] Writers of letters frequently begin by apologizing for using an ostracon,[77] indicating the element of status that use of other writing materials implied, a status conferred in part simply by the fact that ostraca were free, while the other media cost money. Papyrus and parchment were the media of choice for more formal documents—letters, legal documents, literature, and a wide range of quasi-literary magical, medical, scientific, and scholastic texts. Papyrus and parchment were more flexible, allowed (either by pasting sheets together or binding them together into a codex book) for much longer texts, and permitted (at least in the hands of some scribes) greater legibility by virtue of their smoother surfaces.

The thousands of texts, mostly in Coptic, that survive from Jeme and environs immediately raise questions about the levels of literacy in the town, but the evidence that they present on this subject is ambiguous. Scholars have at times interpreted the extensive nature of the Jeme documentary corpus as evidence of widespread literacy, but such generous estimates are questionable.[78] The texts themselves, as we will see in chapters 2 and 3, frequently refer to the illiteracy of the people for whom they were written. As in other ancient cultures, varying degrees of literacy existed at Jeme, ranging from professional scribes who read and wrote for a living, to individuals who could only read or write with some difficulty, to those who could only recognize and sign their own name, to those relatively few who were entirely literate. Even those who could not read or write often had aspects of their lives, activities, and transactions documented in written texts. One can argue that such texts do not represent the lives of all of Jeme's inhabitants and especially exclude those at the lower end of the economic scale. This is certainly a consideration with the textual evidence, as it was with the artifactual record, and needs to be borne in mind when looking at the sources; the textual record may well miss many levels of transactions and activities. This is especially an area of concern when looking for evidence that concerns the lives of women, as we are about to do—women tend, in

[76] Contrary to the impression given in Brown 1991, literary ostraca are relatively uncommon compared to other kinds.

[77] See the catalogue of occurrences of this common feature of Coptic letters in Biedenkopf-Ziehner 1983, 28–31, 211.

[78] For the most optimistic view, see especially Steinmann 1974, but note the more realistic verdict in Bagnall 1993, 258 and the references there.

many premodern cultures, to lead lives that are less well documented by texts than those of men. The textual record from Jeme too is obviously incomplete: we have, on the whole, a series of chance survivals of individual texts and groups of documents, and these are often in far from perfect condition. So the fragmentary nature of the textual evidence from Jeme as well as its potential biases must be taken into consideration when examining these sources. This being understood, however, there is still a wealth of information to be obtained by examination of the extensive textual remains of the inhabitants of Jeme.

The great majority of the thousands of texts from Jeme are from daily life and in Coptic—documentary texts that record the activities and lives of at least a portion of the inhabitants of the town. Lists, accounts, memoranda, receipts, letters, contracts, wills, sales, and other legal documents provide the names of the people of Jeme as well as the details of the significant events of their lives. One of the core groups of such texts from Jeme is the substantial archive of legal documents on papyrus and parchment deposited at the Monastery of Phoibammon for safekeeping and found there in the early nineteenth century (*P.KRU* and various other scattered texts);[79] these texts will provide the starting point for chapters 2, 3, and 4 to follow. Other important groups of extant Jeme documents in less formal texts on ostraca include the archive of a moneylender's family, which will be examined in detail in chapter 5, as well as hundreds of individual texts. Obviously, the significance of individual documentary texts varies depending on the kind and nature of the text and its length. A chatty letter (relatively uncommon, alas) or a lengthy, complex contract may provide more immediately accessible information, but even terse and formulaic texts like tax receipts can, when considered as a group, offer an enormous amount of evidence for some aspect of life at Jeme. At their best, the Jeme documents can present to the modern reader a window into the lives of these long-dead individuals, offering insight into the thoughts and beliefs of the people who produced them. These records have an immediacy and specificity that other sources often lack: in them one can read the lives of individuals as they happened, sometimes in their own words. The nature of these texts, of course, brings about a whole set of special cautions that must be considered when using them as evidence. Aside

---

[79] For discussion of the finding and early history of the Monastery of Phoibammon deposit, see see Godlewski 1986, 161–163.

from the concern raised above that such sources may reflect only certain parts of society and ignore others, documentary texts must also be filtered through sets of biases, those of the original writer, the cultural context, and even the modern editor of such documents. For the study of the lives of women, documentary texts have led to questions of whether the women are indeed writing their texts for themselves, dictating to others who may put their own slant on texts, or having little or no input into the words being ascribed to them. These questions must, of course, be kept in mind, but documentary texts remain in many ways the best sources for the lives and activities of women at Jeme.

A smaller number of the textual sources from Jeme and environs are literary or quasi-literary in nature. Most of these are not from Jeme itself but come from the monasteries of the western Theban area. Their importance for a study specifically relating to Jeme may seem tangential at first glance. But the literary environment of the western Theban monasteries is, in fact, very relevant for an understanding of the Jeme material. It is these monasteries that were responsible for most of the education in the area; in effect, they established and maintained the literate discourse of the region. Moreover, there was considerable interaction between inhabitants of the monasteries and the town, with influences going in both directions that could not help but be colored, to some extent, by the literary environment of the monasteries. Walter Crum, in a masterful study of the literary world of the west Theban monasteries, has given us a vivid picture of the literature available to the west Theban monks.[80] The books of the Old and New Testament of the Bible, of course, were by far the most frequently encountered pieces of literature in this milieu, but a wide range of apocrypha, sermons, homilies, saints' lives, martyrdoms, and a small amount of secular literature also made an appearance. As was common throughout Egypt, magic was practiced in western Thebes, as attested by a number of texts. There is also a certain amount of what one might call scientific literature available as well—medical texts in particular. Under this category one could also group the numerous school and educational texts that survive from the western Theban area, both in Coptic and in Greek.[81] Such educational texts range from simple practice writing letters

---

[80] Winlock and Crum 1926, 196–208, to be discussed more thoroughly in the following chapter.

[81] Discussed below in chapter 3.

and learning the alphabet to complex mathematical and literary exercises. These texts are valuable for what they show of the processes of learning for people in and around Jeme and of how attitudes could be shaped by the prevailing literate culture.

As the documentary texts from Jeme are so extensive and form the basis for most of the chapters that follow, it is perhaps best to begin our study of the lives of the women of Jeme in chapter 1 with a survey of the available literary sources. Not only does this have the advantage of beginning with a smaller and more discrete corpus, but it also has the advantage of indicating how women fare in texts that might be seen as more "theoretical" in nature, at least in terms of the daily lives of the women at Jeme, before viewing their lives in practice through the documentary texts. The literary texts available to the inhabitants of Jeme and environs provide the conceptual backdrop for the evidence of the documentary sources, often highlighting the gap between the ideals of the literary authors for the conduct of women's lives and the realities of women's lives as they played out in the theater of daily life at Jeme.

1

Saints, Sinners, and Women of Jeme: Literary Ideals and Documentary Realities

Although many literary sources relating to the expectations and ideals for women's lives were circulating in and around Jeme in the seventh and eighth centuries, few had any specific connection with the town, and many would have been restricted to a relatively limited audience of literate monks and clerics. We are fortunate, however, to have at least one relevant composition by a writer who lived for a time near Jeme, a homily that may well have been delivered as a sermon to a Jemean audience. The author is Pisentius, who was bishop of nearby Coptos from 599 to 632 but who spent a substantial portion of his life living near Jeme, in nearby monasteries and as a solitary monk living in abandoned ancient tombs in the mountains to the west. In addition to his literary output, Pisentius was also the subject of a biography known in different versions and was the recipient of a number of letters that give some idea of his status in and around Jeme. Taken together these sources relating to Pisentius, literary and documentary, provide insight into the ideals and expectations for women at Jeme but also hint at the ambivalence with which these models were received.

Pisentius was born in 569, somewhere in the district of Armant.[1] His religious training began at an early age: he spent several years at the Monastery of Phoibammon to the northwest of Jeme, served some time at the nearby Monastery of Epiphanius, and later was at the monastery at Tsenti, across the Nile from Coptos.[2] Pisentius became bishop of Coptos in 599 and was closely identified with this city for the rest of his life. Yet, after the Sassanian Persians invaded Egypt in 616, Pisentius fled back to western Thebes, living as a solitary monk (albeit a

---

[1] Gabra 1984 and Müller and Gabra 1991, for biographical data; the brief survey in Winlock and Crum 1926, 223-231 is still valuable, and see now van Lent and van der Vliet 1996 and Fournet 2000, 210-215. Not to be confused with (although perhaps named after) either of the two bishops of Armant named Pisentius, one from the fourth and fifth century (Gabra 1991), the other roughly a contemporary of Pisentius of Coptos (Coquin 1991b).

[2] See Coquin and Martin 1991.

distinguished one provisioned and supported by his followers) in abandoned tombs in the western Theban mountains. His activities during this period are partly documented in a dossier of letters written to him. Pisentius became a widely known figure in Jeme and environs, acting as spiritual advisor and arbiter of local morals, certainly participating in the active monastic life of the region and extending his influence to the town of Jeme itself. He remained there well after the Persians withdrew from Egypt, only returning to Coptos to die in 632. After his death, Pisentius was widely honored and revered in the region and was the subject of a lively biography.

An emphatic exposition of Pisentius's views on the proper conduct of women can be found in his only surviving literary work, a homily on the life of Onnophrios.[3] Such sermons are common in Coptic literature: writers like Pisentius often presented the life of an important saint as an example for the audience to live by. The specific audience in this case is not directly named; the title of the composition is "The discourse that Apa[4] Pisentius of the monastery of Tsenti preached concerning the holy Apa Onnophrios, to the glory of God." From the statements within the sermon, we can see that it is primarily directed to a lay audience; although Pisentius is identified as being of the monastery at Tsenti (near Coptos), the sermon itself was addressed to a more urban and secular audience. It is likely that Pisentius delivered this sermon a number of times, most probably at a church or churches in Coptos and later in Jeme when he was living nearby. While much of the text consists of general exhortation to goodness and saintliness, parts of the sermon are highly specific and include sections directed at women.

[3] Edition in Crum 1915–1917, supplemented by a description of the manuscript in Layton 1987, 152–153 (= no. 133); in the translation that follows, the passages are cited by folio number of the original manuscript. The title and beginning of another literary work by Pisentius are preserved in another manuscript in the British Library (Layton 1987, 204–205 [no. 167.1]), which also contained a text of the life of Pisentius. An apocalypse formerly attributed to Pisentius of Coptos, known only from an Arabic translation, has proven to have been written after the Muslim conquest of Egypt in 641 (see references to this author, now known as pseudo-Pisentius, in Frederick 1991; note also the discussion and translation of excerpts in van Lent and van der Vliet 1996, 207–212).

[4] Apa is a very common monastic title in Late Antique Egypt: see the discussion in Derda and Wipszycka 1994.

Early on in the text, Pisentius gives his rationale for including women in his sermon on the life of an anchoretic monk:

(4) Because of this, then, my beloved children, may everyone emulate the life of the just man and saint Apa Onnophrios, the anchorite blessed by God and man [. . .] For his life is instructional for all races of people and all ages, whether male or female.

Pisentius uses the emphasis on chastity in the life of Onnophrios to bring out those concerns about sexual activity found in his correspondence and biography. The introduction to the topic is badly damaged, but the following is clear:

(7) marriage[. . .] . . . That is to say, that the man keep to his wife and the woman herself to her man and that you be righteous in all your works, so that you, yourselves, will become like the life of this holy one.

Much later in the homily, Pisentius outlines his reasons for marriage as a preventative against fornication and the consequences for those who do not heed his words.

(28) But woe to you who are negligent concerning your own salvation and who continue persevering in their sins until they die. Who is it who has hindered you from taking a wife, O man, so that you stop your fornicating? Or who is it who has hindered you, O woman, from taking a husband according to the law, so that you not find an excuse for fornication? If it is not possible for you to exercise self-control, here is pure marriage established for men: take a wife for yourself according to the law, and woman take a husband for yourself, lest sin take you. Only do not fornicate: for you are wretched, and you will not be able to bear the punishment. O you who defile their bodies through fornication, whether men or women!

Again, it is important to note that Pisentius's concerns and strictures are for men and women equally.

More pointed are Pisentius's exhortations directed at women only, specifically women in the setting of a town, and Pisentius may well have written with the women of Jeme in mind:

(15) Guard yourselves, then, O my beloved ones and my children, in your assembly in the places of the holy ones, on the day of their holy commemoration, lest you not assemble to receive a blessing, only to receive a curse instead of a blessing. Guard yourselves once more, O my beloved children, all wisdom, whether through the sight of your eyes, or through your conduct, or through your speech. Also, as for women who go about unabashedly, their eyes staring unashamedly into the faces of every man: don't go about with uncovered faces—not just here, but also in the streets of your town. For you know now that many times I have warned you, (16) O women, concerning the commandments, but you did not pay attention and you were not ashamed and you did not stop your madness. Now, also, to you I write and beseech and to you I command emphatically in a great instruction in order that no woman at all go outside the door of her house with her head uncovered, nor that she lift her eyes up to the face of any strange man at all. Rather, may you go about on every occasion, O women, with your eyes turned down to the ground, your covering on all sides (of your body) in all propriety. But also, as for your adornment of yourselves, may it become a true measure and a respectability, while you give your hearts at all times to the word of God obediently and you thirst for him at all times. Also, teach your little sons to conduct themselves well and your daughters to love their homes and their husbands. For indeed, the teaching of our fathers is the shepherd of the children into propriety.

Pisentius closes his sermon with admonitions to follow his teachings; again we have the clear description of town life and again the address to the men about the behavior of the women.

(30/31) My brothers, put yourself beyond the wrath of God and be fearful before God. Be fearful, moreover, because of our evil habits and these dirty passions, which were made one with us, so that we may say freely: I will pass through the wall. I am speaking of the wall of passion that surrounds us—that is to say, our own sins. Yes, I beseech you, do not listen to these words only to leave them behind you; don't leave them in the church, the place wherein they have been read out to you, deprived of force. But, rather, go and let us write them upon the tablets of our heart, let us say them every hour, in every house and street and walkway, even in eating and drinking, even in our manual work. Let us proclaim them to our women, our children, our servants and our apprentices, and those who are joined with us.

Pisentius brings his sermon to a close shortly thereafter.

In his homily on Onnophrios, Pisentius clearly divides his seventh-century audience by gender, setting up a bipolar male/female opposition that runs throughout the work. He begins it by declaring his discourse instructive "for all races of people and all ages, whether male or female." Further along, he implores his male audience ("O men!") in juxtaposition to his address to the female portion of his audience ("O women!"); he pairs admonitions to "your sons" with admonitions to "your daughters." This division by biological sex may indeed reflect a literal separation of men and women in Pisentius's audience. Although the evidence for such segregated seating in churches of Pisentius's time is ambiguous, it is (and has been for several centuries) the custom in the modern Coptic church.[5] Beyond this possible literal separation, the male/female division in Pisentius's homily reflects the conception of gender based on biological difference standard in Coptic literature of the seventh and eighth centuries. Indeed, this dichotomy remained a constant from earlier literature; the sermons of the fourth- to fifth-century writer Shenoute, for example, were full of such separate invocations of male and female,[6] and this is founded on still earlier patristic and biblical sources.

[5] See, for example, Khs-Burmester 1967, 20: "The nave . . . was formerly divided into a men's section and a women's section by means of lattice screens. Nowadays, these screens no longer exist. The southern aisle, however, is reserved for women, whilst in the northern aisle men and women may sit together." See also the separate liturgies for the "churching" of women in *P.Lond.Copt.* I 841.

[6] See, for example, the works cited in Wilfong 2002a, 316–318. But note also Shenoute's addresses to an audience, "Whether male or female" (see the discussion in Krawiec 2002, 92–119), as at the beginning of Pisentius's homily.

Pisentius's male/female opposition is aided by the Coptic language itself, which is clearly marked for masculine and feminine (linguistic) gender in many contexts.[7] With regard to human beings, grammatical gender in Coptic almost invariably reflects biological sex as well as socioculturally defined gender. Singular, defined nouns are clearly marked with either masculine (*pe-/p-*) or feminine (*te-/t-*) definite articles, while singular pronominal referents in second and third person are mostly unambiguously masculine or feminine. In addition to gendered determination, certain indigenous words can be marked internally for gender—this is common in certain terms for family relationships that Pisentius used in his sermon (son/daughter: *shêre/sheere*, brother/sister: *son/sône*), as well as for categories of people and for the male and female of certain animals.[8] The Coptic language contains a heavy component of Greek vocabulary items as well (often in somewhat simplified or conventionalized spelling), which are often marked for gender. Even when terms are not internally marked for gender, they are often unambiguously male or female. Thus Pisentius, in his sermon, uses common word pairs—"man/woman" (*rôme/shime*), "male/female" (*hoout/shime*)—to make his basic gender distinctions, and these are, in their context, unmistakable. There are, however, certain subtleties afoot here: even the Coptic-less reader will notice that the words translated as "women" and "female" are the same (*shime*) but that there are separate terms for "man" (*rôme*) and "male" (*hoout*). *Shime* is a more general term, used in a variety of contexts (it can also, for example, mean "wife"),[9] always with female or feminine referent. Indeed, *shime* is the primary indigenous word that is used in Coptic to convey any notion of "woman," "female"; although a more complex Greek vocabulary was available to the Coptic author, it was hardly ever used. *Rôme*, however, is more complicated: although most often best translated as "man," it can refer to males, females, or both. When defined and singular, the

---

[7] The dialect of Coptic used by Pisentius (and the inhabitants of Jeme) was Sahidic, more or less, although note the dialectic peculiarities of the nonliterary texts of this region surveyed in Winlock and Crum 1926, 232–236 and Kahle 1954, 1:48–192. For the following points on (Sahidic) Coptic grammar, see Layton 2000—now the standard reference grammar for Sahidic Coptic, and note the system of transliteration for Coptic examples set out in the "Conventions" section at the beginning of the present book.

[8] For example, "king/queen" (*rro/rrô*) in the first category and "male snake/female snake" (*hof/hfô*) in the second; see Shisha-Halevy 1989, 20 for discussion.

[9] For a discussion (mostly on the orthography) of this term, see Young 1971.

referent of *rôme* is often clarified through the use of masculine or feminine definite articles, but in the case of plural or undefined reference, the gender of *rôme* can be unclear. So, when indefinitely marked, *shime* can only be "a woman," but *rôme*, though commonly "a man," can also be "a woman" or even genderless "a person." The ambiguity is even more pronounced in its prefixal form *rm-*; when prefixed to a place name, it denotes an inhabitant of the place, particularly a person born in the place.[10] Thus in the Jemean corpus, the use of this prefix is split fairly evenly between men and women: for example, Koloje the moneylender is called "the woman of Jeme" (*trm-jeme*), while her son Pecosh is known as "the man of Jeme" (*prm-jeme*). Pisentius's term for "male," *hoout*, is much less ambiguous and well attested in reference to human beings, quite often paired with the corresponding "female." Indeed, the biblical statement of gender distinction that so influenced Coptic writers—"Male and female he created them" (Genesis 1:27)—as translated into Coptic uses *hoout* and *shime*.

Pisentius did not address the men and women of his audience by name, only by these generic gender categories, making his message more general and universal. Had he used the personal names of the inhabitants of Jeme instead, his gender distinctions would have been almost as clear to his audience, for the names used in the Jeme texts tend to be gender-specific and often bear readily identifiable marking of gender.[11] These markings tend to focus on either terminal endings or initial letters of names. The terminal endings are almost always associated with names that come into Coptic from the Greek: names that end in *-os* are usually masculine, and names that end in *-ia* usually feminine, for example.[12] Names marked for gender by initial letters are almost always either indigenous Egyptian names (often those incorporating some form of the definite article or possessive pronoun) or Greek with the Egyptian article or pronoun added. Thus the woman's name Tagape is made up of a Greek word (*agapê*) and the Coptic feminine definite article (*t-*); the man's name Pagape is formed in the

---

[10] The latter point is made explicit in, e.g., *CPR* IV 23.6–7.

[11] For what follows, see the more general study of Coptic names in Shisha-Halevy 1989, especially 20–23, also the earlier study Heuser 1929, and note further the index to Heuser in Brunsch 1984. For names and naming practices in Roman Egypt, see Hobson 1989.

[12] Note, however, the discussion in Clackson 2000, 55 and *P.Mon.Apollo* 25 concerning the name Georgia used for a man.

same way but using the masculine definite article.[13] Some names, however, do not follow the usual patterns. A few masculine names bear predominantly feminine characteristics, and even fewer feminine names bear masculine characteristics. In some cases, this is due to names of one gender being adapted for the other through the addition of possessive pronouns, but in other cases the reasons are less clear. There are a few names that seem "sex-indifferent" or masculine/feminine "double-homonymous"[14]—names that, in effect, can apply to both men and women. The common name Koloje found in a number of Jeme texts illustrates some of the ambiguous possibilities of names in Coptic. It exists in both masculine and feminine forms that are nearly the same; the feminine adds a terminal -e in most cases. There is also a female variant Tkouloje. The name finds its way into Greek as Kolluthos, which is attested only for men. From thence it makes its way back into Coptic as Kolluthos but more often gets shortened to Kolthe or even Golthe, remaining apparently a man's name.[15]

Whether by name or by category, the women to whom Pisentius was speaking were addressed in very specific terms. The tone of his sermon, especially the sections on fornication and on women's behavior, is forceful and direct, clearly intended to prevent or change what Pisentius regards as highly undesirable behavior among his audience. The fact that he considers these injunctions necessary and the way that he phrases them, however, mean that his ideal standard of behavior was probably not being observed—that is to say, he was telling people not to do what they were already doing rather than preaching as a preventative. The extent to which Pisentius could enforce his text on the women (and men) of Jeme is not certain. Although a senior and respected figure by the time he fled to the region, Pisentius was not the head of one of the local monasteries. He sometimes threatened women and men with excommunication to get them to behave as he wanted, but it is not clear whether he could enforce such threats, as could the local bishop Abraham of the Monastery of Phoibammon, for example. Certainly, Pisentius's concerns for women's behavior and its control were shared by this Abraham and many of the other monastic leaders

[13] Pagape is much less common than Tagape in the Jeme texts; see Till 1962, s.v. Tagape, Pagape.

[14] Shisha-Halevy 1989, 22–23.

[15] Till 1962, s.v. Kolluthos, Kuluc, Kuluce, and Tkuloce.

of the area. The texts available in their monasteries show the same kinds of anxieties over women's activity outside the home and a strong desire to regulate women's sexual activity.[16] In some ways, these religious leaders could be seen as the antagonists of our history, attempting to enforce their interpretation of biblical rules for women's behavior and gender relations on a society in which standards of behavior seemed to have developed somewhat differently.

The concerns and urgencies of Pisentius and other contemporary authors to control the behavior of women stemmed, in part, from their conception of who and what women were. In the eyes of authors like Pisentius, women were distinct from men, not only because of physical difference but also because women were considered secondary derivations from men and hence inferior. The specifics of this attitude clearly derive from the work of early patristic authors, in some ways a simplification of the discussion current in the third and fourth centuries on the relative position of men and women with regard to the statement of creation in Genesis cited above.[17] In Egypt, these themes developed and became pervasive throughout Coptic literature, both in translations from the Greek and especially in original compositions in Coptic. The assumed inferiority, weakness, and, ultimately, wickedness of women became a favorite theme with Coptic writers, eventually manifesting itself in a misogynistic strain that reaches an unparalleled climax of virulence in the ninth and tenth centuries.[18] Things had not quite reached this point in the literary milieu of Jeme: women were not generally depicted as deliberately bad so much as the victims of their own sinfulness. Thus the archetypal "bad woman" is stressed in such Jeme texts as an ostracon with the biblical story of woman taken in adultery (O.Brit.Mus.Copt. 20:2), and school texts (such as O.Brit.Mus.Copt. 30:4) cite the dangers of the "wicked women." Indeed, the schoolroom seems to have been a place where such negative stereotypes of women were actively promoted and perpetuated, reinforced with each copying. Young men at the monastery of Epiphanius, for example, may have practiced their Greek on a collection of sayings from the Hellenistic author Menander (P.Mon.Epiph. 619)

---

[16] Discussed in more detail in chapter 3.

[17] Specifically Genesis 1:26–27. See Clark 1993, 117–126 for the patristic evidence.

[18] The "Songs of Good and Bad Women" in Junker 1908–1911, 2:80–87 are striking examples, all derived from passages in Proverbs.

found there: this anthology (known from other manuscripts from elsewhere in Egypt) includes a number of aphorisms about women that parallel the negative attitudes seen in other sources. Overall, the images of women in Coptic literature were not especially positive—women were often described as sources of trouble, disease, and temptation. Usually, these negative portrayals of women were relatively generic—stock figures from the Bible or disapproving generalizations about women. Otherwise, much of the literature stresses the ideals of virginity and purity for women: *Gr.Mon.Epiph.* Ap I H and F are texts on virginity from Cyril of Jerusalem and Severus of Antioch respectively, and the Greek *O.Mon.Epiph.* 600 stresses the virginity of Mary, the mother of Jesus, as does a hymn to Mary in a Greek ostracon from the Theban area.[19] The few individual women treated at all positively in the literature from Jeme and the nearby monasteries were, not surprisingly, the virgin Mary and various female saints; this, again, parallels the usage in early Christian literature, where the archetypes for women are either Eve or the virgin Mary.[20] Even the few women who are described approvingly are treated separately and distinctly from men: their differences are emphasized, and they are textually kept apart.

The virgin Mary was clearly the ultimate of the ideals for women circulating at Jeme and in the local monasteries. Although Mariolatry did not then reach the heights that it did in later periods, the virgin Mary was specially revered and honored. Mary was integral to the church in Egypt, affecting its liturgical texts, its architecture, and its iconography.[21] Marian imagery pervades the liturgy, with a great emphasis on her virginity, her charity, and her role as the mother of God. Though not as extensively developed as in the modern church, the cult of the virgin Mary seems to have had some presence at Jeme and in western Thebes. In addition to the texts mentioned above, there are at least two churches dedicated to Mary in or near the town[22] and another one at Armant commemorated in a Greek graffito at the monastery of Epiphanius (*Gr.Mon.Epiph.* 678). Based on liturgical and iconographic parallels from other contemporary

[19] Leclercq 1912.

[20] Alexandre 1992, 409–410.

[21] See the standard study Giamberardini 1974–1978, especially volumes 1 and 2; also note, for example, van Moorsel 1990, Urbaniak-Walczak 1992.

[22] The church known as "Saint Mary" (*thagia Maria*) in *P.KRU* 38.72, 58.32, etc., and what is probably another institution (*thagia Maria tryga[ta*) "of Jeme" (*P.KRU* 94.62–63); see also the church of Maria in *O.Crum* 36 (at Piohe) and 292 (at Jeme?).

sites, religious services in west Thebes must have been full of Marian imagery and allusion. Even the elaborate bronze dove lamp, already mentioned in chapter 1, from the "small church" at Jeme is inscribed with the words "one God" and "Maria."[23]

Other than the virgin Mary, the major exceptions to the generally negative portrayal of women in the literature circulating in the western Theban area are the lives of female monks. As described at the end of the preceding chapter, our knowledge of the literature circulating at and around Jeme owes much to the masterful analysis of Walter Crum of both the actual fragments of literary texts from the region and the contents of library catalogues.[24] In addition to the brief descriptions of the monastic practices of the sisters of Antony and Pachomius in their biographies, the individual biographies of female monastics, like Syncletica, were known in the Theban area. The Apa Elias library catalogue mentions one work called simply the life (*bios*) of Maria. It is not certain which Maria is meant: Coquin suggests either the life of the virgin Mary or the life of Mary Magdalen. Both of these, however, would be almost certain to have some qualifier after the name, and the chances are much greater that the text actually refers to the life of Mary of Egypt by Bishop Sophronius of Jerusalem.[25] This work is the biography of a prostitute from Alexandria who travels to Palestine, repents of her past life, and goes off into the desert—a standard trope for eastern Christian literature. The Apa Elias library catalogue also lists the life of Macrina, by her brother Gregory of Nyssa;[26] this work, which describes Macrina's life as both a solitary monk and as the head of a religious community, was important in the development of women's monasticism in Syro-Palestine in Late Antiquity. There seems to be no Coptic material relating to a local female saint Dalacina, a Diocletian-era martyr attested in later Arabic sources.[27]

[23] SB XX 14325 and references above.

[24] Winlock and Crum 1926, 196–208. One of Crum's main sources—an extensive library catalogue on an ostracon from a Monastery of Elias—has since been republished in Coquin 1975. Coquin's argument against a Theban origin is unconvincing, all the more because the text is known to have been purchased in the western Theban area at Gurna.

[25] English translation and analysis in Ward 1987, 26–56.

[26] Coptic version not identified; for the Greek version and discussion, see Albrecht 1986.

[27] See Atiya 1991; Dalcina is said to have been martyred with Chanazhum and Sophronius at Luxor on the 20th of Athyr (15 November) in the late third century CE

Regardless whether such literary portraits of women are approving or not, there is a certain consistency in their textual representation of women, as well as in their distinction of women from men. In Coptic literature, men are treated as independent beings, each with a full complement of human features and characteristics. Women, on the other hand, are depicted as miscellaneous collections of attributes and accessories. A graphic illustration of this can be found, for example, in the Coptic account of the finding of the Holy Sepulcher by Constantine I's (legendary) sister Eudoxia. Constantine and the other men are solid, defined characters; Eudoxia, however, is more an absence than a presence. Her depiction in the story is more the account of the furnishings of her room and her clothing than a depiction of her as a person. When Constantine approaches her to kiss her in greeting, his attention is directed to her eyes, mouth, breasts, and hands, never to Eudoxia herself.[28] Thus, for example, we find the treatment of the virgin Mary as a collection of body parts equated with religious symbols in *P.Lond.Copt.* I 178 and even the reduction of women to constitutent parts in Pisentius's homily on Onnophrios translated earlier (where women are admonished as to the conduct of their body parts: head covered, eyes turned down, sides covered, hearts given to God). This sort of breakdown of women into separate body parts, which is a motif throughout much of Coptic literature,[29] extended into the realm of science. In Coptic medical texts, men are taken as the norm, and their bodies are treated as systemic wholes, while women are the exception, and their bodies are broken up into "female parts" (mostly breasts and reproductive organs).[30]

We find something rather different in the literary portrait of a

---

by the archetypal pagan governor Arianos, well known from other martyrdoms and also historical sources.

[28] See Wilfong 1998c for analysis of this Constantinian legend; a related text is attested on an unusual literary ostracon from near Jeme, *O.Mon.Epiph.* 80.

[29] The main exception, interestingly enough, is in Coptic martyrdoms, where female bodies are treated as wholes and male bodies become disjointed and chopped up into constituent parts. This seems intended as a gesture of contempt on the part of the pagan officials, possibly an attempt to "masculinize" the women and "feminize" the men; for a discussion of the "disjointed female body in Coptic" in general and the implication of the martyrdoms, see Wilfong 1998a.

[30] This is, perhaps, as much a function of the Greek and Egyptian precedents for Coptic medicine as it is of Coptic conceptions of "disjointedness." Again, see Wilfong 1998a.

female monk known in copies from western Theban sources: the life of Hilaria, the legendary daughter of Byzantine Emperor Zeno, ostensibly written by Pambo of Scetis.[31] Not only are fragments of this text thought to come from the Theban area, but it is also mentioned in book lists from the region. The book list *P.Mon.Epiph.* 82 refers to the life of Hilaria directly, and the book list *O.Crum* 458 includes a work called "The Daughter of the Em[peror]" that is likely to be the Hilaria story. Hilaria's biography is of a type common in Near Eastern Christian literature—the story of a woman who disguises herself as a man to become a monk—and is one of the most fully developed examples of the genre.[32] Hilaria's escape from the court of Constantinople and subsequent journey to Alexandria and then Scetis disguised as a man are paralleled in a number of other works. But the account of Hilaria's defeminization during the process of becoming an ascetic monk in the Egyptian desert is uniquely detailed, and the whole story is full of instances of sexual ambiguity of the sort not often found in Coptic literature but part of a distinct genre in Eastern monastic literature.[33] The woman Hilaria, through disguising herself as a man (Hilarion) in order to become a monk, underwent a physical as well as conceptual transformation: her breasts shrank due to deliberate binding, while her menstrual cycle ceased because of her asceticism. But such transformation did not result in her becoming a "man"; her colleagues considered her instead to be a eunuch, primarily because she lacked the facial hair that a (typically unshaven) monk would have normally had. Thus Hilaria, as Hilarion, entered into a category seen as distinct from male and female—a "third sex" for which there was a fairly clear and standard category in the discourse of Late Antiquity: the idea of a separate gender consisting of eunuchs and others who do not exhibit primary or secondary sex characteristics of men or women but give off

[31] Text, translation, and discussion: Drescher 1947, 1-13, 69-82; see also two following notes.

[32] Note the study of stories of women "becoming" men for religious purposes, including discussion of the Perpetua legend and Coptic Gnostic evidence, Castelli 1991, and the discussions of the Hilaria story in Wilfong 1998a, and especially Hotchkiss 1996, 23, 136, where the Hilaria story is placed in context with other tales of cross-dressing female saints.

[33] The scene in which Hilaria (disguised as a male monk) heals her sick sister is likewise unusual for its implications, at least to a modern reader, of lesbian activity and incest; Drescher 1947, 77-81, and note discussions in Wilfong 2002a, 319-320; this episode is discussed from a different point of view in Brown 1988, 242-243.

mixed signals or none at all. The court eunuch was a common figure in contemporary Byzantine literature and historiography, the most visible occupant of this niche of the third gender,[34] but such eunuchs were not, as far as we know, present at Jeme, whether in person or in the literature circulating in the area. Instead, Hilaria became the literal equivalent of what all monastics were said to become metaphorically: "eunuchs for the kingdom of heaven" (Matthew 19:12).[35] The description of God found in a text attributed to Severus of Antioch written on a wall of a monastic cell connected with the Monastery of Epiphanius (*Gr.Mon.Epiph.* Ap. I D) may well be an allusion to another manifestation of the concept of a third gender—one lacking in either male or female characteristics—or even the absence of gender. The author contrasts the Christian God with pagan gods that have male and female forms: in this text the Christian God is neither male nor female. This is exceptional for Coptic texts, in which the Christian God is usually masculine; "Our father who art in heaven" is as male in Coptic as in English. But still, here again there is a third gender, this time apparently entirely neuter and apparently not a category to which women could aspire.

In any case, Pisentius, in his sermon on Onnophrios, was not concerned with nonstandard gender categories or relatively esoteric understandings of the gender of the Christian God but rather with the daily behavior of the women and men in his audience. The literary representations of women covered so far concern, on the whole, exceptional individual women of the past or negative portrayals of women in general and do not tend to show contemporary women in the course of their daily life. For such literary images, however, we may turn again to Pisentius, this time to the vivid life of Pisentius by his followers. This biography exists in at least two versions in Coptic (one in the Sahidic dialect and an apparently later version in the Bohairic dialect) and later went on to be translated into Arabic and even Ethiopic (it was being recopied in Arabic as late as the eighteenth century).[36] The biography of Pisentius devotes much attention to his time in the

[34] Ringrose 1994 and Tougher 1997; for general discussion of the phenomenon of the "third sex," see Herdt 1994.

[35] See the discussion in Krawiec 2002, 126–132.

[36] See Gabra 1984 for detailed analysis of the various traditions through which this work passed and extensive bibliography; note also the survey in van Lent and van der Vliet 1996. One Arabic version is available in O'Leary 1930.

mountains to the west of Jeme as a solitary monk and refugee from the Persian invasion. The narrative follows the usual pattern of such works in Coptic: a series of episodes designed to show the virtues of the holy man, with major life milestones recorded and a generous helping of miracles. Pisentius's life is, perhaps, more vibrant and entertaining to a modern reader than most Coptic saints' lives. One of the best-known (and most interesting) episodes recounts the story of Pisentius finding an ancient Egyptian mummy: he revives the mummy, who repents of its life as a pagan and tells of the torments of hell that it is enduring.[37] This episode and others provide a wealth of circumstantial detail that helps us flesh out the setting of Pisentius's exile in western Thebes. The biography, moreover, shows Pisentius in select interactions with the women of Jeme and environs, providing another perspective on his ideals for women and their behavior as articulated in his sermon.

As depicted in the biography, Pisentius's interactions with women were limited and often indirect—the message is that he had little to do with them in the normal course of events, and this is in keeping with the general injunctions that monks (and presumably their superiors) should avoid contact with women as a means of avoiding temptation. The most direct interaction that Pisentius has with women is in connection with the healing of illnesses (remembering that one of the goals of the biography was to succeed in attributing miracles to its subject). In the biography the stories of healing are used to show off Pisentius's powers; in these accounts, however, the healing is effected by the actions of the women, while Pisentius remains passive. The Sahidic version includes a woman suffering from an uncontrollable menstrual flow who touches the hem of Pisentius's garment and is healed (32a-b).[38] Less graceful is the action in the Bohairic version: Pisentius flees the sick women who come to him, covering his head and face (avoiding contact with the women as a monk), and the women instead eat the dust from the print of his right foot and are healed.[39] Female animals receive somewhat different treatment: Pisentius touches

---

[37] Appearing in the Bohairic version but not the Sahidic; see the English translation and notes by Battiscomb Gunn in Lewis and Burstein 2001, 101–110.

[38] In the citations that follow, I translate from the Sahidic text in Budge 1913, cited by manuscript folio number; in spite of the flaws of the edition (corrected in part in Crum 1914), this is the most complete Sahidic version of the biography available. Episodes unique in Coptic to the Bohairic version are from Amélineau 1889.

[39] Amélineau 1889, 289–290.

a pregnant ewe, and his hand sinks into its womb; when the lamb is born, it bears the sign of a cross where Pisentius touched it (65b).

Otherwise, women appear in Pisentius's biography in less direct ways, and again in ways that show off his powers and acumen. Thus, an incident involving a shepherd rapist—an act of sexual violence against a woman—is treated primarily as an excuse for Pisentius to show off his supernatural powers: The shepherd came to Pisentius for a blessing, only to be shouted at and called a sinful man by Pisentius, who orders his disciple (and subsequent biographer) John to haul the shepherd away. John asks the shepherd why Pisentius might have reacted so violently:

> (58b) The shepherd answered him, saying: Why did I not die today when I got up from sleeping? Now it happened to me while I was pasturing (my sheep) today among the acacia bushes: A woman that I know passed by on the road. I overpowered her in my foolishness and had sex with her,[40] thinking (59a) that the great man would not know.

When he realizes that Pisentius does know, the shepherd is struck with remorse—at being caught. The story continues with the shepherd giving John some cheeses to give to Pisentius (without telling him whom they are from); John mixes them in with other cheeses, only to have Pisentius pick out those from the shepherd (another amazing feat) and scold John for trying to deceive him. Nothing further is mentioned about the woman.

Another episode in the biography provides insight into the origin of some of Pisentius's attitudes. A father brings his son to Pisentius, who advises that the father take a wife for the son; the father protests, but Pisentius points out that his son has been sleeping with a woman in the village. Pisentius has been informed of the situation by "some men who are worth believing"—an apparent reference to the sort of local information (mostly gossip about the behavior of women) that we know from other sources that Pisentius liked to collect. Pisentius tells the man to marry his son to this woman immediately, politely

---

[40] The Coptic uses a strong, aggressive verb (*amahte*) for the first clause: "I (forcefully) overpowered her," while the verb in the second clause (*shôpe*) is vague, almost euphemistic—literally "I existed with her."

threatening to refuse communion to the son if this is not done (64a–65b) and citing a law from Deuteronomy to justify his stance. Significantly, the quotation (Deuteronomy 22:29) describes what is to be done in the case of a man commiting forcible sexual acts against a woman he is not betrothed to: he must marry the woman and pay a fine to her father.[41] This case helps illustrate how Pisentius's attitudes toward women were shaped by the Old Testament. In other cases involving women, he cites scripture from the Old Testament as well. Perhaps the most striking involves a woman with a jealous husband (69a–74a), in which Pisentius places the burden of proof on the woman. Pisentius tells the husband that, if she bears a male child, she is innocent, but if she bears a female child, he is to throw her out of the house because she must be guilty. As precedent for his test, he cites Numbers 5:12, where the accused woman is to drink "the water of the curse" (*pmoou mpsahou*), whereupon she will conceive a male child (if innocent) or be covered with pustules and leprosy (if guilty). The woman with the jealous husband, being innocent, bears a male child whom the parents name, of course, after Pisentius. This reliance on Old Testament law for his attitudes toward women is in contrast to Pisentius's treatment of men, whose behavior is judged on precedents in the Gospels and Pauline letters. Beside such strong cases, Pisentius's general warnings to young monks about the danger of "the woman who is wicked" in the town (23a) seem almost irrelevant.

We are in the highly unusual position of being able to control the hagiography of Pisentius's biography to some extent with documentary evidence—an extensive dossier of letters to Pisentius and related documents that give a direct window on his interaction with the women of Jeme and environs. Indeed, Pisentius is perhaps the only author of Late Antique Egypt represented by examples of his literary output, biography, and documentary evidence.[42] The Pisentius correspondence was discovered in the course of antiquities hunting in the early nineteenth century; the bulk of this material found its way to the Louvre and, although indifferently published, is a remarkable resource.[43] The

---

[41] If the woman had consented to the sexual activity, the biblical passage calls for her to be stoned.

[42] We have, of course, documentary texts and literary output for the sixth-century poet Dioscorus of Aphrodito but not the biography, which had to wait until the appearance of MacCoull 1988.

[43] P.*Pisentius*, although not all of these papyri are part of the Pisentius

documents that make up this dossier are mostly letters directed to Pisentius during his refugee period in the Theban area; with a few possible exceptions,[44] the letters are not by Pisentius himself. Unfortunately, few of the letters are intact, and many are mere scraps. Taken with the biographical texts, however, these letters give a vivid insight into aspects of life in western Thebes in the seventh century and, of the more than sixty letters in the corpus, roughly a third concern women in some way. A few are known to have been written by women,[45] while the rest are written by men about women. Not surprisingly, a number of the letters relate to religious activities and institutions; for example, there is a letter from two women (possibly monastics) offering, "If you want us to bind the young women (in monastic habit),[46] may your fatherly lordship command us and we will bind them until the festival of the cross" (*P.Pisentius* 28). More often, however, the writers ask for help or advice. Later on in this same letter from the two women, they ask Pisentius to accept clothing they have made, expressing concern about their work:

> Have pity then our holy lord father, for indeed you have mercy on us on every occasion and you do it for us also. Now, we are

correspondence, and other documents from the corpus are published separately; see Wilfong 1989, 113–114 for a brief history of the papyri and references and now Van Lent and van der Vliet 1996, and note the photographs in Fournet 2000, 210–215. The main group of these papyri in the Louvre was poorly published in Revillout 1900–1914; a new edition of the entire corpus is being prepared by a group headed by Jacques van der Vliet. For the purposes of the present work, I have also made use (with the kind permission of Jaromir Malek) of the transcriptions by Walter E. Crum in the Griffith Institute, Crum Notebooks 40 (summaries of contents) and 84 (transcriptions and notes). As these translations were made without the benefit of the forthcoming new edition, however, they must be considered provisional. A few pieces outside the core group of Louvre papyri are also relevant: the document in Sottas 1922, the Phillips papyri in *O.CrumST* and *SB Kopt.* I 295, along with others cited in Fournet 2000, 215n51. Several documents from the Monastery of Epiphanius can be identified with varying degrees of certainty as relating to Pisentius of Coptos (see the discussion in Winlock and Crum 1926, 223–231).

[44] *P.Pisentius* 18bis (Crum, Notebook 84, p. 59 suggests that this is in Pisentius's hand); also some of the pieces in the Monastery of Epiphanius texts may be by Pisentius, for which see Winlock and Crum, 1926, 213n29, 225nn3–4.

[45] *P.Pisentius* 28, 30, 39, *SB Kopt.* I 295 and also Sottas 1922 for certain. Other documents may also be from women; the writer's name and other internal markings for the gender of the writer are lacking on at least a third of the corpus as published.

[46] A common way of referring to the investiture of monastics.

your servants, being Tesheere and Koshe. Here are two tunics with sleeves and two wraps(?). I sent them to your holy fatherly lordship. If they please you, have pity on me and accept them— I am Koshe (writing this), for indeed you know that I am very distressed about my handicrafts. Now as for the two hoods that I shall make, I shall send them to you also and they will come with the garments. Now, as for the five tunics, I sent them to your holy fatherly lordship—I being Tsheere, your servant, (and the tunics) being four monastic (?) tunics and one secular[47] tunic. Be so good then my lord father and have pity on me because I am distressed and I am (troubled?) about the wool, which I received because [. . . .][48]

Still more typical are the letters from widows requesting help, usually in reference to financial problems incurred because of their husbands' deaths. Good examples of these are *SB Kopt.* I 295, a petition for help, and *P.Pisentius* 39, apparently a reply to a condolence letter from Pisentius:

I received the writings of your love (*agapê*)—you sent them to my miserableness [. . .] you remember me in my widowhood [. . . .]

Such letters show at least a belief on the part of the female writers in Pisentius's concern about their conditions; this is paralleled in the letters of men who write about women's states of being. Also in this category belongs a tantalizing scrap apparently about the abandonment of a female child: the legible fragments read:

. . . to your lordship, so that you shall hear [. . . namely] a little girl. She is useless [. . .] the one (fem.), but I abandoned the district (?)[. . .] should persuade him and he depart with [. . .] with me to my house. The little girl [. . .] go to the water and I was on the point of death, but I did not approach [. . .] little

---

[47] The word is *kosmikon*, so "worldly, secular," contrasted with *sakho*, in this context probably a monastic official; see the discussion below in chapter 4 and Delattre 2001.

[48] *P.Pisentius* 28 again. The edition in Revillout is completely incorrect; in the Crum transcription (Crum Notebook 84, pp. 44–45) the fragment *P.Pisentius* 34 is joined to the end of this letter.

[. . .] he was not patient, but nevertheless [. . .]want it. May he
abandon her [. . .]. (*P.Pisentius* 13).

One might also add here a reference to a letter about a woman whose
husband is in prison (*P.Pisentius* 5:48–49).

But the letters to Pisentius about women are more concerned with
women's actions than their health. Only occasionally do Pisentius's
correspondents write about women in the religious communities of
the region—where Pisentius's authority and control were most powerful
and where his most immediate interests lay. A complaint about a female
monastic is found in a badly broken passage:

> We inform you, then, [that (the woman does not behave)] like
> a female monastic (*monakhê*) of this [community?] but rather
> like a worldly woman [. . .]. (*P.Pisentius* 56)[49]

Otherwise, both in the letters and in the biography, Pisentius's
correspondents are mostly concerned with women in the secular sphere.
A complicated and badly damaged account (apparently with a reply by
Pisentius himself) concerns a woman whose daughter has been unjustly
imprisoned and who, herself, fights (perhaps physically) with the town
magistrate over the matter.[50] More typical are complaints about women's
behavior with regard to men: one very fragmentary letter is written
"concerning a woman": ". . . namely that she enchanted (*mageue*) the
sons [of . . .]" (*P.Pisentius* 35).

Crimes against women are found in the letters and biography; in
these cases, Pisentius's primary concern is with the criminals (without
exception male) rather than with the female victims. Kidnapping and
rape of women figure frequently in these texts, such as in the fragmentary
letter where some men, possibly the invading Sassanian Persians,[51] are
going "from place to place, forcibly carrying off the daughters of the
men." Two of the letters concern the abduction and apparent rape of a
woman by a shepherd. One document gives a brief narrative:

[49] A few lines down there is reference to something that a young woman did,
again badly broken.

[50] *P.Pisentius* 18, and 18bis for the reply in which Pisentius seems to be forwarding
on the original letter as evidence.

[51] *P.Pisentius* 1; early in the document, they are called *atsoor*, that is "Assyrians,"
and there is a reference to the "daughter of the Euphrates."

A man among us, a shepherd [did something] and he carried
off a young woman with violence, while her parents [. . .] his
house. Her parents left, crying out [. . .]. (*P.Pisentius* 54)

The breaks in the text become longer, but it appears that the writer of
the letter becomes involved, retrieving the girl and restoring her to her
home. Later on, the parents are evidently asked if they want to throw
the girl out of the house, apparently because her chances for marriage
are ruined.[52] Another very fragmentary letter may be concerned with
the same shepherd but does not mention the fate of the woman
(*P.Pisentius* 55).[53] One is, of course, reminded of the incident involving
the shepherd rapist in the biography of Pisentius; although the details
as reported do not precisely parallel the events in the letters, there may
be some connection between these episodes.

The behavior of women and men in relation to each other occupies
most of the space in the correspondence devoted to women. Betrothals
and marriages are a common topic: in one letter, the writer is a go-
between who arranges that Psmou "give his daughter to" Hjil's son "as
wife."[54] Hjil and Psmou "pray together" to signify agreement, as
described in a subsequent letter.[55] In addition to the daughter, the same
Psmou also had a son, who was having some sort of problem with the
dowry for his prospective wife.[56] In a scrap, possibly a query as to the
propriety of the action, a man is described as being married to (Coptic
hmoos mn, literally "dwelling with"—not an unusual way of indicating
marriage in Coptic documents) his niece—more specifically, his brother's
daughter (*P.Pisentius* 26). After marriage, the subsequent behavior of
wives was a topic of censure. One letter describes how a woman's
"husband found her in the courtyard with a man, (namely) her lover"
(*P.Pisentius* 38). Pisentius advised "don't hinder her husband from
reconciling with her," and the writer adds, "So, I did not hinder [him.]"

---

[52] The passage is very broken: possibly read the phrases "for i[f you?] want to cast
her out," followed by a long break, then "concerning the ma[tter, for] who will become
husband [to her?]"

[53] For the traditional role of shepherds as disruptive elements in Late Antique
Egypt, see Keenan 1985.

[54] *P.Pisentius* 16; the letter is written to Pisentius by the go-between.

[55] *P.Pisentius* 15.

[56] *P.Pisentius* 19; the Coptic word used is *skhat*, discussed below in chapter 5, but
the precise problem is unclear.

An officially mandated reconciliation did not always work out, as in a follow-up letter regarding advice

> that she reconcile with her husband [. . . to] compel that she reconcile. But he left with his men, for he could not persuade her. When I saw, then, that she would not be reconciled, I wrote for your orders and I excommunicated him since the little fast. (*P.Pisentius* 18ᵗᵉʳ)

The fact that the man is being punished indicates that the writer saw him as being at fault in the matter, but the fact that the man has gone with a group of others suggests that the persuasion involved might be closer to what we might call coercion. Part of the urgency in the correspondence for reconciliation of broken marriages seems to have been to prevent the potential aftermath of separation:

> She departed from him up until now. Now, then, she gave birth in this month. He (the husband) came to me, saying: "It is not mine, namely the little girl that she bore but whom she conceived in secret from me. For indeed it is only six months since I reconciled[57] with her." Now, look, I sent him to your fatherhood. Be so merciful as to listen to him so that he may tell you his story. As for what you will decide, write it to us. (*P.Pisentius* 17)

Complaints about spousal behavior are found from the woman's side too but less frequently.[58]

Much of Pisentius's correspondence is concerned with marital problems and shows a great insistence on reconciliation when possible to avoid divorce. Pisentius amassed an enormous amount of intelligence—one is tempted to call it gossip—about not only his correspondents but also their families and neighbors. Indeed, he seems to have encouraged his correspondents to report on the activities of others—given the number of people who seem to have come to him for

---

[57] Literally, "cohabited with."

[58] *P.Pisentius* 14 (a woman having some sort of problem with a husband in a very fragmentary passage at the beginning), *P.Pisentius* 41 (fragmentary reference to a woman cast out by her husband, possibly involving the same Elias from the preceding text?).

advice and help, he seems to have commanded a sizeable network of information about the inhabitants of Jeme and environs. This makes the snippets that we get in his now very fragmentary correspondence all the more tantalizing and, ultimately, unsatisfactory for understanding the lives of the women of Jeme.

But it is in the Pisentius correspondence that we begin to see the activities and even the actual voices of the women of Jeme, filtered, it is true, in many cases by a scribe or reported second-hand, but still we begin to hear women speak in something of their own words. Fortunately, we are not reliant only on the Pisentius dossier for our information: it is, in fact, some of the least direct evidence we have. In succeeding chapters, we will see women's lives more directly through the documentation of their activities in and around Jeme. Pisentius's sermon, his biography, and his correspondence have set up the patterns by which women were expected to live, but the direct documentary sources will show how these lives actually played out.

2

Elizabeth and an Abigaia or Two:
Some Women of Jeme

Legal documents of the early eighth century relating to a woman named Elizabeth and her niece Abigaia provide perhaps the best introduction to the realities of women's lives at Jeme.[1] Elizabeth was probably born around 680 to a man named Epiphanios and his wife Maria, who also had another, perhaps older, daughter named Tshenoute. Tshenoute married a man named Samuel, who was a deacon—a church official— and they had a daughter named Abigaia, who was probably born around the year 700. Tshenoute and Samuel also had two sons, probably born sometime after Abigaia's birth, named Stephanos and Chareb, the latter being named after his paternal grandfather. Elizabeth, meanwhile, had married a man named Loula, and they had a son named Georgios. (See family tree in fig. 3.) All of these people were inhabitants of Jeme, most if not all having been born there. They may not have been the highest elites in Jeme society, but they owned a certain amount of real estate and moveable property (as we will see shortly) and seem to have been relatively comfortable by Jeme standards.

At some point around or after 700, Elizabeth's husband Loula died and she married again: her second husband was a man named Abraham, son of Theodoros. Abraham stands out from the rest of the extended family in that he came from Syene, the major city considerably to the south (about 175 kilometers) of Jeme. Abraham moved to Jeme when he married Elizabeth but had to return to Syene at least once after the marriage to take care of business interests, and his parents remained there. Elizabeth and Abraham had at least two children, a son Isak and a daughter Kyra, possibly more, while

[1] The following information is drawn from the Coptic documents translated below. These documents were the subject of an essential study by Arthur Schiller (Schiller 1952), which has been a crucial resource for this chapter. The reconstruction of the family history that follows, however, is that of the present author, giving a number of details not found in Schiller's study and differing in a number of points of interpretation. The translations of individual documents in Till 1954 and Till 1964 provide, in many cases, much better readings than Schiller.

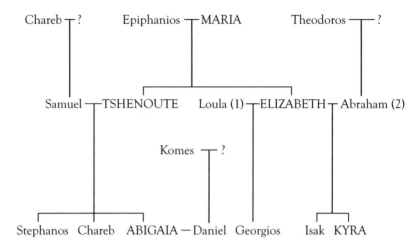

Fig. 3. Family tree of Elizabeth and Abigaia (women's names in all capitals)

Abraham may have acted as stepfather to Elizabeth's son by her first marriage, Georgios. Meanwhile, Elizabeth's niece Abigaia eventually married a Jeme man named Daniel, son of a man named Komes. (Again see the family tree in fig. 3.)

Sometime in the early 700s or 710s, the first in a series of events occurred that eventually resulted in a dispute within the family: Elizabeth's father Epiphanios died. After her father's death Elizabeth brought her widowed mother Maria to live in the home she shared with her husband Abraham and her children. This arrangement came about in part because Tshenoute, Maria's other daughter, had also died by this time, leaving Abigaia without a mother. Abigaia's father appears not to have remarried and instead became a monk in the western Theban hills. Elizabeth's husband Abraham had to go back to Syene to deal with the sale of a house and other property inherited, apparently, from his mother, whose name is not known. Whatever the precise source of the house, he sold it for a substantial amount of money and further managed to sell some of the moveable property from this inheritance to a man who lived across the river from Jeme at Nê (Thebes).[2] Abraham gave a portion of this money to his father Theodoros for an offering (on behalf of his dead wife?), but the rest

[2] The specific amounts of money involved, and their buying power, will be discussed below.

he brought back to Jeme for himself and his wife Elizabeth, who used some of the money for the support of her mother Maria and her son Georgios by her first marriage. Georgios seems to have reached majority around this time, since Elizabeth had to help him pay taxes (normally only levied on adults). She also paid other expenses for him, including the hiring of a blacksmith for him at Klusme—quite a distance away, suggesting that Georgios had done considerable traveling at some point.

Sometime before or in the year 719, Maria died. Upon her death, property belonging to her (including property inherited from her husband) needed to be divided among her heirs. Of immediate and particular interest was a house—probably Maria's most valuable possession—that was to be divided between Maria's daughter Elizabeth and her granddaughter Abigaia. The division of this house was outlined in a long legal document of settlement,[3] drawn up in Abigaia's name. The document itself (*P.KRU* 35) was a long papyrus roll, 144 cm long by 18 cm wide, made of nine sheets of papyrus pasted together and inscribed in ink in 115 lines of Coptic, with a fragmentary protocol in Kufic Arabic script and in Greek at the beginning.[4] This document is part of an archive of legal texts that were the first Coptic texts from Jeme to come to the attention of scholars. This archive, consisting of papyri and parchments deposited for safekeeping in a wooden chest in the Monastery of Phoibammon and later abandoned, was discovered in the ruins of the monastery between 1850 and 1855 and subsequently dispersed on the antiquities market.[5] The document that Abigaia drew up on 6 October 719 begins with a pious invocation of the trinity; following that, the document proper begins:

[3] The standard reference for the law and legal procedure underlying the documents to be studied in this and following chapters is Steinwenter 1955, noting also references in MacCoull 1991. Although not specifically concerned with Coptic documents, for references on women and the law in Byzantine/Late Antique Egypt, see Arjava 1996 and especially the monumental study Beaucamp 1990 and 1992, taking into account the comments in Bagnall 1995. For legal settlements in Late Antique Egypt, see the essential work on the subject, Gagos and van Minnen 1994.

[4] This was standard in Coptic legal documents on papyrus or parchment from after the Muslim conquest of Egypt; these protocols are often helpful in dating texts.

[5] These documents were collected together in Crum and Steindorf 1912 as *P.KRU*. See Godlewski 1986, 55ff., where the problems with this find are summarized and conclusively settled. For a recent, detailed analysis of two legal documents from this find, *P.KRU* 22 and 29, with valuable references and observations, see Richter 1998.

On this day, the eighth of Phaophe of the third indiction year,[6] before the most honored and exalted Biktor, son of the late Thomas, and Ananias, son of the late Abraam, the *lashanes*[7] of the Kastron Jeme,[8] in the district of the city of Armant: greetings.[9] I, Abigaia, daughter of Samuel, deacon and monk of the mountain of Jeme,[10] my mother being the late Tshenoute, with Daniel, my husband, agreeing in everything, (we being) people of the Kastron Jeme in the district of the city of Armant: we write to Elizabeth, daughter of the late Epiphanios, her mother being the late Maria, being people of the Kastron Jeme in the same district. We make this settlement with each other and we provide the ones who will sign below with trustworthy and believable witnesses for them; these who will act as witnesses to this settlement (do so) at our own request: greetings. (*P.KRU* 35.6–22)

So here we have the introduction to the individuals involved in the division, as well as provision for the witnessing of the document.

Abigaia's document continues with a description of the portion of the property going to Elizabeth, along with her rights regarding it:

Since at this time we agreed unanimously among ourselves to divide the house of our deceased one among ourselves in this manner, so that the portion of each will be evident, and we indicated them for you, namely, Elizabeth, the sister of my late

---

[6] Events in legal documents were most commonly dated by their timing in a fifteen-year administrative cycle known as the indiction. Although this was usually adequate for the needs of the people involved in the transaction, it can be a source of considerable frustration for a modern reader attempting to date a particular document. A handy table of indictions and their correspondence to the years of the Jeme documents can be found in Till 1962, 237–239.

[7] The *lashane* was the town magistrate/administrator; at Jeme there were usually two *lashanes* at any given time.

[8] See the discussion of this term in the introduction as an indication for the community at and around Jeme.

[9] It is common to find Jeme legal texts such as this document written using some of the conventions of letters; hence the greetings here.

[10] This signifies that Samuel was a monk in the west Theban mountains but does not indicate for certain whether he was part of an organized monastic community or a solitary monk living in an abandoned tomb.

mother. You have received the room beneath the stairs and the room whose door opens north onto the stairs, and you control the whole veranda, whose door opens north onto the stairs, and the entire grain storage area,[11] which is above the veranda, up to the top. As for the one who wants to build, it is his [sic] to the limit, and he can bring his staircase up to his portion. The outer door, the foyer, the water-holder,[12] and the stairway are common areas between us, unless building is carried out on the house: if building is done, then each one will bring his staircase to his portion, in such a way that we are each satisfied with the two portions. (*P.KRU* 35.22–38)

So Elizabeth receives four specifically identified rooms of the house for her portion.

This is an appropriate point to examine, a bit more thoroughly than in chapter 1, the layout of a Jeme house.[13] Figure 4 shows a hypothetical reconstruction of the house divided between Elizabeth and Abigaia.[14] The house is entered by a foyer that contains a large holder for water jars (specified as being held in common. The foyer leads to a staircase, also held in common, that leads to the other parts of the house. Downstairs we find rooms below street level. Of these, Elizabeth is specifically ceded the space beneath the stairs. This may not seem like a desirable part of the house, but, in fact, it was an important space especially associated with women—an area traditionally identified as the place where women go when they are menstruating— which will be discussed in more detail below. Above that was a room, identified by the Greek term *symposion*, literally a dining room, but more likely to be a combination of reception room and dining room.[15]

[11] Schiller translates this as "threshing floor" (Schiller 1952, 338), which is literally correct but extremely unlikely to have been located above a veranda in a private house! Till's "Speicher" (Till 1954, 112n24) is more probably correct here.

[12] Schiller translates "conduits" (ibid.), apparently envisioning a house with indoor plumbing, but this is more likely to be the stands for water jars with channels for saving the runoff from condensation. These are common in Jeme houses; see the examples in Hölscher 1954, 59–60 and plate 36.

[13] For houses and their parts in Roman and Late Antique Egypt, the essential reference is Husson 1983.

[14] This figure is a composite of various houses from the Jeme excavation designed to incorporate the different features found in the house described in the documents.

[15] See Husson 1983, 267–271 for this term in the Greek papyri.

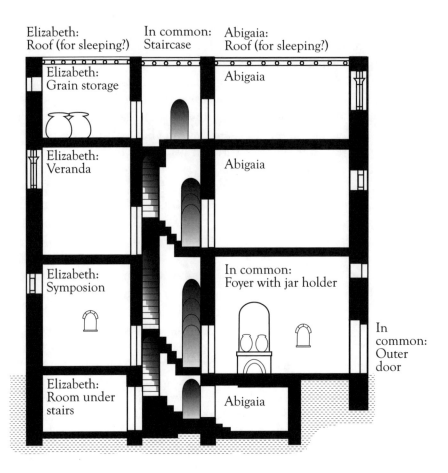

Elizabeth:
Roof (for sleeping?)

In common:
Staircase

Abigaia:
Roof (for sleeping?)

Elizabeth:
Grain storage

Abigaia

Elizabeth:
Veranda

Abigaia

Elizabeth:
Symposion

In common:
Foyer with jar holder

In
common:
Outer
door

Elizabeth:
Room under
stairs

Abigaia

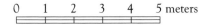

0   1   2   3   4   5 meters

Fig. 4. Reconstruction of the house divided between Elizabeth and Abigaia
(a composite based on houses in Hölscher 1954)

Above this was a veranda—a roofed open porch that would have been a pleasant place to sit and/or sleep—and above that was a grain storage area at the top of the house. Opposite these were two larger rooms that presumably made up Abigaia's share. The women would have also had the roof space, which may have been used for sleeping in warm weather. The asymmetrical arrangement of longer rooms on one side of the staircase than the other is common among Jeme houses. Given the hypothetical reconstruction in figure 4, Abigaia receives fewer rooms than Elizabeth, but Abigaia's rooms are larger, and each woman has nearly equal floor space. This space is typical of Jeme houses: just under 650 square feet (70 square meters), nearly 800 square feet (90 square meters) if one counts the roof space. The settlement clearly envisions that Elizabeth might have wanted to separate her portion of the house from Abigaia's, as there is a provision for making a separate, external staircase to Elizabeth's rooms that would lead down to Kulol Street. Although such an external staircase might protrude significantly into the street, a glance at the map of Jeme shows that this would not necessarily have been a matter of concern; it might have been possible to modify the existing staircase with an exit to the street with minimal inconvenience to anyone.

Abigaia goes on to state the precise location of the house:

> These are the boundaries of that house on the four sides: South: the house of the late Souros, East: the house of Philotheos, North: the house of Antonios, son of Paulos, West: Kulol Street and the Authentes Gate.[16] See, these are the boundaries of that house in the four directions. (*P.KRU* 35.38–42)

This identification of the location of the house was clearly required in a legal document such as this to make sure that there was no ambiguity; we have already noted (in the introduction) the use of street names at Jeme. The identification of the boundaries by the owners of neighboring houses, street names, and landmarks is entirely typical of Jeme documents.

Finally, Abigaia has noted further common property, although this has clearly required some negotiation:

---

[16] This street and gate are known from other Jeme documents, again illustrating the practice of naming streets at Jeme (Timm 3:1018–1019).

> The wall that is between will be held in common between us up to the top (lit. wind): I was paid a gold tremis (for my rights) for the southern part and the northern part in the way we agreed among ourselves. (*P.KRU* 35.43–46)

This seems to refer to a wall between the two sets of rooms. Abigaia has received a relatively small sum of money for ceding complete control over the wall, but it is not entirely clear why; perhaps the wall was primarily in contact with Abigaia's portion, while Elizabeth's rooms were bounded by the walls of the common staircase. And again, she has allowed for the possibility of further building by Elizabeth:

> You, Elizabeth, may go through the door into the grain storage area, which is over the veranda, (but) when you want to build onto the grain storage area, it is you who are in charge. You may take the stairs within the door of the grain storage up to the top. (*P.KRU* 35.46–50)

This provision may suggest that the grain storage area is not as accessible as it could be; perhaps this staircase is an improvement discussed by Epiphanios and Maria but never carried out.

The document continues with standard assurances as to the endurance of the settlement agreement, as well as the mutually satisfactory and voluntary nature of the agreement:

> You, Elizabeth, daughter of the late Epiphanios, from now, have and will have control over these portions of the house yourself, and your children, and your grandchildren, and all those who will come after you, to give them away or to bestow them or to sell them. We are satisfied with each other in every way concerning every settlement in every thing, I desiring (it) and agreeing, without any falsehood, fear, violence, coercion, deception, harm, seizure, fraud, there not being a bit of coercion put on us, but in our decision we make a declaration to each other about the inheritance of the house of our deceased ones, as it was left to us. (*P.KRU* 35.50–63)

The clauses disclaiming any threat of violence or coercion are standard in Jeme contracts and could easily be taken as mere formula; as we have seen in the Pisentius correspondence, however, the possibility of these forms of persuasion was perhaps not so remote, and thus these clauses may have served a very real purpose. These statements are followed by standard clauses asserting that Abigaia and those connected with her will never dispute the agreement, on penalty of a fine:

> It is not permitted that we, or child of ours, or heir of ours, or even a legal representative of ours, bring charge against each other at all. As for the one who will challenge or undertake to disturb this settlement, he shall have to pay four ounces of gold, equaling 24 solidi, of pure gold, by the standard of the Kastron Memnonion. (*P.KRU* 35.63–69)

The fine set for attempting to dispute this settlement is substantial. The solidus (plural solidi),[17] alternately known in these documents as the nomisma and holokottinos (and roughly equivalent to an Arab dinar), was the largest denomination of coin in use at Jeme, typically specified as a gold coin. A solidus equaled three tremisses (also gold), and one frequently encounters fractions of the tremis as well. Smaller denominations include the carat (kerat, keration: usually referred to in Coptic documents as a bronze coin and usually reckoned at the rate of 24 carats = 1 solidus), the *she* (a smaller denomination bronze coin, usually reckoned at 10 to 12 to the carat, so 240 to 288 *she* to the solidus),[18] and the *cor* (960 or thereabouts to the solidus). One solidus was a substantial amount of money (frequently the amount of a year's taxes), and 24 solidi could easily have bought Elizabeth's entire portion. As we will see below, however, it is debatable whether such fines were ever assessed and paid—the amount may be symbolic more than a realistic threat.

Abigaia continued the elaboration of her oath:

[17] Stefanski and Lichtheim 1952, 3–4 for all monetary matters that follow, except where noted; terminology for denominations of money have been standardized, as noted in the Conventions section above. For the solidus/nomisma in earlier Greek papyri, see also Maresch 1994.

[18] For the *she*, see also Brunsch 1979, where 286 is presumably for 288.

> After these things that I have entered into, I have commanded
> the power of this settlement and every thing written in it. Upon
> all these things we swear by the holy, same-substanced trinity,
> and the power, and the strength, and the endurance of our
> lordly rulers, these who are established through God, that there
> will be no disturbance of this settlement and everything written
> in it. (*P.KRU* 35.69–76)

Abigaia swears by "the holy, same-substanced trinity," an unequivocal
assertion of Monophysite belief that would have been highly
controversial a hundred years earlier under Byzantine rule. After the
Muslim conquest, however, this statement of Monophysite belief was
standard in Jeme contracts. Although Abigaia has here sworn a solemn
oath with great religious implications, we will see that this may not
have held much meaning for her.

Finally, the document gives the formal agreement of Abigaia to the
terms of the settlement:

> Being assured, then, with each other, we establish this
> settlement document in duplicate: it will be certain and valid,
> in every place that it is shown. We have been asked and we
> have declared. We have made it public in the month of
> Phaophe, day 8, in the 3rd indiction (= 6 October 719),
> beginning with God. I, Abigaia, daughter of Samuel, the monk,
> with Daniel, my husband, agreeing with me in everything, do
> agree to this settlement, the oath and the fine, and everything
> written in it as set forth before. I Johannes, son of Lazaros,
> wrote for them since they cannot write. (*P.KRU* 35.76–86)

Note the notice of making the agreement public on a specific date—
this is essential in that it makes the settlement and its terms known
beyond the signatories. Abigaia has identified herself as agreeing to the
settlement, along with her husband. But also note the following line:
the signature of a scribe who wrote for Abigaia and her husband because
neither could write. It is not particularly uncommon in Jeme legal
documents to find both men and women being unable to write and
using scribes to write for them.

Following Abigaia's affirmation, we find a long series of witness

statements—these are reproduced below in full to give an idea of the
number of witnesses involved in such an agreement, as well as an idea
of the makeup of a typical body of witnesses:

> I, Pesentius, son of Stephanos, act as witness. I, Johannes,
> son of the late Biktor, act as witness. I, Pshere, by God's grace
> the most humble priest and hegumen of the Holy Church of
> Jeme, act as witness. I, Petros, son of Andreas, act as witness.
> I, Athanasios, son of the late Jeremias, act as witness to this
> settlement. I, Andreas, son of the late Lazaros, write for him
> and act as witness to this settlement. I, Komes, the most
> humble priest of the (Church of the) holy Apa Patermouthios
> of the Kastron Jeme, I act as witness. I, Peshate, son of the
> late Elias, act as witness. I, Kostantinos, son of the late
> Solomon, the *apolashane* (i.e., former *lashane*), act as witness;
> Komes, the most humble priest, asked me and I (also) wrote
> for him, because he cannot. I, Petros, son of the late Komes,
> the *apolashane*, act as witness; I, Andreas, son of the late
> Lazaros, wrote for him because he cannot write. Psate, son of
> Pisrael: I acted as witness. I, Ananias, son of the late Abraham,
> act as witness. I, Komes, son of the late Hatre, act as witness.
> I, Epiphanios, son of the late Zacharias, act as witness. I,
> Johannes, son of Lazaros, have drawn up this document with
> my own hand. (*P.KRU* 35.86–112)

Many of these individuals are known from other Jeme documents; Psate,
son of Pisrael, and Johannes, son of Lazaros, in particular are known as
scribes at Jeme, and Johannes himself is responsible for the writing of
the body of this agreement. Those who have occupations listed are
priests and ex-administrators, and the others may be scribes or other
officials. Twenty percent of these witnesses cannot write (including one
of the former *lashanes* of Jeme!). They are, as far as we can tell, all locals,
inhabitants of Jeme. None of the witnesses are women.

The witness statements form the conclusion to the settlement
proper, but there is a further clause appended:

> We, Abraham and Daniel, have [. . .] with each other: that
> which came to us through the repair of the common wall of

the house of Antonios that we built [. . .] as set forth above.
(*P.KRU* 35.113–115)

The statement is fragmentary, but the gist seems clear: the two men attest
to repairs that have been made to the wall in common between the house
shared by Abigaia and Elizabeth in the agreement and the house of
Antonios to the north. Although the names Abraham and Daniel are
extremely common at Jeme, it is likely that they are the husbands of
Elizabeth and Abigaia respectively—perhaps they undertook repairs needed
for the safety of the house in the settlement. Clearly, this statement was
considered important enough to append to the legal document, in case
there would ever be dispute over the house and its wall.

    This, then, was the settlement of 719 between Abigaia and Elizabeth.
The document is presented as a first-person statement from the mouth
of Abigaia and, although much of the text is clearly standard boilerplate
legal text, there are phrases, particularly in the description of the family
relations involved, that may well reflect the actual sentiments, perhaps
even the actual words, of Abigaia herself.

    We do not hear from Elizabeth herself with regard to the agreement
of 719; the first text we have from Elizabeth's point of view comes from
May or June of 723 and provides a great amount of information about
Elizabeth and her family (*P.KRU* 68). Now that we are familiar with the
formulaic text of these documents, we will content ourselves with
excerpts from the relevant document:

> I, Elizabeth, daughter of the late Epiphanios, my mother being
> Maria, from the Kastron Jeme, in the district of the city of
> Armant . . . (*P.KRU* 68.3–5) I write to my husband Abraham,
> the son of Theodoros, man of the city of Syene, who has taken
> me as his wife in Jeme: Greetings. (*P.KRU* 68.11–13)

In these terse words of identification, we get a brief outline of some of
the major events in Elizabeth's life: the death of her father and her
marriage. She addresses her husband throughout the document:

> In those troubled years which are past, you, my husband
> Abraham, went south to Syene, your city. You sold your house—
> the one that came to you from your parents—and you received

57 solidi of gold: (equals) solidi 57, pure (gold). You brought them to me with the entire wealth of your parents, including iron, bronze, from the most valuable to the cheapest. A quantity of the division (of the parents' property) you sold to Johannes, son of Pkalearios, of Nê, and you received another 5 tremisses for them. All of this makes just one tremis short of 59 solidi. Then need arose, and you gave 6 solidi to your father for his offering. Now, I swear by God, the great king of the great and fearful judgment bench, who judges each one, whether what they have done is good or evil: except for these 6 solidi that you gave to your father because of his urgent need, you have not kept back anything from me up to the amount of a tremis, but rather we have received them ourselves together, me with you, and Maria, my mother, as she had become old, and Georgios, this one whom I bore with my first husband Loula. And as for him, Georgios, I paid his tax from this money and hired a smith for him at Klusme. (*P.KRU* 68.26–41)

We get a detailed account of the financial transactions of Elizabeth's second husband Abraham, involving a substantial inheritance from his mother and various other transactions. The "urgent need" of Abraham's father to make an offering is unclear but may well be connected to the death of his wife—perhaps this was a funerary offering he wanted or felt compelled to make for her. In this instance, and in the case of Elizabeth's taking in of her elderly, widowed mother Maria, we see an emphasis on the care for aging parents. With the addition of her son Georgios from her previous marriage, Elizabeth had a full household. One gets a hint (amply confirmed later) that Georgios was somewhat of an unusual burden on his mother—certainly his need for a blacksmith at Klusme, near modern Suez, suggests that he may have been sent away in an ultimately unsuccessful attempt to establish him in a profession.

Elizabeth moves on to the main point of her document in the following lines:

So I write to you, Abraham, my husband, that you might act as owner in full ownership of my house, this one that came to me from my late parents Epiphanios and Maria, and my unworked

plots of land in the town and in the countryside, moveable and
unmoveable property, as well as all the furnishings in the house,
the yard, and in the workshop: in iron, in bronze, in wood, and in
pottery, from the smallest to the largest, from the most expensive
to the least, from a [. . .][19] to a needle, and you will exercise
ownership over everything as I have said above. (*P.KRU* 68.47–54)

Elizabeth's allotment of her entire property to her husband is striking
first in that it allows her to enumerate it: not only the house divided
with Abigaia but also unworked land in town (presumably vacant lots)
and countryside (so farm land lying fallow), along with substantial
property and furnishings, including things from a workshop of some
sort, in all sorts of materials. But the main point of the document is
that she is transferring her property to her husband upon her death, so
that the present document functions as a will that will also serve to
protect her property while she is still alive. But her concerns are not
entirely for property here, as Elizabeth also takes care to make provision
for the treatment of her own body and soul after her death:

When I die (lit. go in body), the first (thing) for you will be to
take care of my (burial) clothes and the holy offering in the
way of every Christian woman. (*P.KRU* 68.64–66)

Here we have the funereal expectations of a woman of Jeme laid out
neatly for us: proper burial attire and offerings, presumably to be made
in a local church. This may well be the kind of offering that caused
such an urgent need to Abraham's father.

Elizabeth's document, now clearly a will, continues, and it is in the
following lines that we get a clear picture of why she was drawing up
this document and what her fears might have been regarding the
disposition of her property:

But concerning my son Georgios, whom I had with Loule,
since I have declared, by God, above that we have paid each
other the money for expenses, there being no deed of security

---

[19] *P.KRU* 65.61 contrasts a needle with a piece of land, so perhaps restore something
similar here, although *P.KRU* 36, translated below, in a similar context has "humblest
pot and needle."

between us: I paid the tax for him, and hired the laborer for him, and (paid for) all the rest of his troubles, apart from the bridal gift that I made for him. God knows that from this day I have carried out fully for him (the inheritance) on behalf of his late father Loule down to the (smallest) bronze keration, and god knows that from this day he has received from me another 10 solidi, and a tremis. I, and my husband, and my small children—see—I owe them (i.e., the husband and children) and God knows that I have done enough good for him (Georgios) until he has grown up and left me and left me in debt. He will not be able to presume (to do anything), now or any hour or any time, whether when I am dead or while I am alive, and he will not be able to proceed against my husband Abraham, or any man (of his), or child or wife, or any other one of his, or any representative from him. (*P.KRU* 68.68–80)

Whether these were the words that Elizabeth dictated directly to a scribe or the scribe's own rendition, it is impossible to miss the exasperation of Georgios's much put-upon mother or her disappointment at how the son of her first marriage turned out. Her concern is now very clear: to protect the inheritance of her husband Abraham and, perhaps more importantly, that of her two children by Abraham.

This document continues with a clause outlining the fine for attempting to upset it: the phrasing is similar to the earlier document, as is the amount of the fine: 24 solidi. Elizabeth concludes with her statement of agreement, as did Abigaia in her document. But Elizabeth adds an interesting detail about the process and, by implication, about herself:

I, Elizabeth, daughter of the late Epiphanios, my mother being Maria, being the one who made the statement written above, I agree. They read it to me in Egyptian; I heard it and I agree to it. (*P.KRU* 68.95–99)

Clearly, Elizabeth told the scribe her wishes, and he wrote up the document based on this, perhaps taking down her words verbatim. The reading aloud of the document to her, her hearing it and agreeing to it show a multistage process in which the document can not only be checked but also, essentially, performed and made public. The specification that the document was read in Egyptian is equally interesting: it is not surprising to note that "Egyptian" (i.e., Coptic) is the language of this document, since very few documents of any sort in Greek (the only other serious possibility) are known from Jeme in this period. It is the insistence on Egyptian that is interesting; even if some or most of the participants involved were bilingual, Coptic would be the language that most, if not all, spoke in everyday life.

The document concluded with the signatures of witnesses and scribe; it was drawn up by a different scribe (Abraham, son of the late David) from the one who wrote Abigaia's earlier document, and only one witness (Komes, son of the late Hatre) was the same. Elizabeth's will had fewer witnesses than Abigaia's settlement (only eight including the scribe) but included among them an arch-priest, Patermouthios, who also wrote for one of the other witnesses.

Elizabeth's move in drawing up a will to protect the property she wished to go to her husband and their children was partly, as we have seen, motivated by her concerns about her son Georgios from her first marriage. But the timing of this document may also have been prompted by a dispute with Abigaia over property inherited from Maria. At some point in the same year that Elizabeth made her will in favor of her husband, Abigaia, her two brothers Stephanos and Chareb, and their father Samuel instituted proceedings against Elizabeth:

> In the sixth (indiction) year now past, under the most honored Athanasios, son of the late Georgios, and Biktor, son of the late Joseph, the *lashanes* of the Kastron, we instituted proceedings against you concerning this inheritance from the late Epiphanios and the late Maria, our parents, whom we have named above. We were each awarded (portions) under Psate, son of the late Pisrael. After we received (our) awards, the most honored Athanasios and Biktor, the *lashanes*, brought about a settlement between us concerning this inheritance of those deceased ones we named above. We drew up a document of settlement with each other, and you reached a settlement with us about all the goods, from great to small, down to the humblest pot and needle, and we drew up a settlement with each other through the notary of the Kastron, according to

the law of the Kastron, so that we would not proceed against each other over any of the things received from this inheritance of the late Epiphanios and the late Maria. (*P.KRU* 36.16–30)

The dispute and settlement appear to be over moveable property rather than real estate and so do not seem to concern the house already divided between the two women in the settlement of 719. In any case, the settlement under Psate, son of Pisrael, did not last; Abigaia and her family brought proceedings against Elizabeth and her husband in 724, occasioning the document quoted above and here:

In this seventh (indiction) year in which we are now, we instituted proceedings, saying: we cannot release you[20] from the oath, unless you, with your wife Elizabeth, want to carry out completely the oath with us, that was connected to the award. Afterwards, then, we proceeded against you on the pretext of this oath in this manner. We repeated the cause of the dispute before the most honored Athanasios and Biktor, the *lashanes*, with some other ones of the great men. You wanted to carry out the oath completely with us, according to the way that we said, without any obstacle, with great rejoicing and without any blame. When you wanted, then, to persuade us in this (matter), in the way we have been able to state above, and when we saw you wanting to carry out the oath with us, as we have said, after you then went into the church of Apa Biktor and began to swear, the great men came into our midst. They persuaded us and we released you from the oath. We made a request of you, and you paid a half solidus of gold to us, with a tremis, equaling ⁵/₆ of a gold solidus, from hand to hand. After you had paid over this ⁵/₆ solidus, praise be, you asked to receive from us this document of guarantee. (*P.KRU* 36.30–46)

The settlement concludes with similar language to the settlement of 719,

---

[20] The "you" is masculine singular, but it is hard to tell if this indicated that the document is addressed to Elizabeth's husband Abraham, since he would ultimately, in light of the document of 723 quoted above, be owner of the disputed property, or if it is simply a generic (or accidental) use of the masculine pronominal referent.

with fines of 24 solidi stipulated and the usual witness statements. The fact that the present document is in reaction to an apparent violation of an earlier (now lost) settlement from 723 leads to questions of whether these very large fines stipulated in the legal documents were regularly enforced. One would expect some reference to a payment of a fine if it had in fact been paid, especially as it would indicate fault of the fined party.

At the same time that Elizabeth was having trouble with her niece Abigaia, she was also having further trouble with her son Georgios from her first marriage. Clearly there had already been issues with Georgios, as was seen in the will Elizabeth made for her second husband Abraham, in which she was at great pains to protect her property so that Abraham and their two young children would inherit. Georgios clearly felt that Elizabeth owed him property from the inheritance of his late father Loule, while Elizabeth clearly felt that she had already done quite enough for this now adult son from an earlier marriage, paying his tax and helping him out in other monetary ways. Whatever the precise nature of the dispute, by 724 it was resolved in a settlement Georgios made for his mother:

> I write to my beloved mother Elizabeth, the daughter herself of the late Epiphanios, her mother being Maria, and Abraham, her husband, son of Theodoros in this same Kastron: greetings. Since after the death[21] of my late father Loula, and now in this seventh year, I instituted proceedings against you, my beloved mother Elizabeth. I came against you under the most honored Athanasios and Biktor, the *lashanes* in (the Church of) the victorious martyr Abba Kyriakos, in this same Kastron. . . (*P.KRU* 37.5–16)

The expressions of filial love are standard, although not for that reason necessarily insincere. Georgios continued his account of the settlement:

> On that day, you carried out the oath completely with me in the Church of the holy Kyriakos. After you carried out the oath with me, I received and was satisfied with you about the things belonging to this entire inheritance from my late father Loula, (being) gold, silver, clothing, bronze—all the goods from marriage

[21] Literally "sleep," a common euphemism in Coptic (Crum *Dict.*, 224a).

gift, bridal gift, yearly subsistence allowance, and anything that
came in to me from my late father. You fulfilled the conditions
of the oath with me concerning the things received from my late
father, whom I have named above. Now I will not be able to
proceed against you for anything that came from this inheritance
of my late father Loula and my late (grand)parents, or anything
that comes from their entire inheritance, or to say that I have
any pretext (to go into proceedings) with you or to go in against
you according to any cause or pretext, neither me, nor brother,
nor sister, nor first cousin nor second cousin whether on behalf
of my father or mother against you: you, Elizabeth, or son of
yours, or brother, or sister, or first cousin, or second cousin, or
near or distant relative, or stranger, or household member, or
any other one of yours, on any cause or pretext. And I will not
be able to proceed against you in or out of court, or in the city,
or the district . . . (*P.KRU* 37.17–48)

The document concludes with the usual clauses, and a fine of 32 solidi,
somewhat larger than in the earlier cases, is stipulated. Note the reference
to an oath carried out in the Church of the holy Kyriakos: this may be
the name of one of the smaller churches at Jeme or a church at a nearby
monastery.[22] The swearing of oaths in churches (to be discussed at greater
length in chapter 5) was common at Jeme.

Matters in Elizabeth's family seem to have calmed down for a time—
perhaps all the property was finally settled, although it may be that we
simply lack documentation of further disputes. Elizabeth continued to
live with Abraham and their children Isak and Kyra for a time after the
tumultuous years of 723–724. At some point probably not long before
the year 738, Elizabeth died. Georgios then instituted proceedings
against his stepbrother and stepsister Isak and Kyra, and their father
Abraham, to claim some inheritance from his mother. On 26 February
738 Georgios drew up a settlement document:

I, Georgios, son of the late Loula, my mother being the late
Elizabeth, man of the Kastron Jeme in the district of the city of

---

[22] Probably not the so-called Monastery of Cyriacus noted above in the introduction
and recently discussed in Bács 2000, which was not large enough to have its own
church.

Armant, write to my beloved siblings Isak and Kyra and Abraham, man of Syene, their father (*P.KRU* 38.10–14). In this time, I instituted proceedings with you, Isak and Kyra, and Abraham your father, concerning the inheritance of my late mother Elizabeth. God-fearing great men, with God's help, mediated between us over this entire inheritance in all things: gold, silver, bronze, iron, smithing tools,[23] built houses, and vacant lots, from moveable to unmoveable (property), from small to great, everything and every matter of the inheritance of my late mother Elizabeth. I reached a settlement with you, such that the great men were satisfied in the manner of the agreement between us in all things. I have received and was paid by you for the inheritance of my late mother Elizabeth. (*P.KRU* 38.18–31)

The document stipulates a fine of 36 solidi, the largest yet seen in these documents, and closes with the usual clauses and witness statements. The inheritance from Elizabeth seems extensive: Georgios specifies houses, vacant lots, gold, silver, and other metals, as well as smithing tools. The latter is interesting to find coming from his mother. Perhaps it is connected with Elizabeth's hiring of a smith for her son earlier on, and maybe she even bought the tools to set Georgios up in a trade; these may well be part of the furnishings of the workshop mentioned in Elizabeth's will of 723. It is unclear what Georgios inherited and what he was paid for; given the earlier documents, one would not expect that he would inherit anything. The implication of Elizabeth's earlier statements about Georgios was that he was both greedy and persistent, and it is entirely possible that Abraham and the children paid him, not because he had a right to anything from Elizabeth's estate but simply to make him give up and go away. It certainly seems appropriate that our dossier on Elizabeth ends with the settlement of her estate; her immediate family disappears (or, at least, has not been identified) from the documentation after 738.

It is ambiguous whether her niece Abigaia appears in other documentation. Arthur Schiller posited a second marriage for Abigaia and identified her with the Abigaia who is also wife of Zacharias and mother of Abessa and Takhum.[24] If this identification is correct, one

---

[23] Cf. Till 1954, 122n35 with reference to Crum *Dict.*, 363b.
[24] See Schiller 1952, 343–350.

could trace Abigaia's descendants down to her great-grandchildren, indeed could trace the fate of the house divided with Elizabeth down this far, but it seems more likely that we are dealing with two different Abigaias.[25] The transactions involving this second Abigaia and her descendants can be summarized briefly (see family tree, fig. 5). The Abigaia who was married to Zacharias had two daughters, Takhum and Abessa, to whom she left a house. After Abigaia's death, Abessa apparently sold the house for 12 solidi to a man named Daniel but failed to consult her sister and coowner Takhum. Takhum sued in 737/8, and Daniel returned her portion of the property for what he paid for it (*P.KRU* 47). Then Abessa sued to get back her portion from Daniel; Daniel again returned the portion for its purchase price, but Abessa had to pay an additional amount ($^5/_6$ solidus), presumably for reneging on the deal (*P.KRU* 25). Dissatisfied, both sisters disputed with each other over ownership of the parts of the house in 740. The matter was submitted to the "great men" of Jeme, who called in an inspector and subsequently divided the house between the sisters. Each sister filed a document of settlement (*P.KRU* 45, *P.KRU* 46). Abessa's daughter Tsherkah/Thekla and her son Senout/Arsenios[26] are the next generation represented in the texts. Although none of their transactions relates to the house, which appears to have gone to Abessa's daughter Tsherkah, both she and her brother are active in various real estate transactions. In one fragmentary text from around 735 (*P.KRU* 28), the two buy a yard with a storehouse adjoining a property of their father's. A few years later (*P.KRU* 50), the brother and sister received a fourth of a portion of a neighbor's property in resolution of a dispute; the property had been redeemed from a monastery. They also receive shares of property in another settlement, possibly a year later (*P.KRU* 48). Having succeeded in obtaining all this property through litigation in collaboration with her, Senout then sues his sister over the relatively small amount of 4 tremisses, but settles for 1 $^1/_4$ tremis (*P.KRU* 56). This archive reaches its last generation in Tsherkah's daughter Tagape by her first husband. Sometime in the mid-eighth century Tagape makes

[25] Till (1962, 49) treats these as two separate women; the dates in the documents relating to the descendants of Abigaia, wife of Zacharias, seem hard to reconcile with Schiller's reconstruction.

[26] These children are known by both Egyptian and Greek names; see Hobson 1989 for references to this practice in the Greek papyri.

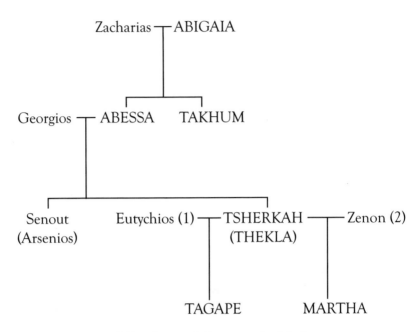

*Fig. 5. Family tree of Abigaia, wife of Zacharias
(women's names in all capitals)*

a settlement with Tsherkah's second husband, Zenon, about inherited property: they both get a room each in a house, and Zenon then sells Tagape his room (*P.KRU* 26). Later on, Tagape's half-sister, Martha, daughter of Tsherkah and Zenon, cedes to her all of a house and its yard, except for a sixth that was retained by Martha—the room under the stairs (*P.KRU* 24). Furthermore, they divide the furnishings of the house "whether gold, or silver, or brass." In Schiller's reading of the family trees, the house is familiar, since he identifies it as the very house inherited by Abigaia and Elizabeth, but, again, this interpretation of the documents is not certain. Even if there is no connection, the papers of the descendants of Abigaia, wife of Zacharias, show the same kinds of transactions as the Elizabeth/Abigaia papers.

3

Elizabeth and Abigaia in Context:
Women's Lives in Family and Community

The documents of Elizabeth and Abigaia raise a number of issues important for understanding women's identities and roles in family and household at Jeme. In all cases, the women are identified first and foremost by their own names—an integral part of their identity as individuals. The set of proper names available to the inhabitants of Jeme was apparently somewhat restricted, though: one might encounter several Elizabeths and Abigaias at any given time.[1] Therefore it was common to find individuals further identified by the names of family members. The names of a person's parents were most common, especially in legal texts. More formal documents tend to spell out the relationship explicitly; thus Elizabeth identifies herself at the beginning of her will as "Elizabeth, daughter of the late Epiphanios, my mother being Maria" (*P.KRU* 68.3–4). This sort of identification by both parents is the custom in the formal legal documents from the Monastery of Phoibammon deposit, but one parent's name usually suffices for less formal documentation, such as that found on ostraca. In most such cases the father is preferred, although a significant minority of cases cite the mother instead. Less formal legal documents also tend toward abbreviation in the identification of parentage, either using a contracted construct form of the term "son/daughter of" or simply using the genitive between the names of child and parent. In certain exceptional cases, a grandparent's name is tacked on to the parent's name by an additional genitive; in most cases this is the name of a paternal grandmother.[2]

---

[1] It is tempting to suggest that the available names for women were even more restricted than the names for men: about 10% of the names known from the Jeme texts (as opposed to known individuals) are women's names. This may, however, reflect biases in the textual evidence—the percentage is suspiciously close to the percentage of known women in legal documents (12%) discussed below.

[2] See the naming of Koloje's grandmother Katharon in *O.Medin.HabuCopt.* 50 and 51, to be discussed in chapter 5. Another paternal grandmother appears in *O.Medin.HabuCopt.* 134 (also appearing in the earlier *O.Medin.HabuCopt.* 104 as mother). Again, note Hobson 1989 on naming practices in Roman Egypt and the anthropological literature on the subject.

In addition to parents, individuals are often identified by other relatives. Sibling relationships are commonly noted, especially in the more formal legal documents like those from the Elizabeth/Abigaia archive. Sibling identifications are usually made in addition to parent names, but, especially in cases involving lists of individuals with the same parents, the sibling identification can be used to cut down on repetition. In especially complex cases, more distant relationships between participants are sometimes pointed out for clarity; thus Abigaia, after providing a statement of her aunt Elizabeth's parentage in the introduction of *P.KRU 35*, goes on to describe her as "the sister of my mother" in the body of the text, explicitly indicating the family connection. Identification by children is uncommon; in a few cases (notably the list of sureties *P.KRU 119* discussed below), the child's name is listed, then "his father Hemai" or just "her mother" with no name given.

These terms of family relationship are reliable for showing a biological relationship when they occur in legal texts and in other official or semi-official documents. Beyond legal phraseology, explicit statements of these family relationships are rare, but addresses and casual references in terms of the relationship are common. Private letters, in particular, abound in such terminology but must be used with great caution in most cases because of the extended use of these terms to express relationships within the church. Patterned on forms of address found in the Coptic translation of the New Testament, "father," "mother," "son," "daughter," and especially "brother" and "sister" were used freely in letters to describe nonbiological relationships "in Christ."[3] These terms expressed religious relationships on levels similar to the family position—respected seniors were addressed as parents, juniors and inferiors as children, and relative equals as siblings—but do not necessarily reflect actual familial relationships. Without other evidence, it is impossible to know for certain whether the writers of letters are using these terms to describe family relationships, religious relationships, or both. Thus in a letter, the well-known monk Frange first addresses "his beloved good lord brother Apa Theodoros" and then goes on to

---

[3] These metaphoric uses of terms of family relationships are found already in Pharaonic (e.g, use of "brother" and "sister" as terms for "husband/wife" or "lover" [Robins 1993, 61–62]) and Graeco-Roman (in a usage that parallels more closely the Coptic texts [Hobson 1989, 172–173]) Egypt.

greet "my God-loving sister Koloje and Pecosh" (*O.Medin.HabuCopt.* 139). "Brother" in reference to Apa Theodore is almost certainly a relationship in religion, but without certain knowledge of Frange's paternity,[4] it is impossible to know whether he is actually Koloje's biological or spiritual "brother." The same is true of cases in which women address bishops as "my father" or monks address women as "my daughter"; these can be terms of religious respect between spiritual inferiors and superiors (and vice-versa), or they can conceal actual family relationships.[5] In some cases, circumstantial evidence can help, but for the most part it is difficult to be certain.

The only family terminology completely reliable even in private letters is that of spousal relationship; the terms for "husband" and "wife" are not (at least, in the Jeme material) used to describe spiritual relationships. With these relationships, the problem is in the ambiguity of the terminology itself. As indicated in chapter 1, the Coptic word for "wife" *shime* is also the word for "woman." In theory, confusion is possible, but in most of the Jeme texts it is generally clear what is meant: *shime* as "wife" is normally limited to instances in which it is followed by a male name ("wife of X") or when it is preceded by a possessive article (invariably "his wife" or "my wife"). Thus qualified, "wife" can be used independently of the woman's name; women are frequently identified only as "my wife," "his wife," or defined solely in terms of their husbands, such as the "wife of Solomon" in *O.Medin.HabuCopt.* 152 or "wife of Pecosh" in *O.Crum* 289.

The terminology for "husband" is more complicated. As with "wife," the word for "man" can also mean "husband," although this is primarily a literary usage and not found in the Jeme corpus; this is also the case of the use of "brother" to mean "husband," which is even rarer.[6] The

---

[4] Frange's parentage is a problem. Is he to be identified (as is tentatively done in Till 1962, 78) with the witness Efranke, son of David in *P.KRU* 38.69, which dates to 738? (This is the document discussed above in which Georgios settles with Elizabeth's husband and children.) This papyrus was thought by Crum to be lost but is, in fact, Oxford Bodleian Library Ms. Copt. a 6(p). Unfortunately, examination of the witness statement of Efranke has so far proven inconclusive: it bears some resemblance to the distinctive hand of Frange's correspondence but also some points of dissimilarity. It may be that Frange had a more formal hand for legal documents and used a slightly different spelling for his name.

[5] Same-sex addresses (men calling a man "my father/brother/son" or women addressing "my mother/sister/daughter") are similarly ambiguous.

[6] This apparently occurs in the (probably) west Theban ostracon *O.CrumST* 34;

word *hoout* (normally meaning "male") can also be used for "husband," and is found as such occasionally in Jeme legal texts. The most common word for "husband" at Jeme is an unambiguous term with no other connotations: *hai*. Thus Abigaia refers to her spouse as "Daniel, my husband"; her aunt Elizabeth's second husband is referred to as "Abraham, my husband" by Elizabeth and "Abraham, her husband" by Abigaia and her relatives, all using *hai*. Like "wife," *hai* can be used independently of the husband's name, but the husband is not usually identified solely in terms of the wife.

The family relations by which women were identified defined key relationships in women's lives at Jeme. Throughout the life cycle, women were part of their families except in the most unusual circumstances. A woman's complex of relations with her family began at birth, expanded, diversified, and continued through her life, and even continued past her death. A very fragmentary document from the Monastery of Epiphanius seems to highlight the significance and persistence of women's relations with their families, although its precise nature is still uncertain. It is apparently a register of marriages, childbirths, and other family information (*O.Mon.Epiph.* 99–100);[7] it is so badly broken that not a single line of it is complete. Nevertheless, what remains of this text gives a useful insight into many aspects of the family of the women of Jeme. As it exists now, the ostracon *O.Mon.Epiph.* 99–100 consists of two fragments of pottery, probably two separate columns that once joined. The beginning appears to be complete; without preamble or introduction it launches directly into the first entry. Each entry begins (and ends?) with a cross, and the general scheme seems to be three or four lines of text per entry. A consecutive translation of this broken text is impossible, but it is possible to detect the overall pattern. Women and their husbands are identified by name (fathers too apparently in some cases); the husband sometimes is described as "taking" (*fi*) the wife in marriage; sometimes the wife's relationship to someone else is noted. The husband is then said to have begotten (*jpo*) a child—always a girl in the cases where the information survives. A few passages can be translated very tentatively:

the text is, however, literary and the context (and actual meaning) somewhat unclear. Note also the non-Theban inscription of Drosis, now *SB Kopt.* I 784.11: granted, this use of "brother" for "husband" is in a lacuna, but the restoration *pe[s s]on* seems certain.

[7] These two fragments were doubtless once part of the same ostracon and will be treated as a single text.

+Elizabeth [. . .] . . . who begot Tano[. . .] . . . the wife of Pap[. . .]
and the wife of Biktor from Belate, and the wife of [. . .] . . . the
sister of Andreas [. . .] he begot Theudote . . . to her.
(*O.Mon.Epiph.* 99.1–9)
+[. . .] took the sister of [. . .] (in marriage) . . . he begot a
daughter [. . .] took her (in marriage), and he begot Da[. . .] . . .
his sister, the wife of [. . .] (*O.Mon.Epiph.* 100.10–14)

Thus, *O.Mon.Epiph.* 99–100 appears to be a record of the major family
roles in certain women's lives: mother, sister, wife, daughter. The reason
for the compilation of the document is obscure; Crum has suggested it
is a register of marriages and resulting births.[8] The presence of the
ostracon at the Monastery of Epiphanius suggests that it was deposited
there as a formal record and/or for safekeeping, just as the large group
of legal documents was deposited at the Monastery of Phoibammon.

Other than this register of births, the Jeme corpus records few details
about the birth of children. From elsewhere in Egypt, there are
numerous texts relating to women's reproductive health.[9] The concerns
in these texts are for maintaining the health of the mother, decreasing
the pain of birth, guaranteeing a live birth, maintaining the infant's
health, and maintaining the mother's ability to produce milk through
care for the breasts. In general, it seems likely that women nursed their
own children; there are apparently no equivalents in Coptic to the
Greek wet-nursing contracts found in Roman Egypt.[10] The early years
of childhood were dangerous ones for the child for childhood illnesses
were common and frequently fatal; parents sometimes even promised

---

[8] Crum and Evelyn White 1926, 177; "register of female births" would be more
accurate, given the apparent absence of male children.

[9] Relevant medical texts are surveyed in Till 1951, 21–22, 26–28, with texts
translated 112–113, 132–134, while relevant magical texts are translated in Meyer and
Smith 1994, 83–90, 95–97, 120–128, 270–273 (from the western Theban area), 304–
310, and 326–341 (note spell at the end on page 341). To some extent, this separation
of texts into categories of "medical" and "magical" is a modern construct: this distinction
would not have been so clear to the inhabitants of Jeme.

[10] The Greek papyri are published in *C.Pap.Gr.* I, where most of the women acting
as wet-nurses have Egyptian names. Wet-nursing is common in Egypt in earlier periods
as well (Robins 1993, 117–118), and one wonders if the apparent trend away from this
practice has something to do with the coming of Christianity and the increasing
emphasis on the motif of the virgin Mary nursing the infant Jesus, for which see now
Bolman 1997.

their sick children as donations to local monasteries in the hope that they would survive.[11] Often, the child's illness was seen as a form of possession.[12] Parents were sometimes blamed for the fatal illnesses of their children, as in the letter O.Mon.Epiph. 209, in which a man writes about children dying because of the sins of their parents. This also seems to be the case in a letter of a woman named Esther to a monk (O.Mon.Epiph. 194), in which she complains that she bears children but they die. Esther thinks she is doing something wrong and asks the monk for a rule (*entole*) whereby she can live, blaming the death of her children on her own behavior. Other than this, few details are known about early childhood at Jeme. The evidence suggests that parents thought of names for children before they were born: a letter from the monk Frange asks Pisentius and his wife to name their child Longinus if it turns out to be a boy (O.Crum 394).

A preference for male children over female children is clearly marked in the documentation;[13] but it is doubtful that this preference manifested itself in the disposal of female infants, as is found in Graeco-Roman Egypt.[14] Aside from a possible reference in a very broken Pisentius letter,[15] there is little evidence for the outright abandonment of children, male or female, which is not surprising. The social historian John Boswell has pointed to the child donation contracts alluded to above (P.KRU 78–103), a form of Coptic legal text peculiar to the Jeme corpus, as evidence of "the most humane form of abandonment ever devised."[16] It is unlikely that parents avoided becoming attached to their very young children because of high infant mortality, as has been suggested in the past for many premodern societies. The expressions of regret and concern over serious childhood illness in the child donation contracts (examples of which are translated below in chapter 4) and Frange's prenatal concerns suggest considerable attachment on the part of Jemeans to their children. Indeed, we have already seen evidence of

[11] See the narrative accounts of child donations translated below in chapter 4.

[12] See Hall 1905, 175, with Winlock and Crum 1926, 163 and also P.Mon.Epiph. 250.

[13] O.Crum 394, for example, and the statements of the child donation contracts translated below in chapter 4.

[14] Apparently from the earlier Greek practice; see, e.g., Rowlandson 1998, 171–172, 235.

[15] P.Pisentius 13, translated above in chapter 1.

[16] Boswell 1988, 237–238; see further references and discussion below in chapter 4.

such attachment in the Elizabeth/Abigaia papers in Elizabeth's concern in her will to protect the inheritance of her young children.

The Jeme documents give little insight into the events of childhood at Jeme; the material culture is only slightly more helpful. Aside from one very badly damaged representation of a female child of relatively elite status,[17] we have a few possible artifactual remains of childhood—clay figures from the Medinet Habu excavations that seem likely to have been used as toys.[18] Childhood was the time for formal education—training to read and write, mostly—for the few who received it, but the precise circumstances of education at Jeme, especially as it related to women, are unclear.[19] Much education was carried out at the monasteries—the numerous school texts from the Monastery of Epiphanius and Monastery of Phoibammon are ample witness to this[20]—but the extent to which inhabitants of Jeme could or did avail themselves of instruction in the monasteries is unknown. The illiteracy rates seen in the Elizabeth/Abigaia papers, not just among the contracting parties but also among the witnesses, suggest that the percentage of Jemeans who received formal education was not high.[21] At any rate, women would not have been welcome at the all-male monastic communities where reading and writing were taught, and this suggests that the education of women probably took place privately.[22] It is certain that at least some women learned to read and write somewhere: a large number

---

[17] The painting of the daughter of Elizabeth, donor of the St. Menas murals in the church in the small Ptolemaic temple at Jeme: see figure 6 and the disucssion at the beginning of chapter 4.

[18] Oriental Institute Museum numbers 15533 (unpublished) and possibly 14607 (Hölscher 1954, 58 and plate 34F). For these and other possible toys, see the forthcoming corpus of figurines from the Medinet Habu excavations (Teeter forthcoming).

[19] For education in Graeco-Roman and Late Antique Egypt in general, the essential reference is Cribiore 1996.

[20] The corpus of known Coptic school texts is available in Hasitzka 1990, with additional texts in Cribiore 1996, and see also now Cribiore 1999. It is sometimes hard to tell which of these texts is from western Thebes; also some of the texts identified as Theban in Hasitzka 1990 are likely to be documentary (for which see the review Wilfong 1993). The provenance of excavated texts, e.g., *O.Medin.HabuCopt.* 212 and *O.Mon.Epiph.* 576 and 611-620, is, of course, certain.

[21] The only substantial work on literacy at Jeme is Steinmann 1974, but his estimates are wildly overoptimistic (see references in Bagnall 1993, 257-258).

[22] A school text with several epistolary phrases was found at Jeme (*O.Medin.HabuCopt.* 212): it includes a number of the addresses used to women, some qualified as "my sister."

of letters and documents were written to and by women from Jeme, and, although it is possible that most were, in fact, written and/or read for the women by scribes, for practical reasons this is unlikely to be true for all.[23] The education of women was rarely discussed and when it was, the writer's attitude is usually ambiguous. A Coptic translation of a statement attributed to Diogenes, from an anthology of aphorisms and sayings, bears this out:

> Diogenes the philosopher saw a girl being taught to write. He said: "Behold a knife being sharpened." (Till 1960, 268)

The quotation likens the educated woman to a sharpened knife, but it is hard to tell whether this is intended as positive (education as a weapon) or negative (educated woman dangerous or harmful like a sharp dagger).[24] Once taught to read and write, women could continue to use this ability throughout their lives. In *O.Mon.Epiph.* 386, Tatre and Katharon write to Moses, asking him to send them a portion of the *kanôn* (apparently, in this context, scripture); Tatre writes "in her own hand," as she puts it, thereby asserting to her monastic correspondent that she will be able to read whatever he may send her.

Beyond reading and writing, female children were also taught crafts and trades. Aside from the letter asking that a daughter be instructed in "work" from Syene,[25] we have a formal contract (probably from western Thebes if not from Jeme) whereby a girl will be taught weaving:

> It is I, Sara, daughter of Manna, who writes to Maria, saying: From today, it being the 26th of Mesore, I give to you my daughter Tapnoub for (learning) weaving so that she spend two years with you and that you teach her for 3 carats. If you

[23] This question is a complex and hotly debated one that cannot be dealt with here; in general the trend among scholars is to assume that documents were written by scribes unless specifically described as otherwise (see, e.g., Bagnall 1996, 24–25). It is difficult to imagine, however, some of the documents in the Koloje archive to be discussed in chapter 5 being written by a scribe, for example, or the woman Anna commissioning a scribe to write her graffito near the Monastery of Epiphanius in her name (*Gr.Mon.Epiph.* 646). In some cases, such as the letter *O.Mon.Epiph.* 386, discussed below, women are explicitly described as reading and writing.

[24] I owe recognition of this ambiguity to Professor Edward Wente.

[25] *O.CrumVC* 19; now = *Pap.Eleph.Eng.* E19.

do not teach her in this manner (?) in two years, you shall pay 6 carats. (*SB Kopt.* I 045)

This contract indicates that the girl was being trained either for a trade or for housework, although given the length of time involved, the former is more likely.

Little more is known about children's lives at Jeme. Three children seems to be the average family size among the contracting parties in the Jeme legal documents from the Monastery of Phoibammon deposit (e.g., Elizabeth and her three children, Abigaia and her two siblings), but this evidence can be ambiguous. The transition from child to adult does not seem to have been marked by any formal rites of passage as it was in (pagan) Roman Egypt,[26] and it is unclear at just what age this was considered to occur. Certainly there was some tie to the reaching of sexual maturity, which in women would be marked by the onset of menstruation. The Jeme documentation is silent on this subject; the only thing that we really know about menstruation is that it seems to have some connection with the room beneath the stairs that is frequently mentioned in legal documents involving houses. In earlier Demotic sources, this room of a house is explicitly described as the place where women menstruate, and there is evidence that special menstrual space existed in Egypt in earlier periods.[27] Although the Jeme documents do not specify that this part of the house was connected with menstruation, we will recall the special emphasis on the room or space beneath the stairs with regard to women in documents we have already looked at. This room is ceded to Elizabeth in the division of the house with Abigaia (*P.KRU* 35), while from the archive of the family of the "other" Abigaia, Martha retains it in the division with Tagape (*P.KRU* 24). Clearly this space had some special significance for women, if only residual from earlier times.

After a woman's passage into adulthood, commemorated or not, Jeme women were, in general, expected to marry and raise a family. Not all women did so: this was also a point at which a woman could,

[26] See Montserrat 1991. It is possible that the female orant figurines (see plate 2) that were found at Jeme, almost always in broken condition, may have been ceremonially broken in some kind of rite of passage for women, but there is, as yet, no evidence to support this (see discussion in chapter 4).

[27] See Wilfong 2000.

for example, enter a monastic house, but the evidence shows that few women at Jeme pursued this option. There is no direct evidence for typical ages at marriage at Jeme; it is generally assumed that this was not too far from the usual ages at marriage in later Roman Egypt (late teens for women, early twenties for men).[28] Part of the difficulty in determining anything about marriage at Jeme is the lack of documentation: the corpus has yielded no marriage or divorce contracts and only a terse document of divorce from the Monastery of Epiphanius (*P.Mon.Epiph.* 270, translated below). Indeed, marriage and divorce contracts are rare in Coptic anyway; for more than a 700-year period, fewer than ten such documents survive,[29] and the general impression is that, as in earlier periods, marriages were only documented in exceptional circumstances.[30] Incidental reference to marriage is much more common in the Jeme texts, but usually this consists of writers simply noting their spouses' names. Initiation of marriage seems to have been a matter of choice; Pisentius's sermon on Onnophrios appears to indicate some theoretical latitude in choice of spouse, but his correspondence also includes letters referring to a marriage arranged by the parents (in this case the fathers) of the bride and groom, possibly through a third party.[31] The will *P.KRU* 67 allowed its author, the monk Paham, to express his concerns at not being consulted on his son's choice of a wife (and also, incidentally, articulate the general concern over virginity in unmarried women):

> As for my eldest son, Papnute, he took a wife against my wishes. I wept very much (over this), but his way did not go smoothly from the time that he married her, fights and disturbances having taken place in his affairs. They came south, and they told me the cause (of the troubles): her virginity had not been

[28] Bagnall and Frier 1994, 111–118. For marriage in Roman and Late Antique Egypt in Greek documentation, see Rowlandson 1998, 312–335, and in the context of Byzantine law, see Grubbs 1995, 99–101, 144–146, 152–153 and Arjava 1996, 111–156.

[29] See Till 1948 for a listing and Green 1993 for a recent discussion and listing of relevant Arabic language evidence; see also Rowlandson 1998, 212–217, and note Steinwenter 1955, 20–22 for the legal background of the Coptic documents.

[30] See Gagos, Koenen, and McNellan 1992 for unwritten marriages in Graeco-Roman Egypt.

[31] *P.Pisentius* 15 and 19, discussed above in chapter 1.

intact. I said that I did not have anything to do with him because he did not listen to me. (*P.KRU* 67.19–23)[32]

In another case (*P.Ryl.Copt.* 139, possibly not a Jeme text), either a dowry or a bridal gift (or both) is arranged between the groom's father and the bride's mother. As these documents show, a dowry was negotiated before the marriage.[33] The actual ceremony probably included a feast; in her will Elizabeth refers to "the wedding which I gave for" her son (*P.KRU* 68.71), while in *P.Ryl.Copt.* 139 the groom's father and bride's mother agree to hold the wedding together and to divide expenses between them. There is no documentation of the ceremony in church that is a prominent feature of modern Coptic practice, but the documents just cited do attach importance to some sort of ceremony. Documentation of the marriage was apparently only necessary if there were potential problems or unusual circumstances in relation to property.

Life within the marriage can only be glimpsed through incidental references and from documents that record what happened when things went wrong. The general impression is that women had widely varying degrees of autonomy within the marriage; there are women who stay strictly within the family circle, but there are also women involved in complex business dealings outside the home with no apparent reference to a husband. The ideal of married life as set by Pisentius was for the woman to stay home, obey her husband, and care for her children. This ideal is promulgated by other religious writers as well and even appears in documentary evidence. Thus in a case where a man and wife are detaining another man's young wife (their daughter?), the writer tells the couple:

> If you still do not teach this man's wife that she agree to obey him like every woman and do his bidding, know that I shall excommunicate you as long as she continues to be in this disturbed state. I have written this once again to you! (*O.Crum* Ad 13)

Note also the case in *O.Mon.Epiph.* 161, in which a woman has

---

[32] See Rowlandson 1998, 214–215 for more on this document.
[33] The terminology and nature of dowries and bridal gifts in the Coptic documents will be discussed further in chapter 5.

abandoned her husband and gone to Coptos to stay with another woman; the writer asks that she be refused communion, presumably until she returns to her husband. Religious authorities in west Thebes felt that they had a right and even a duty to interfere in marital disputes of the secular community; this is why so much of Pisentius's correspondence is concerned with the marital problems of his "flock."[34]

When pastoral efforts were insufficient to reconcile married couples, divorce was the result.[35] There are even fewer documents of divorce than marriage in Coptic,[36] and again they seem to record exceptional circumstances; more often divorce is mentioned but not elaborated on. In spite of Apa Abraham's threat to excommunicate men or women who divorce for any reason other than adultery (*O.Crum* 72), we find divorce occurring for a number of reasons. It could be initiated by either party, as the cases noted by Till show. In theory, divorces were "no-fault" in modern legal terminology, mutual agreements between the divorcing parties. In practice, men more commonly took the initiative in divorce, and some of the documentation shows divorce as simple abandonment of a wife by her husband. A terse record of a divorce comes from the Monastery of Epiphanius, written on the back of a letter (*P.Mon.Epiph.* 270).[37] The divorce is simple and straightforward, perhaps merely a memorandum noted down by someone rather than a legal documentation.

> Shenetom, the fisherman, son of Pecale, from Pashme (near the Monastery of Epiphanius), has thrown out his wife Tegoshe and taken (as wife) Teret, daughter of Komes, son of Pares, and given his (Shenetom's) daughter to her (Teret's) son in marriage.[38]

[34] For Bishop Abraham's efforts in this direction, see Krause 1956, 61–63, 151–176.

[35] For divorce in Late Antique Egypt from the Greek documents, see Bagnall 1987, Rowlandson 1998, 208–212; and for its context of Byzantine law see Grubbs 1995, 238–242 and Arjava 1996, 177–189.

[36] Again, see Till 1948 and Steinwenter 1955, 20–22.

[37] The text on the front includes very fragmentary references to a woman going to Jeme and marital problems; perhaps this bears some relation to the divorce recorded on the verso.

[38] We see here also the pattern of cementing one new relationship with another. By marrying off his daughter to the son of his new wife, Shenetom binds his daughter to the new wife, at least potentially alienating her from her biological mother, the abandoned wife.

This relative informality of divorce and remarriage is attested in other Coptic documentation, and, again, the main problems occur when there is property to divide or when support of a spouse, most often a wife, was an issue (we will return to the issue of support in chapter 5).

Theban religious officials such as Abraham and Pisentius showed a great deal of concern over the maintenance of marriages in their domains and used such powers of persuasion as they had to prevent divorce. But even more troubling to them were manifestations of women's sexuality outside of marriage. This concern can be seen as the culmination of the earlier writings of such figures as Pachomius, Horsiesios, Shenoute, Besa, and Moses of Abydos/Balliana, in which women's sexual activity was the object of worry and regulation.[39] Unfortunately, most of the evidence for women's sexual lives at Jeme also derives from these very authors—Abraham and Pisentius (or more precisely, in the case of Pisentius, his correspondents and biographers). The women themselves were entirely reticent on the matter in their correspondence; of course the fact of women having children and their ages are evidence of some sort of sexual life, but we get nothing of the women's own understandings and perceptions from these bare facts, and we are left with mostly negative evidence. The great concern in both Abraham and Pisentius was the prevention of extramarital sex. Pisentius's correspondence contains instances of extramarital affairs by women (especially *P.Pisentius* 38, excerpted above in chapter 1), as well as those by men. In all cases, his concern is that the spouses reconcile.

More transgressive, in the eyes of writers like Pisentius, were the aspects of women's sexuality that took place outside of both marriage and private life. Prostitution was just such an activity. Frequently used in literature as a symbol of the lowest possible depravity to which a woman could sink,[40] prostitution haunted the writings exhorting women to chastity and faithfulness to their husbands. Actual evidence of the practice of prostitution in Late Antique Egypt is much rarer.[41] From Jeme and environs, we have one possible reference to a woman having

[39] See Wilfong 2002a for a survey of all but the last of these authors and their work on related subjects; and note Arjava 1996, 193–229 for the general background in the Late Antique world.

[40] See, for example, the stories cited in Ward 1987.

[41] For the evidence from fourth- to sixth-century Egypt, see Bagnall 1993, 196–198 and Montserrat 1996, 106–135.

run off to Kos to become a prostitute (*P.Mon.Epiph.* 269)—this after participating in a murder. The text is badly broken, however, and it may be that the woman was either escaping to Kos to avoid punishment for the murder of her husband or simply going off to Kos for an extramarital affair. It is not out of place to wonder whether prostitution existed at Jeme itself; it was a phenomenon of towns and cities in both literary and documentary sources, with women operating out of "houses" in urban environments. Although not as large as Coptos to the north or Armant to the south, Jeme could conceivably have supported a house of prostitution. Other expressions of female sexuality doubtless existed at Jeme but do not appear in the evidence. Erotic activity between women is primarily known from monastic literature in Late Antique Egypt.[42] Not only do Horsiesios, Shenoute, and Besa warn women's monastic houses against it in their letters, but there are also incidental references in their writings and a record of women being punished for having sex with each other at Shenoute's monastery.[43] In this latter case, the women (Taese and Tsansno) are said to have gone to each other "in friendship and physical desire," there being no more explicit terminology in Coptic to describe lesbian activity.[44]

This adversative use of the term "friendship" in Coptic is not limited to the case of Taese and Tsansno; Horsiesios rails against "friendship" as a euphemism for homosexual relations, and it does not get favorable mention in other religious writers. In general, this seems to have been a usage specific to monastic communities; friendship between men in secular life was, in certain contexts, seen as desirable and its neglect a source for reproach.[45] Women are often seen in business relations with nonrelatives (see discussion below in chapter 5), but we find little explicit reference to extrafamilial, nonbusiness friendships between women at Jeme, although one can infer friendly relations between neighbors to a certain extent from legal documents such as the ones in chapter 2.

The insistence in the work of religious writers that a woman's main social relations be within her family, especially with her husband and children, is, to some degree, reflected in the documentary evidence.

---

[42] But note the Egyptian sources from the later Roman period discussed throughout Brooten 1996 and Montserrat 1996, 158–161.

[43] Discussion and references in Wilfong 2002a.

[44] Again, Wilfong 2002a; for the Coptic evidence for male homosexual activity, see now Behlmer 2001 and also Wilfong 2002a, 313–321.

[45] References in Wilfong 2002a, 313.

Both women and men retained an especially close relationship with their mothers long after childhood; relations between fathers and adult children seem more complicated, usually around issues of control and inheritance. Relations between siblings as adults were often quite close; the frequent tandem actions of Abigaia and her siblings and the siblings of successive generations are mirrored in many other legal documents of the Monastery of Phoibammon deposit. This was, no doubt, encouraged and to some degree forced by the frequent joint ownership that came about through inheritance. Indeed, inheritance of jointly owned property also resulted in close ties between aunts and uncles and their nieces and nephews, Abigaia and her aunt Elizabeth being a notable instance. It is difficult to trace specific living arrangements within this set of family interactions; children moved out of the parental house at marriage, but domiciles could include unmarried sisters or aunts, less often male relatives. In general, parents maintained their own household as long as was possible, but, as in the case of Elizabeth's mother Maria in *P.KRU* 68, would come to live with their children if they were unable to care for themselves. In some cases, children had an incentive to care for their elderly parents: note the transaction in *P.KRU* 116 whereby Mariam and her husband Papnute, son of Mathaios, agree to care for Mariam's father Daniel in exchange for Daniel's house. The agreement, drawn up by Papnute in his own hand, calls for the house to revert back to Daniel if they fail to care for him properly.

There are no records from Jeme with statistical information to draw upon like the Roman census documents, but the general impression given by the Jeme texts is that, although mortality for young girls and women of child-bearing age was higher than male mortality at comparable ages, after these points were past, women tended to outlive their husbands at Jeme.[46] This may reflect the actual situation or may also be due to the accidents of preservation of the evidence. It is almost certainly an indication of a tendency in the discourse: the habit of noting the status of a woman whose husband was dead as "widow" versus a relative lack of comparable marking of the status of men as widowers (although these would have been less common). Indeed, the

---

[46] This tends to follow the basic patterns seen in Bagnall and Frier 1994. For a survey of the Roman period material on widowhood, see the monumental study Krause 1994–1995; note also the documents translated in Rowlandson 1998.

state of widowhood and its concerns are the subject of much of the private correspondence of women at Jeme. In nearly all cases, this is because of hardships encountered as a result of being widowed. Such cases occur most frequently in correspondence with religious officials, where the women are writing to get help with the problems caused by the deaths of their spouses. Some of the women whose letters are attested from western Thebes were apparently widowed as a result of the Sassanian invasion of Egypt. One ostracon already mentioned (*SB Kopt.* I 295) is written by a widow whose husband was killed, whose son was injured, and whose cattle were carried off by "the Persians"; her letter is addressed to Bishop Pisentius of Coptos, who, himself, was a refugee from the Sassanian invasion. A similar case is recorded in *O.Mon.Epiph.* 170, in which two women write that the husband of one and the sons of both were killed "by barbarians." The disruption of business caused by the invasion resulted in hardship for the widows; both *SB Kopt.* I 295 and *O.Mon.Epiph.* 300 record the loss of income from husbands' deaths, while in *O.Theb.* 28 a widow bemoans the lack of her husband to till the land that he left her. There are also cases in which widows complain of the behavior of their children after the death of the husband, asking for help in managing them (*O.Mon.Epiph.* 179, for example). Widowhood did not, in all cases, result in dependency and destitution. Among the property owners of Jeme, the widow frequently inherited at least a substantial part of the husband's estate, which was often considerable.[47] Cases of remarriage after widowhood are common in the Jeme documents,[48] and these second marriages, if carried out at a young enough age,[49] often resulted in further children, who could significantly complicate inheritance issues. The will of Elizabeth translated earlier provides an excellent example: Elizabeth had a son Georgios by her first husband Loula; after Loula died, she remarried—to Abraham, with whom then she had Kyra and Isak. After her death, Georgios fought and ultimately settled with her second husband and children from the second marriage.

[47] As in the Elizabeth/Abigaia papers; see also, for example, *P.KRU* 74, in which a widow inherits all her husband's extensive property, and the will of the widow Susanna, who has considerable property to dispose of to her children (*P.KRU* 66 = *P.KRU* 76). For inheritance in general, see Till 1954 (the standard work).

[48] The will *P.KRU* 74, however, apparently makes its bequest contingent on the widow not remarrying.

[49] For earlier Roman period material on this subject, see Hanson 2000.

Elizabeth's will also attests to women's concern about death and its attendant issues: not only does Elizabeth attempt to settle the disposition of her property according to her wishes after death, but she also tries to ensure that she receive proper postmortem treatment of her body and soul. She asks Abraham to see to her burial clothes (and by implication the burial) as well as her holy offering "in the way of every Christian woman" (*P.KRU* 68.64–66). Clearly there were expectations about what was to be done in connection with a death, and Elizabeth's words suggest that perhaps these suggestions had a gendered dimension. In general, references to death and dying are well attested at Jeme, most often in the form of wills or in donation documents. The imminent death of children is, we have seen, a constant of the child donation contracts and illustrates graphically some of the attitudes of Jemeans toward death. The effect of the death of men at Jeme on the survivors can be seen in the letters of widows described above, but comparable references to the deaths of women are rare. One example is the letter of a woman written to a monk about the death of her mother (*O.Mon.Epiph.* 489), but this gives little information on the impact of such an event. We see a bit more of the impact of a woman's death in Elizabeth's will, in reference to the death of her unnamed mother-in-law: not only were there property matters to be taken care of that necessitated Abraham's return to Syene, but the dead woman's husband also had urgent need for 6 solidi—a not inconsiderable sum—apparently to provide for his dead wife's funerary offerings. The nature of these offerings is not entirely clear, but it seems that they would enable the saying of prayers and/or performance of a religious service in memory of the dead woman.

We sometimes get information about the effects of death upon the women who were dying from their own words; the donation contracts that record deathbed bequests usually contain a short narrative of how the dying person came to make the gift. In one, Anna, mother of Johannes, described the deathbed suffering that led her to donate property (her memorial) to the Monastery of Paul of Kulol for charity:

> Now, I myself was this wretched woman awaiting her hour of death. Because of the great sickness into which I had fallen, I knew that I was approaching my end: as the holy prophet has

said it: "*Lord, show me my death.*"[50] Now when, according to the will of the good God, he made me fall into this sickness in which I shall pass away like all my forefathers, I was afraid, being on my bed, and I tossed and turned continually. I could not see anywhere to support my head, so that I could find some rest in a comfortable place. Then God put it into my heart to donate this little memorial to the holy Monastery (of Paul) which I mentioned at the head of this deed: first, may his prayers and his holy dignities be favorable to me before the judge of truth, and that my little memorial be preserved for the sake of the great charity which is now done for the poor who pass by the holy monastery. (*P.KRU* 106.57–77)

Anna goes into great detail about the nature and disposition of her donation: again, an example of a Jeme woman determined to spell out her legacy to the community as well as her family.

Once dead, the body would be prepared and then buried; Elizabeth's will implies a special funerary costume of some sort, perhaps something along the lines of the elaborately decorated textiles known from so many burial sites in Late Antique Egypt.[51] The bodies of the dead of Jeme were buried in an area to the northwest of the town, near the church built on the ruins of the Ay and Horemheb temple and in the midst of earlier pagan burials of the Roman period—near enough to the town to be visited as a devotional act and to be seen when traveling to the nearby monasteries.[52] The burials were made in small pits that were oval, rectangular, or sometimes in a vaguely human shape; some of the pits were lined with stone.[53] Unfortunately, not a single grave of the Jeme cemetery received any sort of formal recording before the burials were plundered,[54] and consequently there is little information on the precise treatment of the bodies. There is some parallel material

[50] Quotation of Psalm 38:5.

[51] Rutschowskaya 1990 for basic references on the very extensive literature on "Coptic" textiles.

[52] See Hölscher 1932, plate 34.

[53] Hölscher 1954, 56–57.

[54] This was already the case in Winlock and Crum's survey (1926, 5), which was based on information from excavations in 1911–1912. Much of the cemetery fell outside the Oriental Institute's concession, so it was not within Hölscher's area of excavation. In 1992, nothing could be seen of the Jeme burial ground.

from the nearby monasteries,[55] but since these were burials of monks, the disposition of their remains was probably not typical of that of the average Jemean. Moreover, these monastic sites have yielded no female bodies, so they are of little help in determining the details specific to women's bodies. The loss to scholarship of the bodies of the Jeme inhabitants is considerable: these remains may have enabled palaeopathological investigations that would have told us much about the health and lives of the people of Jeme, in addition to illuminating burial practices. Instead we are left with empty graves, along with a knowledge of the legacies some women of Jeme left to their families and to their community.

In life, the women of Jeme were not simply limited to their household, dealing only with family members and staying within the home. These women were active on many levels in the public life of Jeme and environs: in their immediate neighborhoods, in their communities, in the western Theban area in general, and even outside the region. The Elizabeth/Abigaia archive shows a relatively restricted field: the women's documented interactions and business dealings are mostly within the family and concern a fairly small group of properties. But, at a minimal level, we also know something about the women's neighbors: the initial house division implies at least the passive interest, if not the active involvement, of the neighbors enumerated in this document. The relatively close quarters at Jeme would have made the neighbors on Kulol Street aware of the comings and goings at Elizabeth and Abigaia's shared house, for example, or the repairs done by Abraham and Daniel, and the proposed external staircase for Elizabeth's portion would have certainly attracted the attention and discussion of the near neighbors. The preparation and implementation of these documents involved the services of witnesses and scribes who were not related to the family, travel at least to the churches where the agreements were made, and, in some cases, recourse to the "great men" of Jeme for the settlement of disputes. Elizabeth's marriage to a man from Syene and her son Georgios's activity in Klusme, too, indicate that these women would have had contacts well beyond Jeme. All of this suggests a world at odds with Pisentius's admonitions (discussed in chapter 1) that women restrict their activities to their homes only, and it is

---

[55] See Winlock and Crum 1926, 45–50, Bachatly 1981, 28, Bács 2000, and the comprehensive study of a single body in Castel 1979.

instructive to see how the women of Jeme existed as members of a larger community.

We have seen how Elizabeth and Abigaia were identified in their legal documents by their own and their family names. They are also identified by their communities: Elizabeth, in her will, identifies herself as being "from the Kastron Jeme in the district of the city of Armant" (*P.KRU* 68.3–5) while Abigaia, in the initial house division from the archive, identifies herself and her husband and family, as well as Elizabeth and her family, as "people of the Kastron Jeme in the district of the city of Armant" (*P.KRU* 35.14–15). This is standard practice in the formal legal documents from the Monastery of Phoibammon deposit—true for both men and women. In less formal documents, one often finds an abbreviated form of this identification. Thus in the archive of the woman Koloje to be discussed in detail below in chapter 5, we find Koloje described simply as "the woman of Jeme," sometimes qualified as "in the district of Armant" (in, e.g., *O.Medin.HabuCopt.* 72). That this is not peculiar to Jemeans is clear from other documents, such as texts from the Koloje archive where women are identified as "the woman of Petemout," as well as, of course, Elizabeth's husband Abraham, who is usually described as "the man of Syene," even though he no longer lived there. Such identifications by place appear primarily in legal documents, where one's place of residence and/or origin had some significance; these designations do not usually appear in private letters but are instead indicators of community membership in documents of a more public nature.

Although identified as members of a community and inhabitants of a region in legal documents, women were not permitted the same roles in these realms as men. Women were excluded from official and administrative activities: we do not, for example, see women as officials, witnesses, or scribes in any of the Elizabeth/Abigaia papers. Women were barred from participation in public administration. There is no attestation of women holding official position in Jeme, in the western Theban area, or in the district as a whole: the highest office of pagarch at Armant down to the office of *lashane* at Jeme and the various subordinate local positions were held exclusively by men in both the documentary and literary evidence from the time. As we have seen, the Jeme legal texts record many otherwise indeterminate officials known simply as the "great men of Jeme,"[56] but there were not, at least officially, any "great women" of Jeme. This situation does not come as a surprise, given the norms of Late Antique Egypt as a whole and the official policies of successive Byzantine, Sassanian and Muslim administrations regarding Egypt. Nevertheless, certain traditions of female administrators in the region have been preserved in Arabic sources, centering on a woman identified as the "daughter of the Christian Caesar" named Tharzah, who is said to have ruled Luxor at the time of the Muslim conquest.[57] Although we have no contemporary confirmation of this legend, it does present at least a perception that women once held administrative power in the Theban area. But the Jeme texts themselves show no trace of this kind of role for women.

Even lower-level positions in the town bureaucracy seem to have been closed to the women of Jeme. Although at least some women at Jeme were likely to have been literate, they could not function as official scribes for (or witnesses to) formal legal documents. Coptic documents from elsewhere attest to women holding the title *sakho*, which has traditionally been translated as "great scribe" but may instead be a title for a craft worker.[58] As we have seen, women did act independently in legal contexts: Elizabeth initiated her own will, dictated it to a scribe, and approved it, while Abigaia, although acting with her husband, seems to have been the driving force in the house settlement made with Elizabeth. Women certainly appear in legal documents with great frequency: in the 123 legal documents from the Monastery of Phoibammon deposit, about 12 percent of the individuals (excluding witnesses and doubtful cases) that appear are women. These women did not write or sign their own documents, but even many of the men involved could not do so either. Women may have acted as (uncredited) scribe to less formal and elaborate legal documents frequently found on ostraca—these will be discussed in chapter 5. But again this implied no official status.

[56] Although it is theoretically possible to read the Coptic for "great men" (*noc nrôme*) as a non-gender-specific plural (i.e., "great people") that could include women, the evidence does not permit this; see Steinwenter 1920, 43–44 for this and the parallel term "great sons" (*noc nshêre*), which is clearly masculine.

[57] See Legrain 1914, 63–72. These legends are part of the complex of stories about Luxor's "patron saint" Abu'l Haggag that Legrain recorded. (I owe this reference to Lanny Bell.)

[58] See Delattre 2001; S. J. Clackson has also addressed this matter in a forthcoming article on Coptic texts from Oxyrhynchus.

The official status of women within the community of Jeme can be summed up by two documents: a communal agreement (*P.CLT* 6) and a listing of guarantors (*P.KRU* 119). The former document, a formal agreement among a group of Jemeans to divide duties imposed on the community, contains no mention of women, this silence an eloquent statement of women's exclusion from official public roles. The latter document, however, includes women: in an official listing of guarantors and the persons they are standing surety for, women appear on both sides of the list. This list shows women functioning as a part of the community in both an economic and legal capacity. Through each of these documents it is possible to trace both the official exclusion from public office and the semi-official inclusion of women in the public life of Jeme.

The communal agreement *P.CLT* 6, dating to either 724 or 739,[59] is a document in which a group of citizens from Jeme agrees on how to divide up naval duties imposed on the community by the Muslim authorities. *P.CLT* 6 is otherwise unparalleled in the Jeme documentation, but its original editor cited a number of parallels from elsewhere.[60] This agreement is an all-male document: the signers and (in the case of illiterates) scribes are all men and are identified only by their fathers' names. The document is signed by only eighteen men; either these were the only men responsible for these particular duties at this time or, more likely, the signatories represent a subset of the total of Jeme men liable for these duties. In either case, this document does reflect the general exclusion of women from such official responsibilities at Jeme.[61]

This exclusion is paralleled in the general exclusion of women from taxation that is found in the Jeme documents. The evidence for taxation

[59] See Till 1962, 44 for these dates.

[60] Schiller 1932, 56–57, citing *P.Lond.Copt.* I 1014 and *P. Lond.* IV 1542, neither of which includes women. Given the regularity with which the Muslim authorities imposed duties on local populations, agreements like *P.CLT* 6 must have been quite common.

[61] This may not have been the case elsewhere: see the roughly contemporary *P. Lond.* IV 1488 (and also Bell and Crum 1910, xxxii for commentary thereupon), where women are included in a list of conscripts in an eighth-century papyrus from Aphrodito. Much of the conscription at Aphrodito was naval, but it is unclear what the women in the case are to be doing. Other documents from the corpus refer to a woman as a *pistikos*, which the original editors read as "ship's captain" but could also be an agent: see, e.g. *SPP* X 29, where a *pistikos* is a spokesman for the Arab administration on tax collection. (Thanks to S. J. Clackson for this reference.)

at Jeme is primarily limited to incidental mentions of the payment of taxes and the receipts issued to the taxpayers.[62] A fairly large number of the latter exist; most of these tax receipts were written on pottery of a specific type between the years 695 and 735. Of the hundreds of published tax receipts from Jeme and environs,[63] only a few are receipts of tax paid by women. This is not surprising: the majority of these receipts are for the poll tax or head tax (*diagraphon*), which was levied only on adult males.[64] One of the receipts of tax paid by a woman (*O.Crum* 428) could be interpreted as an exceptional case of poll tax paid by a woman, but the text is ambiguous as to the type of tax being paid. In it, Athanasia, daughter of Konstantinos, pays 1 gold solidus in the first payment of the tax cycle. These "payments" are usually for poll tax, but there are enough uncertain cases in the corpus that it is impossible to say that Athanasia is indeed paying poll tax.[65] Two other receipts for tax paid by women are unmistakably for tax on land (*dēmosion*). In *BKU* I 84,[66] a woman named Thellina pays half a gold solidus for her land tax, while in *O.CrumST* 83, two women, Tagape and Thentia, pay 16 (?) carats (= $^2/_3$ gold solidus) as their share of the land tax. In the latter case, the shares are due, perhaps, to joint ownership of property of the sort we saw with Elizabeth and Abigaia; the two women would have shared ownership of the property being taxed with at least one other individual. These two tax receipts from women come from the relatively small number of receipts for land tax from Jeme, and the precise mechanics of its assessment are not clear. The poll tax is by far the more common, and this is something that women were definitely excluded from.

---

[62] For the complex subject of taxation in Egypt after the Muslim conquest in general, see Baek Simonsen 1988 and the references therein; note also the works cited in the following notes.

[63] See now the listings in Worp 1999 and Poll 1999; note also the earlier work Kahle 1974, Hintze 1974, Gascou 1979, and Boud'Hors 1996.

[64] See Bell and Crum 1910, xxv, 173 for the evidence for this. The citation of *P.Ryl.Copt.* 322 on behalf of this may not, perhaps, be such good support; rather than a reference to women's exemption from poll tax, this text seems to show that a man has made women his heirs and that they were exempted from tax demands as a result (see below).

[65] Another possibility would be to read the name as Athanasis, that is, the man's name Athanasius; this is suggested by Crum but not very strongly. Alternatively, Athanasia could be paying poll tax for a deceased male relative; for examples of this see Bell and Crum 1910, 173. *O.Crum* 428 is dated by Walter Till (1962, 64) to 720.

[66] See now Hintze 1974, no. 17.

Aside from the tax receipts, however, in most cases where women are found paying taxes, they are actually paying them for a male relative. A good example is the ostracon discussed above (*SB Kopt.* I 295), where a woman complains that, although her husband was killed during the Sassanian invasion, she was still held liable for his land.[67] She had to borrow money to pay the land tax (*dêmosion*) on this land; when she was unable to repay it, the (male) moneylender carried off her remaining cattle. Women also paid the taxes of male relatives under more favorable circumstances. We have already seen this in the will of Elizabeth, where she states that she has paid the "taxes" (*dêmosion*, but in a more generic sense) of her son Georgios, an act mentioned twice in her descriptions of what she has done for this problem son (*P.KRU* 68.40,70). While these texts do not reveal much about the taxation of women, they do show how women could, and at times were required to, take over for men as taxpayers[68] but were in general excluded from regular, communal taxation, just as they were from the naval duties levied on the community in the agreement discussed above.

We can contrast this situation with the list of guarantors *P.KRU* 119, a document that shows women acting as part of the community in a different way from the communal agreement. This text is a listing of some 39 lines; on each line there is the name of one or two individuals, followed by an abbreviated word and then another name. Although somewhat ambiguous, the wording of the various entries implies that the first names are the guarantors and the latter the persons being guaranteed, the entries to be translated "X the guarantor of Y" or "X guarantees Y."[69] Women appear on both sides of the list, as guarantor

[67] Disagreeing with Drescher 1944, 93, who takes this as a reference to the woman's duties of farming state land; the parallels he gives are much earlier than the present text.

[68] The case in *P.Ryl.Copt.* 322 mentioned above could be read as the case of a man distributing shares of his estate so that women do not have to pay tax on it. "Since Mena had given the women shares of his, we exempted them from (literally 'erased them regarding') demands (of taxation) against them." Reading *krerês* for *klêros* "shares" requires less emendation than Crum's *klêronemos* "heirs" and makes better sense. If this is the case, the officials seem well aware of the stratagem involved, since *P.Ryl.Copt.* 322 is a letter between officials.

[69] The latter seems more likely by completing the abbreviation as a verb—*antiphô(neue n)* or something similar. Till's standard work on Coptic surety documents (Bürgschaftsurkunden) considers *P.KRU* 119 "unklar" (Till 1958, 218), an opinion reflected by his translation of the text in the posthumously published Till 1964, 196–

and guarantee; of the 92 names in the list, 11 are women, making up about 12 percent of the total, a proportion already noted for women in the formal Jeme legal documents in general. In some cases women act with reference to relatives, but in other cases they guarantee or are guaranteed by nonrelatives. The fact that women are acceptable as guarantors highlights the other side of their public life at Jeme: excluded from certain official functions and obligations that were imposed from outside the community, women were not excluded from acting in extrafamilial roles within the community.

Indeed, we see the women of Jeme participating in the life of their community in other, often very visibly public, ways as well. Given the importance of religion in daily life at Jeme, it is not surprising to find the women of Jeme very active in this sphere. In some ways, their participation in the religious life of the community parallels their involvements in the secular sphere: although barred from official positions in the religious hierarchy, the women of Jeme found many significant unofficial roles in the religious life of their community. The women of Jeme who filled the different religious roles available to them will be the focus of the next chapter.

197, where he merely gives the two groups of names separated by "(*antiphônêtês*)." In the relevant entries in Till's prosopography of Jeme texts (1962), however, he seems to have tacitly accepted the view expressed here.

4

Donors, Monastics, Worshippers:
Women's Lives and Religion

The private lives and public acts of women at Jeme were both intimately connected to another aspect of Jemean life: religion. Indeed, the most conspicuous public acts of women in the town were religious in nature, pious donations to local religious institutions. Although these donations could be highly visible indicators of economic and social status, in the context of Jemean society they were probably seen even more as religious acts, as conspicuous markers of devotion. These various donations to religious institutions are perhaps the best-documented manifestations of the wide range of activities that the women of Jeme participated in as part of the religious life of their town. As we have seen, the church and its authorities exercised a substantial influence, even control, over the lives of women at Jeme, but these women were not merely passive recipients of instruction from religious leaders. Although barred from formal service in the priesthood, women participated in the religious life of Jeme, and their lives centered on the church and its activities.

One woman's donation to a local church may have given us our only identifiable portrait of a woman of Jeme. In the small Ptolemaic period temple to the east of the monumental Ramesses III gateway that was reused by the inhabitants of Jeme for a church is a series of murals showing various scenes from Egyptian Christian hagiography.[1] These murals have been very badly damaged over time—no complete figures or inscriptions survive—but enough remains to show that one long wall of the church was given over to a mural devoted to Menas, one of the most beloved of the Egyptian saints.[2] The mural shows Menas in various situations relevant to his life: Menas and his tomb, Menas with camels (he is particularly associated with camels), Menas performing a miracle involving bricks of gold (?), Menas apparently raising the dead. To the

[1] See the facsimiles in Edgerton 1937, plates 98–101 and discussion in Wilber 1940; location noted by number 8 in the map in figure 2.
[2] The literature on Menas is extensive; for a general survey, see Krause 1991, and note the stories about Menas in Drescher 1946.

95

a
         b

Fig. 6a–b. Mural of Elizabeth and her daughter
(after Edgerton 1937, plates 91 and 98) (a) and reconstruction (b)

extreme right of the scene are two female figures (the only two figures definitely identifiable as women in the entire church, see fig. 6a), identified by a Coptic caption above the figures as "Elizabeth and her daughter . . ."[3] Elizabeth and her daughter are represented with their arms raised in the traditional attitude of prayer (the "orans" or "orant" pose); as one would expect, Elizabeth is considerably taller than her daughter. Little is preserved of these images apart from their hands, which seem to show that the skin tones were indicated with the same yellowish (now greenish) color used for the background, and their clothing, which is depicted in tones of light to dark red. It is possible, based on parallels in the other murals in the chapel, to attempt some general reconstruction (fig. 6b), but much remains unclear.[4]

The figures are not, as far as can be determined, part of the immediately adjacent miracle scene: they are clearly isolated from the action of that scene and set apart at the end of a long wall. This is not surprising, as no one named Elizabeth (with or without a daughter) is known to have been connected to the life of Menas. Bearing these factors in mind, the author of the primary study of the Menas mural concluded that the woman named Elizabeth was, in fact, the donor of the chapel—the person who paid for the mural in which she was shown (Wilbur 1940, 98). And indeed, this is really the only explanation for these figures that makes sense. Elizabeth stands off to the side, observing the events from the safety of her position as donor but not participating.

[3] The earlier commentator (Wilbur 1940, 98) notes the traces of an "illegible word or words" following "Elizabeth and her daughter" but does not state the obvious conclusion that these traces once gave the name of the daughter, possibly beginning with "M," so "Maria" being the most likely, although there are a number of other possibilities (e.g., Martha, Martyria, Makrina, etc.). Although this inscription is primarily known from the color facsimile of the Menas mural (Edgerton 1937, plate 98), there is a somewhat better black and white photograph of it in the documentation of the much earlier Demotic graffito directly under it (Edgerton 1937, plate 91 showing graffito 341), which may repay further study.

[4] In particular, it is ambiguous whether these figures of Elizabeth and her daughter originally had haloes or nimbuses around their heads, like those figures participating directly in the scenes of Menas and his miracles. Wilbur, in his reconstruction, showed them with nimbuses (1940, figure 1), but I am not convinced that the black mark between Elizabeth's head and hand is the remains of a nimbus: the nimbuses that are unambiguous elsewhere in the mural are colored gray, but there is no trace of this color around Elizabeth's head, nor is there a trace of any sort of nimbus where one would expect it to the left of the head of her daughter. This absence of haloes on these figures reinforces the identification of these as donor figures.

She prominently displays not only her own wealth in being able to commission such a mural but also her piety, as witnessed by the commission itself, her depiction, and the respectful attitude of prayer in which she stands. Further, Elizabeth displays her daughter before her and, in doing so, makes a statement about her daughter's status and piety as well. Although the figures are badly damaged, we can see fragmentary details that, when taken with the other better preserved figures in the murals, enable us to be reasonably confident of the restoration in figure 6b. Although far from realistic portraits, the images of Elizabeth and her daughter are the only representations of real women (as opposed to abstracted ideals) to survive from Jeme.[5]

Elizabeth's murals are the only known remains of a woman's donation from Jeme, but we have records of many other religiously motivated donations. Commemorative offerings to the memory of one's parents were a common feature of western Theban religious life, and several documents record women's participation in this custom. The purpose of such offerings was either to provide furnishings for a church or monastery or to pay for special commemorative services, or both. One text (*O.CrumVC* 88) is a letter from a woman apologizing for being absent from her home because she had to go to church for her mother's commemoration day. That such offerings were expected is evident from *O.CrumVC* 85, a letter to a woman upbraiding her for neglecting the commemorative offering for her mother. In another document (*O.CrumVC* 70), Rebecca writes to a priest concerning problems with the memorial offering for her parents, instructing him to sell a donated censer if the money is needed instead.[6] In addition to commemorative offerings, one finds outright donations of property to religious institutions, some of which were made by women. In one document (*O.Brit.Mus.Copt.* 66:2), a woman

---

[5] Indeed, it is very tempting to identify this Elizabeth with the woman from the Eizabeth/Abigaia papers discussed above in chapters 3 and 4. The name Elizabeth, of course, is far too common to permit this; the Elizabeth of the archive would have presumably had the funds to make such a donation, but in the absence of further evidence it is impossible to support this suggestion. The only slight indication in favor of an identification might be the name of the daughter in the mural, if she was named Maria (as the traces suit): the archive Elizabeth's mother was named Maria, and the naming of children after grandparents was common. But we have no record of a child named Maria for the archive Elizabeth, so this is hardly conclusive evidence.

[6] A number of censers of varying degrees of elaborateness were found in the Medinet Habu excavations; see Hölscher 1954, 63 (metal) and 77–78 (ceramic).

donates land obtained from her father to the Monastery of Pisentius, listing the boundaries of the property.

More elaborate and substantial are the donations recorded in the documents from the archive of Jeme legal papers found in the ruins of the Monastery of Phoibammon—the same source as the Elizabeth/ Abigaia archive. Indeed, the legal documents that record donations provide some of the most vivid accounts of women's involvement in local religious life. Like the Elizabeth/Abigaia papers, the donation documents are highly formulaic and follow a set structure,[7] but they also provide important details that enable us to reconstruct something of the lives of the women involved. Very often these texts provide narratives of events that led to these donations; although mediated through a scribe in all cases, these texts may well preserve the women's own accounts of their lives. A substantial donation of property is preserved in *P.KRU* 106, partly translated in the previous chapter, a testamentary donation of a house and a portion of another by Anna, mother of Johannes, from 735. Anna provides a short narrative of the circumstances of her donation, describing it as a deathbed act of piety, and her intentions as to the use of her donation: to contribute to an ongoing charitable effort toward the poor ("that my little memorial be preserved for the sake of the great charity that is now done for the poor who pass by the holy monastery"). Like most such donations from Jeme residents, the gift is made to one of the nearby monasteries of western Thebes; in the case of Anna it is the Monastery of Paulos of Kulol, while other donations from women go to the better-known west Theban monasteries of Phoibammon and Pisentius.[8] In some cases, the value of the donations is not large—note the one tremis donated by Tsyros, daughter of Takhum, to the monastery of Apa Psate in *P.KRU* 54—but these were still treated seriously and scrupulously documented.

To modern readers and scholars, the Jeme contracts documenting the donation of children to local monasteries (*P.KRU* 78-103) have provoked the most interest and discussion.[9] In these contracts, parents donate male children, usually at a very young age, to the Monastery of

[7] For a detailed analysis of the formulae and structure of these documents, see now Biedenkopf-Ziehner 2001.

[8] The former was the recipient of most of the donated children from Jeme to be discussed immediately below, while the latter received a piece of land in *O.Brit.Mus.Copt.* 66:2 from a woman who had inherited it from her father.

[9] For a recent discussion of the legal implications of these documents and an

Phoibammon to serve the monastery; when specified, their duties most often include the tending of lamps. The parents usually made these donations in gratitude for the healing of a sick child or some other perceived divine action. In a number of instances, parents have attempted to go back on an initial promise to donate, only to have their child become dangerously ill. These contracts frequently include, imbedded in the midst of the usual legal phraseology and formulae, brief but vivid tales of childhood sickness, parental love, and uncertainties over the act of donating a child for religious service. Three of these contracts, in particular, give an unparalleled insight into the conflict that three women felt between their duties toward their children and their God.

In the year 766, a woman named Tachel, daughter of Sophia, prepared a contract to donate her son Athanasios to the service of the Monastery of Phoibammon (*P.KRU* 86). She did so in conjunction with her sister Elizabeth; there is no mention of a husband, either in the legal formulae of the contract or in Tachel's account of her son's birth and early life. The usual interpretation here is that Tachel's husband had died or left her, but it is, of course, entirely possible that Tachel was instead an unmarried mother.[10] In any case, the implication is that Elizabeth had helped her sister raise the child, hence her participation in the donation. The circumstances surrounding the birth of the child and the donation are described in the contract:

> Since, in that time in which we were, a male child was born
> to me, Tachel, woman and free-woman,[11] in his seventh

extensive listing of earlier scholarship, see Schaten 1996; note, in general, the discussion in MacCoull 1979 and Thissen 1986, and for a detailed discussion of the legal formulae and personnel of these documents, see now Biedenkopf-Ziehner 2001, 5–46, 69–94. These texts are among the few Coptic documentary sources to receive attention from historians outside the areas of Egyptology, Papyrology, and Coptic Studies—see, for example, the discussion in Boswell 1988, cited above in chapter 3.

[10] Certainly there is good precedent in Demotic documents for the dedication of children to religious institutions in these circumstances: note the dedications of children with named mothers and fathers known as Buirekhirenef (i.e., "I don't know his name"); see Thissen 1986, 124–128 and DePauw 1997, 136–137.

[11] *Teshime auô eleuthera*: for this last term, see Steinwenter 1955, 16–17. In this context, it is presumably in reference to Tachel's ability to enter freely into this contract; see further below.

month.[12] I promised him as servant to the holy Monastery of Phoibammon in the mountain of Jeme, so that, if God would keep him from death, I should give him to the holy monastery. Afterward, when God caused that this little boy, whom I named Athanasios at the holy baptism, grow and get bigger, my lost reason cast me into a great sin. Concerning this little boy, I plotted that I should not (have to) give him to the holy place. When God saw the lawless thing I did, he cast the little boy into a great sickness, which became so great that it was reckoned by everyone who saw him that he had died. When I remembered the sin and the reckless thing that I had done, I once again called upon the holy one in his monastery: "If you will call upon God and he bestows on this boy a cure, I will put him into the monastery forever, according to my first agreement." (*P.KRU* 86.17–32)

Athanasios's premature birth clearly caused concerns for his survival, hence Tachel's promise that he be donated to the Monastery of Phoibammon. Most, if not all, of the surviving child donations were made under similar circumstances, in the hope of protection and/or healing for newborns and very young children. The actual handing over of the child to the monastery did not, however, take place until the child was old enough to take on simple duties. The time between the initial promise of the donation and the point at which a child could enter the monastery was clearly a difficult time for the mother. In the case of Tachel, she became so attached to her son that she neglected her promise. The child became ill, which Tachel interpreted as punishment for her neglect of her promise. The conflict between her obvious attachment to Athanasios and her feelings of guilt at not honoring her promise to God is evident in her characterization of her desire to keep her child as losing her reason. Tachel renewed her promise

---

[12] Till's translation (1964, 163) takes the phrase "in his seventh month" as going with the following clause—a statement that Tachel made her promise when the boy was seven months old. But one would expect a different verbal construction if that were the case; grammatically it makes more sense to read this adverbial phrase as the end of the preceding description—a reference to a premature birth that may account for the health problems that follow. For the idea common in Greek medical writers that a seven-month premature child would survive but an eight-month premature child would not, see Hanson 1987, Rowlandson 1998, 292–294, and the references there.

in the hope that Athanasios would survive. The text does indeed go on to describe his recovery, and Tachel's description of her fulfillment of her promise reads simply but poignantly: "I lifted him in my hands and brought him to the holy place" (34–35). The remainder of her document is full of standard legal formulae and witness statements.

A similar case appears in a document drawn up some time after Tachel's (*P.KRU* 79). In this text, Kalisthene[13] describes the circumstances of the donation of her son Merkoure to the Monastery of Phoibammon:

> I reflected that I am a sinner dwelling on the earth like all my ancestors. (So) I made a decision and donated my beloved son Merkoure to the holy chapel of the holy Apa Phoibammon of the mountain of Jeme in order that he become a servant in the holy place forever for the health of my sinful soul and that of my late husband. I will inform you precisely: When the merciful and pitying God gave the child to me, afterward, when the little one approached adulthood, the good God brought on him a very hard and heavy sickness, so that I should abandon him as dying. Then we called upon the God of the holy Apa Phoibammon: "If you will grace him with a cure, I will donate him to your altar, and he shall be a servant of God in return for the good things that you did for me." (*P.KRU* 79.13–29)

Kalisthene is more specific than Tachel about her marital situation: her husband is dead, and she is acting alone, although her concern for her husband's soul shows him still to be in her thoughts. Like Tachel, Kalisthene has made an initial promise to donate her son to the monastery and then neglects it: her son is described as approaching adulthood when he is stricken ill and Kalisthene reminded of her promise. Exactly what age is implied by this wording is unclear: the boy could be approaching puberty or, and this is probably more likely, approaching an age at which he could make decisions about his own life, so in his later teens. Again, the contract concludes with standard

---

[13] Kalisthene does not give a parent's name, although a gap is left for its insertion. Her name is given later in the document as "Talistene," again with a gap for a parent's name; given her indecisiveness about the spelling of her own name, perhaps Kalisthene intended to check on the spelling of a parent's name and never did so. Alternatively, she may have been an orphan, although one would expect some reference to this status, or, perhaps most likely, she may have been illegitimate herself.

formulae and witness statements: these donation contracts are considered as legally binding as any other.

In a third example, drawn up in 771 (*P.KRU* 81), a woman named Staurou, daughter of Peshate, donated her son Andreas to the Monastery of Phoibammon:

> When my good God commanded and a male child was born to me, I called his name Andreas. God commanded and brought a sickness upon him because of the gravity of my sins. (So) I took him into the holy Monastery of Apa Phoibammon, the honored martyr, which is located in the mountain of Jeme. I put him before the altar, and I called on (God) with prayers and supplications: "If you will bestow a blessing on him for me before Christ, (and if Christ's) pity reach him and (Christ) has mercy on him, I will make him a servant in your holy monastery, and he will serve the holy monastery either with his body or render his duty to the lamp of the holy monastery." (*P.KRU* 81.15–23)

Staurou's narrative gives a vivid picture of her taking the sick child into the monastery's chapel and placing him on the altar—physically treating the child as an offering for his own healing. Again, there is no reference to the father of the child, who is presumed dead or missing; Staurou's naming of the child by herself strongly suggests that the father was dead or absent before the child's birth. Staurou's attribution of the boy's illness to "the gravity of my sins" may well suggest that she was unmarried at his birth. In this contract, Staurou is specifically described as being unable to write, and a priest Theodoros writes for her. This narrative is followed by the usual witness statements.

It may be significant that none of these three women is described as being from Jeme itself: Tachel was from Apé (modern Luxor) across the river, while Staurou was from Psoi but staying in a monastery in Apé, and Kalisthene may have come from much farther north.[14] Other child donors from the Jeme contracts come from outside of Jeme as well: Maria from Tout in *P.KRU* 95, Thomas from the district of Shmin (= Akhmim) in *P.KRU* 99, Zael from Armant in *P.KRU* 80. Although

---

[14] See Winlock and Crum 1926, 105 for discussion of where the district of Primide may be.

the majority of child donors in the contracts seem to come from Jeme, the donations coming from outside are suggestive. It is possible that the Monastery of Phoibammon was specially linked to child donations: we lack documentation of this sort from monasteries elsewhere in Egypt. If Tachel and Staurou[15] were, in fact, unwed mothers, this might suggest that the Monastery of Phoibammon was widely known as an institution where illegitimate children could be safely placed.

Although we have looked in detail at the cases of three women who have donated their children, it is important to bear in mind that in the majority of cases from the Jeme documents, children were donated by their fathers, or by their fathers in conjunction with their mothers; in the latter cases, the narratives are from the fathers' point of view, with the mothers simply agreeing to the contracts. In one case (*P.KRU* 101) a grandfather donates his grandson in the absence of nearer relatives. The precise nature of these donations is not entirely clear: Some contracts (e.g., *P.KRU* 89.17–18) draw a parallel between the donation of the child and the biblical story of Anna's donation of her son Samuel to divine service in gratitude (1 Samuel 1:27–28).[16] Certain contracts state explicitly that the child's status is "like that of a slave bought with money" (*P.KRU* 82.15–16) and to last "forever" (ibid.), so the emphasis on the status of the donor Tachel as a "free-woman" (*eleuthera*: *P.KRU* 86.19) seems all the more significant.[17] Whether this all is to be taken literally and how the donated children's status was affected when they reached adulthood have been the subject of much discussion[18] and are beyond the scope of the present study. Of more relevance for our investigation into the lives of the women of Jeme is the fact that these contracts record only the donation of male children. Since the documents all come from the Monastery of Phoibammon, a men's monastic house, this is not particularly surprising but does raise the question of whether there were comparable institutions to which girls could be donated, indeed whether there were women's monastic houses at all among the many monasteries near Jeme in the western Theban area.

Women's monasticism was certainly well established in Egypt by

[15] And possibly Maria from *P.KRU* 95, but the beginning of the document, with the narrative of the circumstances of the donation, is missing.

[16] See discussion in Biedenkopf-Ziehner 2001, 43–46.

[17] See Steinwenter 1955, 16–18.

[18] Again, note the references in Schaten 1996.

the seventh century. They are attested as monastics in Egypt as early as monasticism itself: a number of women who lived as ascetics and hermits are known from the third and fourth centuries CE.[19] Pachomius, the originator of community-based monasticism and author of the earliest known rule for monastic behavior, is credited with founding the first women's monastic community for his sister Maria near his own monastery in Tabennisi in the mid-fourth century.[20] Pachomius later founded a second women's community nearby, initially supervised by a man but later placed under the direct authority of an elder woman, known as the "old woman" or the "mother." Pachomius did not write a separate rule for women but placed them under the same rule as that of the men in his own monastery. In addition to devotional exercises, this rule prescribed manual work and obedience for the monastic population. Pachomius's successors Theodore and Horsiesios carried on the Pachomian tradition of supervising women's communities. Probably the best-known women's community of this period was at the White Monastery, home of the famous author and abbot Shenoute and his successor Besa, at ancient Atripe.[21] A Coptic biography of Shenoute claims that the women in the community totaled 1,800, compared to 2,400 men—clearly a very substantial population. Shenoute's writings and, to a lesser extent, those of his successor Besa frequently addressed specific issues relating to women's monastic communities. Other religious communities for women were founded in southern Egypt, such as the one at Balliana, known from the writings of its superior Moses. In general, women's religious communities from the fifth century onward were often regarded as sources of potential trouble that required constant supervision. The roots of these negative attitudes toward women's communities, however, are already found in the Pachomian and Shenoutean writings, with their emphasis on regulation and control of women's behavior.[22] In spite of these attitudes, women's communities continued to grow.

After the fifth century, the documentation of women's monasticism becomes increasingly sparse. Although Coptic monastic literature was far from dead, its emphases and priorities had shifted. Monastic themes

[19] See the overview in Elm 1994, 227–228, 253–282.
[20] For the early history of these communities, see Elm 1994, 283–296.
[21] See now the essential study Krawiec 2002.
[22] Again, see the discussion in Wilfong 2002a.

still appeared in literature, but they were generally biographies of single figures rather than the collected anecdotes of several individuals or the pastoral letters that provide so much of the information for earlier periods. For the study of men's monasteries this is not such a problem: the decline in literary sources is accompanied by an increase in nonliterary, documentary evidence. Unfortunately, the same cannot be said for women's religious communities, and this is nowhere better illustrated than in the material from the western Theban area. Nineteen monastic communities are known by name in the western Theban region from the extensive documentary materials; further, at least eleven archaeological sites in the area are known to have been fairly substantial monasteries, and probably twice as many were smaller monastic dwellings or anchorite cells. Of these, however, none can be definitely identified as a female monastic community; in the absence of inscriptional evidence or physical remains, it is impossible, for example, to say for certain whether a given monastic site housed men or women. The traditional identification of the monastic site of the Roman temple to Isis called Deir el-Shelwit ("the distant monastery") as the site of a women's religious community is unproven and the archaeology of the site itself virtually unpublished.[23] Until definite evidence turns up to identify a particular monastic site as a women's monastery, it will not be possible to discuss distinctive features of such institutions from archaeological evidence.[24] In spite of this uncertainty, there are fairly clear indications in the sources that there were women's monastic organizations of some sort in the western Theban area. Although there is no specific information about the names, location, and organization of these communities, the documentation does provide some information on these institutions and the women who inhabited them.

No definitely identifiable women's monastic communities are named in the Theban texts, and the only direct mention of one is vague. *P.Ryl.Copt.* 330 refers to something happening "because of the house of those female monks" (*etbe pêi nmonakhê*) but gives no name and is in a broken context in a letter complaining about a theft from a monastery and high taxes. An unpublished Coptic stela from the Ramesseum is the tombstone for a woman named Maria who seems to

[23] See Wilfong 1989, 126–127 for bibliography.

[24] A reexamination of the available archaeological material should ideally take into account a gendered perspective along the lines of Gilchrist 1994.

bear the monastic administrative title *hegumene*.[25] The existence of a women's monastic community in the Ramesseum is thus a possibility, although there is no further textual or archaeological evidence.

A number of female monastic superiors with the standard title *amma* or *ama* ("mother") are known from the Theban texts, all, unfortunately, in broken or unclear contexts. In the graffito *Gr.Mont.Theb.* 2918 from the Theban mountain, a "Mother Sophia" is mentioned at the end of a list of seven male monks. *BKU* 121 refers to a "Mother T[. . .]," and *O.CrumST* 195 may also refer to an unnamed "Mother." The lack of named women's monasteries and scarcity of named female superiors in the texts make it possible that Theban women's monasteries were informal communities directly connected with men's monasteries, with no separate government (or name) of their own. This view is made more likely by *O.Brit.Mus.Copt.* 66:1, a letter in which a man thanks Apa Dios (and others) for accepting a girl into a monastery and putting her "under his shadow entirely," possibly in return for a financial consideration. Given the monastic rules and regulations in effect in the Theban area at this time,[26] it is extremely unlikely that the girl was taken into a community of men; she must have been placed in the care of women over whom Dios was superior. Female monks explicitly called *monakhê* appear in some Theban documents. A group of them appear in *O.CrumST* 138, part of which is an account of grain paid to some female monks. Theophile the female monk (*monakhê*) acknowledges receipt of rent for her house over a five-year period from an Apa Basile (probably a priest and not a monk) in *CPR IV* 152. This is significant in that it shows that female monastics, like other women, could own and rent out real property. *O.Brit.Mus.Copt.* 53:6 is the broken beginning of a letter from the female monk Maria "to my beloved brother Isaac." In *O.Brit.Mus.Copt.* Ad 23, the female monk Maria[27] writes to Kyriakos "the anchorite," asking for prayers on behalf of an orphan whose father left him with her. Unfortunately, we have no further information on the care of children by female monks, but, lacking further evidence for such a guardianship

[25] For notes on this unpublished text, see the epilogue below and Wilfong forthcoming; the extremely late date of this piece (891) makes it of limited relevance for the present discussion since it was made long after the western Theban area was generally abandoned.

[26] See, for example, the text cited in Winlock and Crum 1926, 134.

[27] The same woman? The publication gives no photograph of the second text.

role, it is unlikely to be something that a female monk could have undertaken for an extended period. The tantalizingly incomplete fragment *P.Pisentius 56* appears to be a letter of complaint about a woman, who behaves not "like a female monk (*monakhê*) of our [monastery (?)] but rather like a worldly woman (*kosmikê*)." Although this sort of accusation is a common topos in literary texts, this is an unusual example of such a complaint in a documentary text.

Other texts from the Theban area are likely to involve female monks, although the women in them are not explicitly identified as such. In *P.Pisentius 28*, translated in chapter 1, two women, Tsheere and Koshe, write to Pisentius concerning the various garments that they are making for the bishop. Young girls who are required to observe the Fast of the Cross (17 Thoth = 13/14 September) are helping them, and this fact, in addition to the general tone of the letter, makes it likely that these two writers are female monks and the work is being done as part of the handicrafts of the monastery with which they were associated. Another letter from two women who are probably monastics is *O.Mon.Epiph.* 386; in this text the women ask a priest to write out part of an ecclesiastical canon for them. A fragmentary letter from a man to three women, Nonna, Tasia, and Maria (*O.Brit.Mus.Copt.* 47:3), is about people going to Armant and what they told him about another woman called Audoxia.[28] There remain a few additional attestations of women, all unfortunately somewhat ambiguous, in a potentially monastic context that suggest that they may have been solitary anchorites. A tombstone (in Greek) of a woman named Swaei from a tomb in the Valley of the Kings,[29] seems from its contents and context likely to have been made for a female anchorite. A few highly damaged graffiti from the Theban mountain may refer to women,[30] but *Gr.Mont.Theb.* 2955, "Mara (for Maria?) the virgin," is the only one likely to have monastic connotations.[31] Another graffito reads:

[28] Although it is tempting to connect the name of the first recipient of this letter with *nonna* "nun," this word is not normally used in this sense in Coptic, but "Nonna" is well attested as a personal name in Coptic documents (Till 1962, 147).

[29] Hall 1905, plate 9:4.

[30] *Gr.Mont.Theb.* 3677 mentions a "Sare" in a broken context, and *Gr.Mont.Theb.* 3751 could refer to a woman in a damaged passage (if the reading of *sikhime* as an early writing of *shime* is accepted).

[31] If it is not, in fact, a reference to the virgin Mary; unfortunately, the entire graffito is obscure and unclear.

Be so good and pray for me in your (masc.) prayers upon (?)
[. . .] the habit. Your beloved [. . .] that god may show great pity
on my miserable soul, in love. + Anna, the sinner, the vir[gin?
. . .] daughter of Theodosios+. (*Gr.Mon.Epiph.* 646)

It is certainly by a woman, and her reference to the monastic habit
(*skhêma*) in a broken passage may mark her as a monastic or at least
someone aspiring to this position.

Documentary sources from other sites in southern Egypt help flesh
out the picture of female monastic communities in the seventh and
eighth centuries. The Greek documents from the archive of the pagarch
Basilios of Aphrodito show evidence of organized female monasticism;
since the Aphrodito papyri represent an administrative level somewhat
higher than that of the western Theban papyri, they give a useful insight
into institutions not explicitly described in the Theban documents but
present in the region. The relevant documents are the long account
books *P.Lond.* IV 1416, 1419, 1421–1422, which contain registers of,
among other things, the payments of land tax under Governor Qurrah
ibn Sharik to the pagarch's representatives. Among the long registers
of taxes on the landholdings, there are listings of the taxes paid by two
women's religious communities: that of Ama Thekla and that of Ama
Maria. Unlike the larger monasteries entered in the registers, neither
women's community is given a separate section, and neither seems to
have had extensive land holdings. The rates of taxation are consistent
with those for other communities, and the amounts paid show that the
women's communities may have had considerable resources to draw upon.

More vivid illustration of the activities and inhabitants of women's
monastic communities comes from the roughly contemporary
settlement in the Seti I temple at Abydos. This community is known
from both literary and nonliterary sources. A fragmentary series of
pastoral letters from Moses of Balliana to the women living in the
Abydos temple,[32] apparently written at the women's request, combines
spiritual instruction with practical advice. In particular, Moses was
concerned with the virginity of the women, their behavior in relation

[32] Edited and translated in Amélineau 1888, 693–701; in some places Amélineau's
copies seem faulty, and a new edition is needed. Moses's surviving letters to the women
are numbered fourteen through eighteen; numbers one through thirteen have not yet
been identified; see Coquin 1991a.

to the nearby towns, and the manual work in which the women were engaged; he also shows special interest in maintaining harmony within the community and in the women's education and reading. Moses of Balliana lived in the sixth century, but the community remained active through at least the next two centuries, as is evident from a group of more than fifty graffiti from the temple walls.[33] Of these graffiti, many are the usual crosses, scriptural quotations, and prayers found in most Coptic sites. Several, however, list the names of female monks and monastic superiors, and others describe a particular woman as having "done the week(ly duties)."[34] These duties included cleaning, collecting honey, and various other agricultural tasks; the women's agricultural work is further implied in other graffiti recording the dates of the rising of the Nile that often accompany the inscriptions concerning the weekly duties. These activities of the women of Abydos are entirely consistent with the other evidence, literary and nonliterary, for women's religious communities and provide a valuable complement to the western Theban material.

Beyond the actual participation of Jeme women in monastic life as monks, we find them fulfilling significant roles in connection with men's monasticism. This is especially well illustrated in the Monastery of Epiphanius corpus.[35] In these texts, men and women of Jeme and the surrounding countryside interact with the monks of the Monastery of Epiphanius and other desert hermitages.[36] In the largest group of Monastery of Epiphanius texts concerning women, they are involved in supplying the financial and material needs of the monks and the monastery itself. In most of these texts, the women dealing with monks are usually relatives: mothers, sisters, sisters-in-law; substantially more female relatives perform services and get supplies to monks than male relatives.[37] Individual monks, in some cases, relied very heavily on these

[33] Crum 1904, 38–43, plates 25–38. Compare to Piankoff 1958–1960 for the graffiti in the nearby Osireion.

[34] See Crum 1904, 42. These weekly duties are prescribed for men in the Pachomian monastic rules; see Lefort 1956, 32 (no. 111) and 33 (no. 124).

[35] The discussion that follows was originally presented (in a much different form) at the 1993 Byzantine Studies Conference at Princeton University; I am grateful to Roger S. Bagnall and Jennifer Sheridan for their comments and suggestions.

[36] For an essential study of the interaction of monasteries and nearby towns in Late Antique Egypt from the Greek documentation, see Wipszycka 1994.

[37] In some cases, the existence of a family relationship (as opposed to a spiritual one) is uncertain, for the reasons of terminology discussed in chapters 1 and 4. In

informal networks of female relatives for their dealings with the world outside the monastery: they bring supplies, food, and even heavy equipment to the Monastery of Epiphanius. Such transactions are not always done merely out of familial piety: the women often ask for payment for goods. In one ostracon,[38] a woman asks her father for payment on a shipment of dates (from the tone, one gets the impression that this is not the first time she has asked for payment), while another is an agreement between a Mariam and her brother Moses (*O.Mon.Epiph.* 352): she will load a loom on two camels and bring the loom to him if he will pay for the camels' use. There are frequent follow-up letters from the women on the deliveries (*P.Mon.Epiph.* 433 from Tagape). More than that, these women also look after or administer the monks' outside business interests, conveying money to and from the monks, buying and selling goods and property for them, and so on. An apparent interchange of letters between an Epiphanius and his mother records such transactions: Epiphanius writes to his mother Koloje asking about the selling of wine and sending him the profits and other money (*O.Mon.Epiph* 259); in reply, Koloje sends wine and writes to say that she will send money if possible. She also asks Epiphanius to visit David and ask about his property because he (Epiphanius) does not realize that he has been robbed and finally asks him to send her the grain, which she will grind (*O.Mon.Epiph.* 336). Sometimes these actions are to be done in tandem with male relatives as in the case of a monk asking his mother and father to make a payment for him (*O.Mon.Epiph.* 294), but mostly it is female relatives alone. In one letter, a monk asks his brother's wife to check into a dispute over various objects (*O.Mon.Epiph.* 407), while another letter concerns money sent by a woman that turned out to be less than the writer's mother said it should be (*O.Mon.Epiph.* 280). Female relatives perform other services for the monks, such as running errands (*P.Mon.Epiph.* 311 and *O.Mon.Epiph.* 451, done by man's mother), delivering letters (*O.Mon.Epiph.* 343) and messages, and bringing people to see the monks (*O.Mon.Epiph.* 374). Letters commonly contain multiple requests; Epiphanius asks his mother to have a key duplicated for him and deliver a letter (*O.Mon.Epiph.* 397).

---

general, the cases that will be discussed here are limited to those in which there is more reason for assuming a familial relationship than just terms of address.

[38] "Discard" text number VI.14A.153 in the Walter Crum notes.

A number of the women dealing with the monks are apparently not relatives; these women are paid for supplies and for work (the nature of which is not always expressed), so these relations are perhaps more commercial than pious. In these cases, the dealings seem to be less with the individual monks and more with the monastery as a whole. In some cases, women make deliveries directly to the monastery (*O.Mon.Epiph.* 236) of various supplies, and there are frequent if vague references to women buying and selling (*O.Mon.Epiph.* 349).[39] Lists of moneys and goods paid out to women are frequently found in expense accounts (*O.Mon.Epiph.* 519, 530, 532, 533); in one case these payments are made to the women through various men (*O.Mon.Epiph.* 538). The presence of a so-called pawnbroker's journal (*O.Mon.Epiph.* 531), which includes payments to women in grain and money and refers to articles on deposit, at the Monastery of Epiphanius suggests that women's moneylending activities, to be discussed in chapter 5, extended to the monasteries.[40] A woman who sends someone to pick up a candelabrum (*O.Mon.Epiph.* 544) seems to be repossessing it or taking it as a pledge on a loan. In a highly interesting but badly damaged text (*O.Mon.Epiph.* 388) monks write to a woman about a book they have ordered, wanting it to be sent quickly; unfortunately, the text does not specify whether she is copying it, decorating it, binding it, or what. In carrying out these kinds of errands, women managed to participate in men's monasticism by facilitating their monastic activities.

Another form of participation in monasteries and their activities in Late Antique Egypt was religious pilgrimage, and women were certainly active in this regard elsewhere in Egypt.[41] But the evidence from the region around Jeme is scanty: we certainly have no record of Jeme women (or men) going on pilgrimages outside the Theban area. The reasons for this may be purely pragmatic: the western Theban area had such a variety of religious sites that travel elsewhere for purposes of devotional tourism may have seemed superfluous. The region supported at least twelve churches, twenty monasteries and a large number of

[39] Note a similar situation in a text not from the western Theban area: *P.Mon.Apollo* 49, where a woman is supplying wine to the Monastery of Apollo at Bawit.

[40] Of course, such transactions could go in the other direction, as in *P.Mon.Apollo* 33, also from Bawit, where a woman borrows money from a monk at the Monastery of Apollo, who, since lending at interest is forbidden to monks, does not charge her interest.

[41] See, in general, the articles in Frankfurter 1998b.

solitary ascetic monks (always popular objects of religious tourism in Egypt), and visiting celebrities such as Bishop Pisentius of Coptos. Contemporary graffiti show how popular these places and people were with visitors (including at least one woman in *Gr.Mon.Epiph.* 646), and they appear to have sufficed for the devotional needs of the western Thebans.[42] But evidence does not suggest that this was a popular devotional activity for the women of Jeme, who may have been content with their more mundane contacts with the western Theban monasteries.

Participation in donations and monasticism was to some extent exceptional: donations, at least the recorded ones, tended to be special occasions. Only a small minority of Jemean women would have been active monastics themselves, and the number of women who provided support services for male monastics in the western Theban area would have been relatively small. The primary religious involvement of most of the women at Jeme would have been regular participation in religious worship and festivals at their local churches. The great Holy Church of Jeme dominated the entire town, while at least three other smaller churches provided accommodation for worship as well. Although women are never attested as officiating at religious services, not surprising considering their restriction from the priesthood, they certainly participated as worshippers. References in textual material to women in connection with worship at these churches, however, are largely exceptional. There are several references to women causing disturbances in churches, although none of them is explicit as to what was done. In one case (*P.Ryl.Copt.* 280), a woman is punished by having the soles of her feet beaten for causing a disturbance (*skantalon*), but this is not otherwise described. Another disturbance is noted in a very fragmentary letter (*O.Brit.Mus.Copt.* 70:3) about a woman who disturbed (*tarahe*) a church: she is described as going in and doing violence, "and (now) she cries." In some cases, the mere presence of women was considered a disturbance, especially in a monastery of men: in a letter of Bishop Serenianus, he complains that, on the first Sunday of Easter, Papas profaned the Monastery of Phoibammon by bringing a crowd of women into the chapel and administering the sacrament to them.[43]

---

[42] Note the late (tenth- to thirteenth-century) graffiti at the Monastery of Phoibammon (Godlewski 1986, 141–152, numbers 1–8, 10–17, and 29) that are records of visitors to the monastery long after its abandonment.

[43] Winlock and Crum 1926, 134.

The highly fragmentary *P.Pisentius* 43 apparently describes how, on the night of the Sunday of Easter, a woman and her children seized her husband and did something that resulted in a great expulsion (from the church?).

Unfortunately, this material is exceptional by its very nature, and much of the day-to-day involvement of women in religion seems to have gone unrecorded. There are, for example, more than enough references to show that women regularly went to church, but it is not possible to tell how often or what they did there. We get casual references to the observance of religious feasts and fasts (see, again, the letter translated in chapter 1 and discussed above—*P.Pisentius* 28—in which two girls are said to keep a particular feast). Nor is it known whether women participated specially in festivals of female saints, like those recorded in O.*Crum* 26–27. Such details of daily life are not even recorded in literary texts; instead only exceptional circumstances are mentioned in the written evidence, so it is hard to draw any general conclusions.

We also have relatively little information about personal religious devotions and activities in the home. These were a major component of women's lives in Egypt in earlier periods, and many of the traditions established in pagan times survived the coming of Christianity.[44] We find the use of crosses as amulets,[45] and a few magical texts from Jeme,[46] both of which are manifestations of some form of personal devotion, and pious graffiti scratched in the walls of some Jeme houses.[47] The only other evidence that may indicate some kind of personal worship activities are the so-called orant figures found at the site. These small ceramic figures of women with arms raised in the attitude of prayer have been found throughout central and southern Egypt, several during the excavation of Medinet Habu. A single complete example was published in the excavation report (now pl. 2a in the present

[44] See especially Frankfurter 1998a, 131–142.

[45] See the crosses in Hölscher 1954, 64 and plate 39A:1–7 and the unpublished molds for making them alluded to earlier (Oriental Institute Museum numbers 14807–14809).

[46] See the magical ostracon O.*Medin.HabuCopt.* 4 (Brashear 1983) and the magical papyrus Carnarvon from Deir el Bakhit (translated Meyer and Smith 1994, 270–273); other "biblical" ostraca may also be amuletic in nature (e.g., the Jeme ostraca published in Wikgren 1946 with Psalm texts). Recall also the reference to a woman accused of practicing magic on some men in *P.Pisentius* 35, translated above in chapter 1.

[47] Hölscher 1954, 47, figure 54.

volume),[48] while a number of unpublished fragments are now in the Oriental Institute Museum (for example, the three heads in pl. 2b of the present volume).[49] The Medinet Habu orants are very similar to those from elsewhere in Egypt: all were made in two-piece molds[50] of unglazed, fired clay, and most were decorated with paint. The depiction of women in these figures is fairly uniform. The bodies are more or less cylindrical, with a flat base, a ridge marking the bottom of the dress, and some indication of breasts. The arms are upraised, and the hands are usually not detailed.[51] The women are usually shown wearing necklaces, from which a cross often hangs, and have very detailed faces; all bear a distinctive and elaborate triangular coiffure. Surviving orants are usually painted in black and red: the eyes are emphasized, there is usually detailing on the headdress, and patterns are often painted on the trunk and lower body. In places, these bodily decorations clearly represent a patterned dress; more intricate decorations on the wrists of some orants, however, probably represent tattoos.[52] All orant figures are pierced with at least one hole in the top of the triangular hairdo, and many, including all of the Medinet Habu pieces, have an additional hole on either side of the head. The traditional explanation of these holes is that they were for suspension; this may be the case, although the bases of the figures show that they were intended to stand on a flat surface, and the placement of the three holes found in all of the Medinet Habu orants would make suspension very awkward. An alternative explanation is that these holes were used for insertion of other decorative elements, such as jewelry, flowers, or a wreath. The use of the orants as votive figures is fairly well established, although the exact way in which they were used is unclear. That most of these figures, even those that

[48] Hölscher 1954, plate 34D.

[49] Oriental Institute Museum numbers 14641, 14642, and 15539; also note numbers 14643 (body fragment) and 15544 (hand). All of the Medinet Habu orant figures will be published in Teeter forthcoming.

[50] One such mold was discovered at Elephantine, now Coptic Museum 68718, published in photograph in Ballet 1991.

[51] See, however, OIM 15544, which is a carefully modeled hand from an orant.

[52] Montserrat 1996a. The practice of tattooing among Christian Egyptians is poorly studied in general, in spite of its ubiquity among the Copts of the past few centuries. Coptic textual evidence for tattooing is rare; the fifth/sixth-century writer known as Pseudo-Shenoute forbids it outright, as do the earlier canons of St. Basil (Kuhn 1960, 1:24–25 and references therein). Note also the discussion of early Christian sources in Elm 1996.

now appear as complete, have had their heads broken off is suggestive of some sort of ceremonial smashing. Some writers have tried to trace the origins of these statues to earlier pagan Graeco-Roman fertility figures, particularly those connected with Roman period Isis cults.[53] This would not be surprising, especially since there are no comparable statues of worshipping men from Coptic sites. Whatever their origin and use, it is clear that the orants were a uniquely female component of religious practice in the western Theban area.

Beyond worship services, and any personal devotions, probably the most frequent contact most women had with religious institutions was in a legal or economic context. Religious institutions were important registry centers for legal documents: the Monastery of Phoibammon (built in and on the Hatshepsut temple at Deir el-Bahri) was a major center in the western Theban area for the deposit of legal documents. Indeed, most of the Jeme legal documents we have examined so far have come from the deposit of documents at the Monastery of Phoibammon. The register of marriages and births discussed in the previous chapter (*O.Mon.Epiph.* 99–100) likewise was found and presumably deposited at the Monastery of Epiphanius—perhaps for registration purposes or for safekeeping. The most common legal activity in churches and monasteries was the swearing of oaths; in any sort of transaction involving an acknowledgment of payment or receipt of goods, for example, it was customary to swear by a holy place that payment or goods had been received. The large number of such oaths involving women attests not only to women's presence in the church for the swearing of the oath but also to women's extensive commercial activities at Jeme, which will be discussed in detail in the following chapter. To give just one sample oath for now, in *O.Medin.HabuCopt.* 88 the woman Trempou swears by "the holy place" that she has received a dress from the woman Trakote, for which she paid 4 tremisses; the text itself is written by the well-attested scribe Aristophanes, son of John. Clearly, the Holy Church of Jeme (and related institutions) dominated not only the religious life of the town but also its commercial life, as we will see in the archive of a woman moneylender named Koloje.

[53] References in Ballet 1991. There are certainly parallels to the orant figures with pagan associations from later Roman sites like Karanis. See examples in Allen 1985, where there are orant figures both seated (dated to mid-first to early fourth centuries, 2:414–436) and standing (dated to early fourth to fifth centuries, 2:437–457).

5

Koloje the Moneylender
and Other Women in the Economy of Jeme

In the northwest corner of the Holy Church of Jeme behind the nave of the church, a small doorway is carved through the Pharaonic temple wall. This doorway leads outside to an irregular street running northeast, lined with houses. Fifteen meters along this street on the west side is the entrance to a house numbered by the excavators as 34 (see number 2 on the map of Jeme in fig. 2). This is the house where, on 20 December 1929, University of Chicago excavators found thirty documents concerning a woman named Koloje and her family.[1] These texts, all on fragments of broken pottery (see pl. 4a–b for examples), record the business transactions of Koloje, a woman who acted as a moneylender, along with those members of her family who carried out the same business. The Koloje archive provides an instructive example of a woman of Jeme engaged in the town's economy.

Koloje's house was typical of other such Jeme houses: an irregularly shaped mud-brick structure of three or four stories, with two rooms on each level and a stairway between them. Plate 3 shows the house as excavated, while figure 7 shows a plan of the house and its neighbors. The house was one of the earlier structures in the block, with the areas to the west and north vacant; the subsequently built House 31 occupied these vacant areas and necessitated the blocking of House 34's second door. The remaining doorway and the first floor were at street level; below that level was a cellar with a vaulted ceiling. A pottery pipe in the crown of the vault supplied ventilation, allowed for quick disposal of floor sweepings, and possibly permitted a little illumination to the cellar. In the cellar, the excavators found thirty ostraca—broken potsherds used as writing material—documenting the activities of Koloje and family.[2]

---

[1] For the technical details on the reconstruction of this archive, see Wilfong 1990.

[2] Of these thirty ostraca, twenty were published in O.Medin.HabuCopt. All thirty were apparently returned to Egypt, along with most, if not all, of the Coptic ostraca from the Oriental Institute Medinet Habu excavations; the current whereabouts of these ostraca is unclear. From a partial set of photographs in the Oriental Institute Museum Archive, it has been possible to make some preliminary statements about a few of the unpublished pieces from this archive, for which see Wilfong 1990, 177–179.

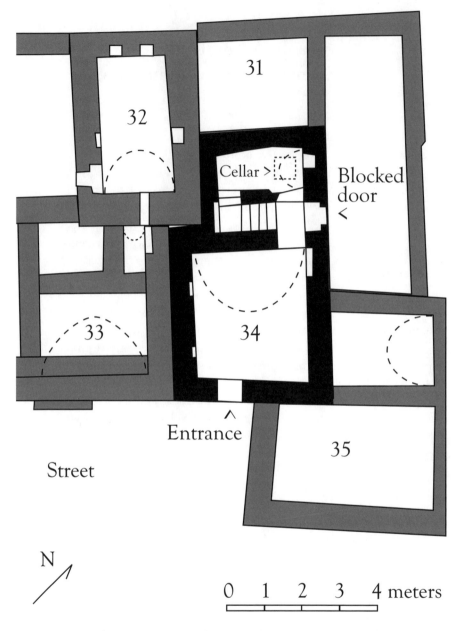

32

31

Cellar >

Blocked
door
<

33

34

∧
Entrance

Street

35

N

0 1 2 3 4 meters

Fig. 7. Plan of House 34 and environs (after Hölscher 1934, plate 32)

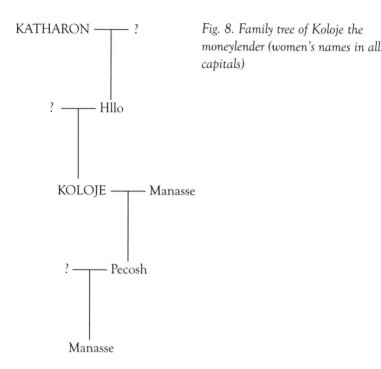

KATHARON —— ?

? —— Hllo

KOLOJE —— Manasse

? —— Pecosh

Manasse

Fig. 8. Family tree of Koloje the moneylender (women's names in all capitals)

They also found a variety of pottery objects: an oil lamp, a single-handled jar, an Egyptian Red Slip Ware bowl, some fragments of stamped Red Slip Ware, and two jar sealings—all of types familiar throughout the site. Less commonly encountered objects from this house were some Pharaonic faience beads (perhaps reused), a decorated bone button, a diamond-shaped oil cake, and a number of bronze rings.[3] It is important, in the case of Koloje and family, to count the house and its contents as an integral part of the "archive." These items and structures, and even the location of the house with respect to the rest of the town, are important attestations of the material context of the archive and, as such, provide information unattested in the textual evidence.

The interrelationship of the individuals named in the texts from House 34 are straightforward, and the family relationships are much simpler to chart than those in the Elizabeth/Abigaia archive (see family tree in fig. 8). Koloje is identified as the daughter of a man named Hllo (sometimes written Phllo), who is himself identified as the son of a

---

[3] My thanks to Emily Teeter for the information on the details of this find.

woman named Katharon. Katharon, thus Koloje's paternal grandmother, also lent money. Recently identified documents from another source appear to show this same Katharon involved in business extending as far north as Fustat.[4] We know nothing of Koloje's father Hllo, apart from his name and his identity as Katharon's son and Koloje's father. Koloje was married to a man named Manasse, known only from the documents of their son, Pecosh, who also lent money and held, at one time, the title of Ara at Jeme.[5] Pecosh had a son named after his grandfather Manasse, a fairly common practice in Egypt; this Manasse the younger also lent money and represents the last generation covered by the archive. The dates of the archive seem to span the later seventh and eighth centuries—perhaps as long as a century or more—with Manasse or perhaps his children keeping the ostraca in their basement until the abandonment of Jeme toward the end of the eighth century.[6]

The earliest document from the archive is from Koloje's grandmother Katharon (*O.Medin.HabuCopt.* 98); although highly fragmentary, this text seems to be an acknowledgment of a loan from Katharon to a man named Johannes. No documents survive from the generation of Katharon's son and Koloje's father Hllo, and the core of the archive consists of the ostraca relating to Koloje. Three of the texts are straightforward loan agreements. The first reads in full:

---

[4] Bacot 1999, where the identification of the Katharon in these documents with Koloje's grandmother is very convincing. The handwriting in Louvre AF 12310 may even be Katharon's own.

[5] See parallels in Crum *Dict.*, 14b; there are sometimes references to more than one Ara of Jeme at a time, and the title always appears in financial or legal contexts, but little more can be said about it at this point. It may ultimately prove significant that the title tends to appear only in transactions recorded in ostraca rather than in the more formal legal documents of the Monastery of Phoibammon deposit, perhaps suggesting less of a formal townwide administrative office and more of a local, neighborhood office.

[6] The documents of Koloje and Pecosh contain apparent references to individuals known from dated documents that suggest a date of late seventh/early eighth centuries for their activities (see Wilfong 1990, 175–176 for comments). Their association with the well-known monk Frange should be helpful in dating, but Frange's own dates are uncertain: it seems increasingly difficult to accept Crum's insistence that he was a witness to the Sassanian Persian domination of Egypt in the early seventh century; see the discussion of Frange's possible dates above in chapter 3. The large quantities of new Frange texts currently being studied by Anne Boud'Hors and Chantal Heurtel may provide answers and aid in a more precise date for Koloje and her family.

Pses, son of Lase, writes: he owes to Koloje, daughter of Hllo,
son of Katharon, one *shokas*[7] of wheat, and I[8] shall give it to
you in Paone together with its interest, which is two *maje*[9] to
the *artaba*, without any objection. I, Pses, son of Lase, agree to
this ostracon. I, Isaac, son of Paul, was asked and wrote (this)
with my own hand, and I am witness. I wrote on the twenty-
fifth of Paone (19 June), under Abraham, son of Atheris.
Matthaios, son of Shai, witness. Mark, son of Samuel, witness.
(*O.Medin.HabuCopt.* 50)

Compared to the Elizabeth/Abigaia papers, this legal text on an
ostracon is much more concise: less introductory formula, more direct
wording of the actual transaction involved, and fewer witnesses. Texts
on ostraca often refer to the ostracon itself as document, as in this case.
The text itself is straightforward: Pses has borrowed one *shokas* of wheat,
which he will repay at an interest rate of 2 *maje* on the *artaba*, so a total
of 4 *maje* in interest, which equals 16 $^2/_3$ percent interest. The repayment
period is not specified but is usually a year. The document is drawn up by
a scribe who also acts as witness. *O.Medin.HabuCopt.* 51 is similar; in it,
Tadore, daughter of Korsyne, owes Koloje one gold tremis, to be repaid
with interest of eight *maje* (of wheat) in Paone, so again late May/June. It
is possibly even written by Tadore ("I, Tadore, agree to this ostracon"
with no scribal statement as in the Pses document above) and is witnessed
by two men. The unpublished text MH 2404 seems to be a loan of a
similar type in which Koloje has lent money to a man, possibly named
Helias.[10] These documents record what appears to have been Koloje's
basic trade: the lending of money or agricultural products at interest.
　　Although none of these loans mentions the deposit of securities as
collateral for the loans, Koloje clearly required this of at least some of

[7] Probably two *artabas* (Stefanksi and Lichtheim 1952, 4); the *artaba* was the
standard grain measure in Graeco-Roman and Late Antique Egypt, but its capacity
varied over time. In the seventh and eighth centuries, the *artaba* was probably more
than the 40-liter *artaba* of the Roman period and somewhat more than an American
or British bushel.

[8] Shifts from first to third (or in this case third to first) person are common in
Jeme legal documents and letters.

[9] One *maje* is a twelfth of an *artaba* (Stefanksi and Lichtheim 1952, 4), so one-
sixth *artaba* here.

[10] See Wilfong 1990, 177 for information on this text.

her borrowers. In two ostraca from the archive borrowers renounce their claim on securities left with Koloje, presumably because they have failed to repay their loans. Thus we get one document:

> I, Mariam, daughter of Pebo, woman of Petemout, write to Koloje, daughter of Phello, woman of Jeme, saying: Seeing that I deposited the chain with you for 2 solidi, now, behold, I declare on this day, which is the fourteenth day of the month of Epiph (8 July), that I have no [means] of proceeding against you on account of it, ever, neither I nor any heir of mine, nor any man acting as my representative. Whosoever shall desire, from today until any time to come, to proceed against you concerning the chain, shall give 4 solidi as a fine and shall come and comply with this release. (*O.Medin.HabuCopt.* 72)

Here Mariam renounces claim on a necklace deposited with Koloje as security for a loan of 2 solidi. It seems probable that Mariam would do this only because she was unable to repay the loan. Since most of the loans in the Koloje archive were due in Paone, it is likely that the date of this document in the following month of Epiph was no accident: Mariam surrendered her security only after it was clear that she was unable to pay the loan by its due date. The fine set for anyone who might dispute the agreement is twice the value of the necklace; this is rather like the fines specified in the Elizabeth/Abigaia papers, and again it is not clear that these were ever paid. The amount of the loan was rather higher than the loans made to Pses and Tadore, which may be the reason for the requirement of a security. The fact that Mariam is from outside Jeme—across the river in Petemout (modern Medamoud)[11]—may also be a factor: perhaps Koloje considered her more of a risk for default.

Even some Jeme borrowers were required to leave security deposits. *O.Medin.HabuCopt.* 73 is presented in much the same terms: Leontios, son of Anastasios, of Jeme, renounces claim to all the securities (1 gold necklace, 2 robes (?), and 2 coverlets) that he has deposited with Koloje for 4 solidi. If anyone, particularly Leontios's heirs, proceeds legally against Koloje for the return of the securities, they will have to pay an ounce of gold (worth at least 8 solidi) as fine. Koloje herself had to

[11] Timm 4:1503–1505.

account for the items left with her as securities, as seen in this document from the archive, an oath (sworn in a holy place, most likely the Holy Church of Jeme just up the street from her house) regarding a security for a loan:

> (Sworn) By this holy place that is here, concerning this gold necklace (deposited as security) for 2 solidi: I have not removed anything from it, for these 2 gold solidi and their interest. (*O.Medin.HabuCopt.* 93; see pl. 4b)

Although Koloje is not mentioned by name, the use of the relatively uncommon word for necklace in this document makes it likely that this text refers to either the necklace of Mariam or the one left by Leontios mentioned above, and thus security for a loan from Koloje.[12] These are almost certainly Koloje's own words and possibly her own handwriting as well; there is no scribal statement on the text.

Another document from the archive probably also records a loan, but it differs from the normal format of such documents. In *O.Medin.HabuCopt.* 52, Daniel writes to Koloje, saying that he owes her either one *artaba* of dates or one *ho* of wheat, to be paid in Thoth (late August/September) of indiction year 15. The document was written by Daniel himself, and there are no witnesses. The absence of both witnesses and any mention of interest, as well as the alternative of commodity to be paid may indicate that this text is a simple record of debt rather than a formal loan. It may also be significant that it is to be paid well after the month of Paone, the traditional month of repayment of loans of agricultural commodities. This Daniel is almost certainly the man of the same name who appears in two other documents from the archive. *O.Medin.HabuCopt.* 66 is an acknowledgment of a loan. In this transaction, Daniel has lent 1 solidus to Paphnute to be repaid with unspecified interest in Paone. The deacon Moses wrote and witnessed the sherd. The name of Paphnute's father (or mother) is lost in a lacuna, but that of Daniel is partly preserved and can be restored as Kalapesios. Unfortunately, the text is very fragmentary, but a mention of Koloje is clear, and it appears that the loan is either being made through Koloje or is to be repaid with interest to Koloje. Either

---

[12] A number of similar oaths exist (e. g., *O.Medin.HabuCopt.* 91, 92, 95) that do not give the name of the writer.

interpretation would, of course, explain why the ostracon was in the archive. Part of the text can be restored with some certainty:

> . . . I appealed to you and you [received for me] a solidus by the hand of Koloje [and she gave] it to you.

The remaining Koloje document from the archive also concerns a Daniel, probably the same man:

> It is I, Pahatre, who writes to Koloje, saying: Since I have settled my business with you, as I sat with you and Daniel, saying: "The solidus is mine, along with the wheat," I said to you: "As for the man who brings this sherd to you, you should give to him the property: it is mine. Don't start legal action!" Farewell. Give it to Koloje from Pahatre. (*O.Medin.HabuCopt.* 151; see pl. 4a)

The purpose of the letter is not entirely clear: Pahatre may be attempting to collect on a loan or could be claiming securities left with Koloje for a loan that has been repaid. The latter seems more likely; in any case this text confirms the existence of some sort of business association between Koloje and Daniel.

Finally, there is an account that may well belong with Koloje's documents. This ostracon reads simply:

> Paphnute, son of Tors
> Kanih of Pashme: 1 solidus
> Tecoshe, woman of Armant
> Paulos, the fisher (*O.Medin.HabuCopt.* 26)

Although there is no heading, it seems likely that this is some sort of account of loans or list of borrowers. Only one name has an amount next to it, and, most likely, this is an account of outstanding loans, on which amounts repaid were to be added later. In any case, it is not hard to imagine how these texts could fit into a moneylender's archive, whether relating to Koloje's transactions or those of her descendants.

Seven of the published documents from House 34 that concern Koloje's son Pecosh can be summarized briefly. *O.Medin.HabuCopt.* 55

records the indebtedness of John, son of Pesenthius, from Terkot to Pecosh for one *artaba* of wheat and its interest of one *ment*[13] of wheat, to be repaid in Paone. The ostracon was written by John, son of Mathusala, in the month of Thoth. *O.Medin.HabuCopt.* 58 and 60 both record loans by Pecosh to Michaias, son of Enoch, also a citizen of Terkot. In the former, Michaias owes Pecosh one gold tremis with one *mosne* of sesame as interest. It is to be repaid in Paone of the fifth year. The sherd was written by Moses, deacon of the Holy Church of Terkot, because "he (Michaias) does not know how to write." In the latter of the two documents, Michaias owes Pecosh one gold solidus and its interest of one *artaba* of sesame, payable in Paone of the sixth year. Again the ostracon was written for him by an employee of the Holy Church of Terkot; it is also witnessed by a number of people, including John, son of Pesenthius, from *O.Medin.HabuCopt.* 55 above. In *O.Medin.HabuCopt.* 59 yet another citizen of Terkot, Andreas, son of Matthaios, owes Pecosh two gold tremisses and interest of eight *maje* of lentils, to be repaid in Paone of the fourth year. The sherd was drawn up by Moses the lector, in Tobe of the fourth year, and is witnessed, again, by John, son of Pesentius. Here Pecosh is given the title Ara of Jeme, mentioned above.

The remaining three documents relating to Pecosh do not record loans as such but instead deal with related matters. In *O.Medin.HabuCopt.* 83, There renounces any claim that she may have had against Pecosh owing to a settlement that they made. The text is not very specific: the claim could be in relation to the repayment of a loan or the return of securities. *O.Medin.HabuCopt.* 70 is more explicit; Pia, daughter of Pelatos, from Petemout declares that Pecosh has returned her securities of 22 cloth items and 15 bronze utensils and that she has no further claim against him. Both of these ostraca also bear the names of witnesses. The text of the remaining Pecosh document, *O.Medin.HabuCopt.* 84, is a brief statement to the effect that a woman's dress, two vessels, and five garments are being held at Pecosh's house until they are called for. Perhaps these are items that were left in exchange for money or goods, in which case this ostracon would have served as a sort of pawn ticket, although, given the other

[13] Seems to be equivalent to two *maje*, so one-sixth *artaba* (Stefanski and Lichtheim 1952, 4).

documents in the archive, it seems much more likely that these were securities for loans that were paid off at interest.

For the last generation of this family, that of Manasse, son of Pecosh, we have three documents from the published portion of the archive. In *O.Medin.HabuCopt.* 54, Tagape, daughter of Paul, from the Roma district (?) of Jeme declares that she owes Manasse one *artaba* of wheat with one *ment* interest, and one *oipe* of sesame with X *maje* interest (amount in lacuna), payable in the coming Paone. It is written by a scribe and signed by witnesses. *O.Medin.HabuCopt.* 96 is a document in which Petros, from Psenheai, relinquishes ownership of securities in payment of a debt. Although the text is fragmentary, it seems that Petros had left a gold necklace with Manasse in addition to 38 and 16 *artabas* of some grain as security for an unspecified loan, and in this document he gives them to Manasse, possibly in payment for a debt. *O.Medin.HabuCopt.* 71 is a receipt in which Joseph, son of Plein, acknowledges the return of a solidus deposited with Manasse and renounces any further claim. Finally, Manasse appears in the unpublished text MH 2417, in which he promises to pay 400 *cor*—a small-denomination bronze coin equal to about $^1/_{40}$ of a carat[14]—to a certain Paulos—perhaps in reference to a loan, although this is not specified.

The transactions recorded in the Koloje texts take place on a different level from those represented in the Elizabeth/Abigaia papers. The actual writing materials should be kept in mind: the Elizabeth/Abigaia papers are on more expensive (as well as durable and permanent) parchment and papyrus; the Koloje texts are on potsherds. Unlike the Elizabeth/Abigaia texts, the Koloje ostraca contain none of the elaborate protocols and attestations found in the other archive, nor did they involve the direct participation of town officials. Rather than the transfer of real estate and large amounts of moveable property, the Koloje texts record transactions on a smaller scale, involving smaller amounts of money. Koloje's ostraca were legal documents in the same way as the Elizabeth/Abigaia papers and reflect in general the attitudes of Jemeans toward legal matters. The feeling prevalent among Koloje and her circle at Jeme is probably best summed up in the letter of Pahatre translated above, where he warns Koloje: "Don't start legal action!" Pahatre's words to Koloje could be taken as a kind of motto for Late Antique Egypt in

---

[14] So 960 *cor* equal a solidus. Manasse's 400 *cor* equal 10 carats, or a little less than half a solidus; see Satzinger 1986, 110 and references there.

general when it came to legal cases. Private settlements and arbitration
of the kind well attested in the documentation of Late Antique Egypt
were preferred over more official remedies for disputes.[15] At Jeme this
would have involved the officials called the "great men," and we have
already seen these officials in action in the documents of Elizabeth and
Abigaia. In more intractable cases, legal action would have to go before
Arab officials, as in *P.KRU* 52, where Petros, son of the late Komes,
described legal proceedings before "our lord [. . .] Souleiman, the most
honored Emir" against Daniel, son of the late Pachom, and Tanope,
daughter of Abraham and wife of the late Solomon, over items they
stole from his house. Souleiman was, in fact, the pagarch, or district
chief, in Armant—a level of official not far below that of the Arab
governor who ruled the entire country—and the case ultimately involved
not only him but also the dioiketes below him and the "great men" of
Jeme. Clearly, this is the kind of legal complication that most Jemeans
liked to avoid, and so arbitration on a local level was a more desirable
means of resolving disputes. It may well be that this system of local
arbitration at Jeme gave women greater freedom of action and recourse
than they would have had otherwise. As is seen in the documents
renouncing ownership of securities, Koloje and her clients seem to
have been able to settle much of their business among themselves.

All the texts relating to Koloje and her family are connected in
some way with moneylending. Most prevalent are the records of loans;
Koloje and her descendants lent money and agricultural products
(mostly wheat), on which they collected interest in either money or
kind (sometimes wheat but also dates, sesame, and lentils). Securities
for loans were deposited with them: jewelry, clothing, and household
items being the most common. Interest was usually about one-sixth of
the amount of the loan, resulting in an interest rate of exactly 16 $^2/_3$
percent (this seems to be the standard interest rate in Jeme loans, as we
will see shortly). Other documents include renunciations of claims,
memoranda about securities, oaths regarding securities, an account,
and a letter. Although the amounts of money and property involved
here, not to mention the fines for disputing settlements, are not nearly
as large as those mentioned in the Elizabeth/Abigaia papers, they were
clearly not trifling matters to the individuals involved in the transactions.
The proceeds of Koloje's business can be seen in the archaeological

[15] Again, see the standard work on settlements: Gagos and van Minnen 1994.

remains in House 34: the relatively high-quality pottery, decorative items of dress, and metal objects.

On the other side of the transactions are the men and women borrowing money from Koloje and her descendants. In fact, in some ways the archive is more informative for the borrowers than the lenders; most of the documents are drawn up by them in the form of first-person narratives and provide information about their special circumstances. Some of the borrowers are from Jeme itself, one woman even living in a named part of the town: Tagape, who lives in Roma in Jeme.[16] Others are out-of-towners: Pia, daughter of Pelatos, and Mariam, daughter of Pebo, are both from Petemout[17] across the river (about 20 kilometers away), and Tecoshe is from Armant, the administrative capital about 20 kilometers to the south; some of the men who borrow from Koloje's son Pecosh are from Terkot,[18] about 30 kilometers away from Jeme, to the south of Armant (see map, fig. 1), while one borrower is from Pashme,[19] probably to the northeast of Jeme across the river and not far from Petemout. None of these towns is more than a day's journey away from Jeme, but a day's journey to or from Jeme would have involved a considerable amount of effort: walking an hour or two to the river and then a boat or ferry trip, or just hours of walking. The simple fact that these people turned to a moneylender of Jeme to borrow from is significant.

The borrowers in the Koloje archive show certain gendered patterns in their borrowing. The women borrow mostly money while the men borrow grain as often as money. The securities left for these loans are the household furnishings and personal belongings of the borrowers. Women's clothing and jewelry figure most frequently as securities in loans contracted by women; but women's possessions are also used as securities in the loans contracted by men (although one does not see the converse). A few of the documents that record borrowing by women are written in the first person with no indication of who is writing, and it is possible that these were actually written by the women themselves.[20]

---

[16] In O.Medin.HabuCopt. 54. This is contrasted to the lender Manasse the younger who simply lives "in Jeme." Note the discussion of the various quarters of Jeme in the introduction.

[17] Timm 5:1503–1505.

[18] Timm 6:2590–2591.

[19] Timm 4:1849–1852.

[20] O.Medin.HabuCopt. 51 and O.Medin.HabuCopt. 72.

In the other cases, the ostracon is explicitly said to be written by a scribe, for example *O.Medin.HabuCopt.* 83. The text is in the first person ("It is I, There, who writes"), but later on that is qualified by a scribal statement ("I, Joseph, son of David, wrote this ostracon").[21]

These documents show the women moneylenders in a variety of situations and activities. On the side of the lenders, Koloje and (probably) her grandmother Katharon lent money and produce to a range of customers, male and female, entirely on their own and independent of parents or husbands. Katharon, in documents from outside the Koloje archive mentioned above, is apparently active and well traveled, going all the way north to Fustat in connection with business with various men and women. Koloje is associated at times in her business with a nonrelated man, Daniel, son of Kalapesios, who borrows from her and with whom she has other business interests. Koloje even lent Daniel money to lend out himself, as we saw in *O.Medin.HabuCopt.* 66 above. Hatre, from *O.Medin.HabuCopt.* 151, may have also been another business associate rather than just a borrower. From a document that is not part of the Koloje archive but apparently involves the same Koloje (*O.Medin.HabuCopt.* 139), we find her in friendly correspondence with the monk Frange, seemingly not a relative, who was living in the desert and part of a lively circle of correspondents.[22] Clearly, Koloje was not restricted to her home and family circle but found clients and associates well beyond it; indeed, Koloje and Katharon seem to have wider connections than their male descendants who also lent money. We see as well that women such as Koloje could and did contract business without reference to male relatives, could associate in business with male nonrelatives, and were able to do business with a wide range of people. Though the documentation is overwhelmingly secular, religion does play an oblique role in these business dealings. Living in the shadow of the Holy Church of Jeme, Koloje used the church as an assertion of her honesty in oaths, while the language of

---

[21] Of the five documents ostensibly written by women, three have scribal statements (*O.Medin.HabuCopt.* 54, 70, 83). The proportion is slightly higher for male borrowers: out of eleven documents, nine were written by scribes, and one is broken where the statement would be. In only two of these cases (both loans by Pecosh to individuals living in Terkot) it is explicitly stated that the scribe (the same man in both cases: the deacon of the "Holy Church of Terkot") was asked by and wrote for the borrower "because he does not know (how to write)."

[22] This document is discussed in chapter 3 above.

religion found its way into the standard formulae used in legal documents. Koloje is often identified as "the woman of Jeme," and in Koloje we have a businesswoman living almost in the literal center of a thriving community. Her activities extended far beyond her immediate circle and even went well outside the boundaries of Jeme itself.

Koloje was far from the only woman involved in moneylending at Jeme. Indeed, a substantial percentage of the moneylenders at Jeme were women: women are lenders in about a third of the loans known from the Jeme texts, with at least ten individual women definitely involved in moneylending.[23] This percentage is considerably higher than the general level of women's presence in the Jeme legal texts from the Phoibammon deposit, in which (as discussed in chapter 3) women represent about 12 percent of the active participants. The women who lend money are attested from the same kinds of transactions as the male moneylenders; they make loans of roughly the same amounts and with the same sorts of interest and securities.

The documents of these other women moneylenders parallel precisely the kinds of texts found in the Koloje archive. Thus two ostraca record loans made by a woman named Tachel to a woman named Maria:

+ It is I, Maria, Daughter of Zacharias, woman of Jeme, who writes to Tachel, daughter of David, of the same town, saying: I owe you a tremis of gold, and I am ready to give it to you at any time that you want, with its interest, without any refusal, and I put in your hands my portion of the field that is below Pshnkoloje[24] as a pledge until I give the tremis to you with its interest. I, Maria daughter of Zacharias, assent. I Elias, son of Johannes, have written this ostracon with my (own) hand on

[23] In addition to Koloje and her grandmother Katharon, we have Maria, wife of Dioskoros (*O.Medin.HabuCopt.* 57), Maria (same as preceding?, *O.Medin.HabuCopt.* 69), X, daughter of Rebecca (*O.Medin.HabuCopt.* 103), Kasia (*O.CrumST* 420), Mariham, daughter of Basilius (*O.CrumVC* 25), Touhore (*O.CrumVC* 36a), Tachel, daughter of David and Parthenopa (Hall 1911 1 and 2), Tsaerbenis, daughter of Ereieus (*O.Brit.Mus.Copt.* 78:1).

[24] Apparently a place, otherwise unattested. Alternatively, it could be a personal name or even an identification by filiation ("the son of Koloje"), in which case it would be understood that the field offered as security is below one belonging to this person. Unfortunately, the name Koloje is common enough that we cannot assume any connection with our moneylender.

the 16th of Epiph (10 July), under Paulos, son of Pses, the *lashane*, (and) I am witness. Elisaios, son of Patermoute: witness. +Kostantine, son of Jakob—witness.

+ I Maria, daughter of Zacharias, the woman of Jeme, write to Tachel, the daughter of Parthenopa in the same town: I owe you a tremis of gold, complete with its interest which is a carat [. . .] . . . other year. I put in your hand my portion of the field that is in Pshoumare with the barns that are in it, until I give the tremis to you. I, Johannes, son of Mathousala, I wrote this ostracon on the 26th day of Pharmoute (21 April). (Hall 1911, texts 1–2)

We see how the terminology and format of the documents parallels exactly that of the Koloje loans. There are some differences here, most notably the use of land as a security for the loan. It is interesting to see the variation in how Tachel is identified: in the first loan, she is identified by her father David and in the second by her mother Parthenopa. We find this kind of alternation in the Koloje archive as well, where Pecosh is identified in one year as "son of Koloje" (*O.Medin.HabuCopt.* 58) and in the next as "son of Manasse" (*O.Medin.HabuCopt.* 60). It is not clear whether there is some purpose behind this alternation, but the inclusion of a female parent or relative (such as Koloje's grandmother Katharon, by whom she is sometimes identified) may have the significance of connecting the current moneylender with a moneylending relative of the past. Even male moneylenders will identify themselves by their female parent rather than the male parent, as is more common—note David, son of Abigaia, who is a lender in *O.Medin.HabuCopt.* 104 and a borrower in *O.Medin.HabuCopt.* 134.

In addition to the documents of the sort found in the Koloje archive, other kinds of text attest to the activities of women moneylenders. Of special interest is a list of loans made by Tsaerbenis, daughter of Ereieus (*O.Brit.Mus.Copt.* 78:1).[25] This list records loans listed by borrower's name, amount, and interest: the loans are all made to men, the loans

[25] This text is badly edited and only available in a poor hand facsimile by the editor, who interprets this text as if it were an account of Tsaerbenis repaying debts to different men. This makes much less sense, however, than taking it as Tsaerbenis's own account of money lent out to various individuals. Proper understanding of this

are all for one solidus, and the interest, which is reckoned as "yearly," comes to 40 *she*.[26] It is not clear whether this means that these were long-term loans on which interest would be paid every year or whether some other arrangement was in place. But it is clear that we have in this document some kind of record whereby Tsaerbenis kept track of her outstanding loans and amounts that would be due to her. Although women never acted as official, credited scribe or witness for their own loan documents, it is possible that documents such as Tsaerbenis's loan register, like Koloje's security statement referred to above, may be in their own hand.

Incidental mentions of women as moneylenders are uncommon in the Jeme texts and always ambiguous. The letter of two women requesting money owed to them by a monk from the Monastery of Epiphanius (*O.Mon.Epiph.* 293) may refer to a formal loan agreement, but it could just as easily be money owed for something the women sold him. In a few cases, men are referred to by the term "moneylender" (*danistês*, from the Greek); it occurs infrequently in the Jeme texts and only in letters, never in the loan documents themselves. Thus the widow's petition to Pisentius discussed earlier (*SB Kopt.* I 295) refers to the moneylender from whom she had to borrow in order to pay tax on her dead husband's land, while in *O.Crum* 189 the writer complains that he is being harassed by a moneylender for the payment of his addressee's debt, the addressee being off in the desert. In both cases, the moneylenders identified as *danistês* are male; the term is never used for the women of Jeme who lend money.

As in the Koloje archive, the general corpus of loan documents and related texts tells us as much, if not more, about the borrowers involved in the loans. As with the lenders, women account for about a third of the borrowers known from Jeme loan documents. Women were more likely to borrow from women than from men (about 60 percent borrowed from women), just as men were more likely to borrow from men than from women (about 27 percent from women). Married

---

document will require a completely new edition; until someone undertakes this, it is possible to make some corrections to the existing edition and interpretation that have been tacitly adopted here: see Wilfong forthcoming.

[26] This interest rate would support a value of the *she* at 240 *she* = 1 solidus, which would give the customary 16 $^2/_3$%; like the carat, however, the value of the *she* seems to have varied somewhat: note the discussion in chapter 3. If, instead, the *she* were valued at 288 to the nomisma, this would make for a lower interest rate of about 14%.

couples who borrowed jointly borrow from women in 75 percent of the cases. The places that borrowers come from in the documents suggest gendered patterns as well: in the Koloje archive, the locations of the borrowers outside Jeme break down by gender: the borrowers from Terkot are all men (who borrow from Koloje's son Pecosh), while the borrowers from Petemout are all women, who borrow from Koloje. This may well be because of specific personal associations of the respective moneylenders. Women also seem to have lent money to monks in the local monasteries, as witnessed in *O.Mon.Epiph.* 531, described as a "pawnbroker's journal" by the original editor: it includes payments to women in grain and money and refers to articles on deposit. In general, the borrowers come from the same range of places as in the Koloje archive: a number from outside of Jeme, all within a 30 kilometer radius of the town.

There are a number of incidental mentions of women as borrowers in other Jeme texts. In *P.KRU* 16 Shenetom hands over his wife Rachel's house to a man in repayment of a loan that Rachel has accepted but failed to repay. *P.KRU* 30 is ambiguous; it is a document in which a man gives his house as security to his wife for 2 solidi of her bridal gift (on which see below), but it is not clear whether he is getting the 2 solidi as a loan from his wife or whether it is an amount he owes her for the bridal gift because he never paid it. In *P.KRU* 53, a woman has borrowed from her son and then repaid him, but this seems less likely to involve moneylending at interest. In some documents, women make payments that may be repayments of formal loans but are not identified as such. Thus, an ostracon in Krakow illustrates such a transaction involving a number of family members:

It is I, Anna, with her children, who writes to, and greets, her beloved mother Hilaria,[27] and her beloved father Makari, and her beloved sister Tshileet,[28] with her husband and children. Now, (as for) you, Tshileet: be so good in the matter of the half tremis you are dealing with and pay it to Petros, as I owe it to him. You have 112 *cor* from my hand. Take them for yourself from [. . .] *SB Kopt.* I 297[29]

[27] Named after the transvestite saint discussed in chapter 1.

[28] Name literally means "the bride."

[29] See also edition in Satzinger 1986, 108–110. There is no stated provenance for this text, but the orthography and grammar are consistent with a west Theban origin.

The 112 *cor* is a bit short of the half tremis owed, but the lost part of the text may have explained where the remaining 48 *cor* was to come from. Anna owes the half tremis to Petros, and it may have been from a formal loan, but there is no way to be certain of this.

In general, the Jeme loans seem to follow the same format regardless of who the borrowers and lenders were: the statement of borrower and lender, the scribal and witness statements, the amount of loan and interest and the security for the loan. From this information we get some idea of the economic impact of the activity of the Jeme moneylenders. Loans were made either of money (with interest in money) or in agricultural produce (with interest in either money or agricultural produce). Many of the loans for money are for amounts usually paid in taxes (which had to be paid in cash); this, combined with the statement in the widow's petition *SB Kopt.* I 295 that she had to borrow from the moneylender to pay her husband's tax, makes it likely that much of the lending was being done so that the borrowers could pay tax. Interest rates are not always easy to determine precisely, but interest tends to equal about one-sixth of the value of the loan, or 16 $^2/_3$ percent. This interest rate was in excess of the officially mandated rates under the earlier Byzantine administration but comparable to rates in other Coptic documentary texts.[30]

We also have a great deal of information about the securities left as collateral for the loans. These securities left and received by women for loans give some indication of the sorts of things owned by women, helping us go beyond the picture of parcels of land and house portions belonging to women seen in the Elizabeth/Abigaia papers discussed in chapter 3.[31] In addition to plots of land seen in the Tachel loans translated above, the securities left by and with women include grain, wine, women's clothing, jewelry, and various household utensils.[32] Certainly, clothing, jewelry, and cooking utensils dominate the possessions of women in lists, accounts, and letters, as well as in wills

---

[30] Stefanski and Lichtheim 1952, 5–6.

[31] See also the list of house owners, half of whom are women, *O.Brit.Mus.Copt.* 82:6. For women as owners of land in Roman and Late Antique Egypt from Greek sources, see Hobson 1983 and Rowlandson 1996.

[32] If *O.Mon.Epiph.* 531, the so-called pawnbroker's journal, is really a record of loan securities deposited with a lender by women, it records deposits and payments of wine, grain, and bread. The women and the writer are recorded as eating these items, so it is uncertain exactly why they were being taken and given.

and as securities in loan documents. The frequency with which women's belongings (especially dresses and jewelry) were left as security for loans by men[33] suggests that at least some of the "women's things" were seen as disposable luxury items that could be used by a husband for collateral.[34] Women could also own the tools of their trade, as in the case of the loom inherited from a mother by a son in *P.KRU 27*.

Women's wills are useful guides to their property;[35] in general the amounts of property and their disposition are comparable to those of men. We have already seen the will of Elizabeth (*P.KRU 68*), in which she leaves her second husband a house inherited from her parents, parcels of land, and household goods. In the lengthy will of Susanna, preserved in two slightly different copies (*P.KRU 66* and *76*), she leaves real estate and household goods to the sons and daughters of her deceased son. The bequest is made by gendered groups; that is, Susanna leaves the house she inherited from her mother to the grandsons and the house she got from her father to her granddaughters. She explicitly refers to and lists "my women's things" (*naeidos nshime*), which she bequeaths to her granddaughters:

> the dyed women's dresses, my colored mantle, an item of clothing, my headscarves (?), a kettle (?), and all women's things. (*P.KRU 76.38ff.*)

Unfortunately, the vocabulary of this list contains words of uncertain meaning,[36] and the last entry implies more unenumerated "women's things," but the overall trend is clear: women's clothing and cooking vessels. Susanna's will contrasts this portion of the bequest with the

---

[33] See, for example, *O.Medin.HabuCopt.* 72, where women's clothing and jewelry are left with Koloje as security for a loan to a man.

[34] Note the earlier document and discussion of a husband's use of his wife's property in Gagos, Koenen, and McNellen 1992.

[35] *P.KRU* 66, 68, 69, 70, 72 (with husband), 76 (parallels 66), for example; also note *O.Crum* 145 is a property division (written on a platter) by a woman, who specifies both where she got her property and to whom it is to go, but it lacks some of the formal features of Jeme wills. See, in general, Till's standard work on the subject (1954, especially 27–56). The wills of men and the general patterns of disposition of property between men and women are also, of course, instructive in this regard. Note, for example, *P.KRU* 43, which explicitly spells out the general practice of dividing property between male and female heirs of the same generational level at a ration of 2:1 male to female.

[36] See the discussion of these terms in Wilfong forthcoming.

"men's things" she leaves to her grandsons; this statement is followed by a list of things (household items such as lamps, boxes, buckets, utensils), but it is not clear whether these are the "men's things" or just other things that the grandsons also receive. Whatever the precise meaning of the term, there is a very clear gender-based division between the grandson's household goods and the granddaughter's bequest. The husband of Tsible in *P.KRU* 69 is to receive 4 tremisses, part of a house, and some land, but he must use the money for memorial offerings for her and sell the house portion to her brother. Tsible also swears that no property that she has inherited from her family will go to the husband. In an apparent case of a woman with no living relatives, Tbases leaves her property to a local official and his son, with the provision that they make memorial offerings for her (*P.KRU* 70). The sole example of a joint husband/wife will from Jeme (*P.KRU* 72) does not preserve the disposition of property. In addition to the surviving wills, there are many references to inheritance from female relatives, especially in the Elizabeth/Abigaia archive. In many cases, this is with reference to property inherited from mothers, where daughters are much more frequently listed as heirs of the mothers than sons.

Less formal documents on ostraca record property division, especially the division of the estate of someone who has died without a will. The mechanics of the procedure of settlement are found in a text in which two lists of household items are given. One is a list of items owned by the writer's father, the other a list of goods given to a woman named Sabek:[37]

Two keys
Three coverlets
Four pillows
Two sheets
One bronze brazier
One candlestick
Two frying pans
One bronze figure
One lion (?) of bronze

[37] My identification of some of these items differs from that of the original editors; again see Wilfong forthcoming.

One strainer
One *xestes* measure
One censer
One sickle
One chain (?)
One handle (?)
One gridiron (?)
Four cups
One basket
One jar
One bronze bucket
One bronze cover
One bronze cup
This is the account of my father's things

Those (things) that have been given to Sabek:
Three dyed dresses
Two cloaks
Two napkins
Eight face towels
One pillow
One sheepskin
Eight dresses
One frying pan
One gridiron (?)
One censer
One bronze figure
One candlestick

This is followed by a note to the addressee:

> I greet your always revered fatherly piety. Be so good as to do this
> for God's sake: make a settlement between my own sister and
> Sabek, and decide their business . . . (O.Medin.HabuCopt. 5)

Even though the circumstances of this case are not certain, the
mechanics are: an enumeration of the disputed property and the use
of outside arbitration. Other settlements take place through agreement

without outside intervention, as in O.*Medin.HabuCopt.* 85, where two people (a man and woman?) divide the property of a deceased woman, one getting the iron furniture, one the wooden furniture, with the bronze articles being shared between them "in common."

Documents relating to marriage provide another useful source for the kinds of property held by women at Jeme. Given the relative paucity of marriage documents, the exact details are uncertain, but it is clear that a standard feature of the marriage was a wedding gift or dowry to the bride, known variously as the *skhat, skhaat, sshot,* or *shat,*[38] which was given either by the groom or by his parent(s).[39] This bridal gift could consist of money (a gold solidus in O.*Crum* 131), household goods (as in O.*Mon.Epiph.* 456), clothing, real property (a house in P.*KRU* 17), or a combination of these—in short, anything that could be conveyed from one person to another. The amount of the bridal gift was subject to negotiation and varies from document to document. There is no evidence that there was a standard bridal gift amount at Jeme of the sort that appears in the known tenth- through thirteenth-century documents, where the value of the gift given to the woman ranges between 80 and 100 gold dinars.[40] In general, the gift was worth much

---

[38] See Till 1948, Till 1954, 7–11, and Steinwenter 1955, 21–22 for details. Another such gift that Crum translates as "dowry" (Crum *Dict.*, 832b), the *crèce,* is known only from literary texts and appears to be given to the bride's parents by the groom or his parents. See Lüddeckens 1960 and Pestman 1961 for the earlier Egyptian terminology.

[39] P.*Pisentius* 19, where the groom's father seems to be arranging the gift; O.*Crum* 131, where the mother gives the son a solidus for it. In O.*Mon.Epiph.* 479 a senior monastic official may be helping to arrange for the gift, an explanation more likely than Crum's interpretation of this broken passage as referring to the *skhat* as being given *to* the religious official. In his commentary on O.*Mon.Epiph* 479, Crum cites a few examples that he interprets as the *skhat* being given to the groom, but none of these is conclusive. In particular, Crum's implication that O.*Crum* 131 is a document in which a mother gives a solidus to the son as *his skhat* does not fit the evidence, which supports the interpretation that she is contributing to the gift that the son will give to his bride (see Steinwenter 1955, 22). Steinwenter sees the *sheleet* that appears in a few Jeme texts (P.*KRU* 37 and 44, for example) as a gift given by the bride's parents to the groom, but this practice is not so well attested.

[40] A dinar being roughly equivalent to the earlier solidus. See the two late documents in Till 1948, both from the thirteenth century, and also the two tenth-century Arabic marriage documents of Copts from Luxor published in Abbott 1941, both of which record bridal gifts of 90 and 80 dinars. In her commentary on the latter, Abbott notes that these amounts are very atypical of the standard in contemporary Muslim documents (Abbott 1941, 60). These amounts may well have

less than this in the seventh-/eighth-century Jeme documents: a solidus in *O.Crum* 131, a courtyard worth 1 solidus and 4 carats in *O.CrumST* 48, and so on. The gift in the seventh-/eighth-century agreement *P.Ryl.Copt.* 139 (possibly not Jemean) is 3 $^{1}/_{2}$ solidi, plus various items of apparel. Another sort of wedding gift, the "outfit,"[41] was apparently supposed to come to the bride from her parents (*P.KRU* 67.59). This gift is something that can be divided (*P.KRU* 37.58, 44.73), but little else is known about it.

The disposition of the bridal gift was left up to the bride, as can be seen from *O.CrumST* 48, in which a woman sells the courtyard she received as a bridal gift from her husband to another man, with no apparent reference to the husband. There is some evidence to suggest that the ability to dispose of the bridal gift depended on the bride's bearing of children. *O.CrumVC* 50 appears to record the resolution of a dispute between Leontius and Martha, husband and wife, possibly now divorced. The text is, unfortunately, quite fragmentary. After a broken passage concerning the division of property acquired jointly with reference to a daughter who has apparently died, the writer turns to the disposition of the *skhat*:

> And concerning the bridal gift: since she has born children for him, she is its [owner, b]ut she must carry the burden of the memorial offering for her daughter and contribute for her burial from [that which she] has received. (*O.CrumVC* 50)

This text implies fairly clearly that, had Martha borne no children, the bridal gift would not have necessarily belonged to her. The insistence on having children is found in documents relating to alimony as well, for which see below. Potential disposition of a money bridal gift is described in a text from the Monastery of Epiphanius, apparently an extract of a document in which a man disclaims responsibility for the way in which a woman might dispose of her bridal gift:

> Lest she make an excuse (?) and she say "Here is the document" or "I myself pay them on his behalf" or "I have made a gift of

---

been intended as an incentive for Christian women to marry Christians rather than Muslims.

[41] *Nouhr ebol*: perhaps "trousseau" would be a better translation?

something from my bridal gift on your behalf." She does not
have any authority on my behalf, because God has persuaded
my heart that my offering and my charity should take place in
my own place, the place of my holy fathers, through the hand
of my (spiritual?) son, according to God. Lest she make an
excuse "I have paid something to a man from my bridal gift"
or "From my bridal gift I have paid on your behalf." See, I
swear in this same oath that she has not given anything on my
behalf from her bridal gift, nor have I said to her: "pay
something from your bridal gift to some man" or "give a gift to
some man." (O.Mon.Epiph. 98)

Although the exact situation in this document is obscure,[42] it shows
both the woman's ability to use her bridal gift and the importance
attached to her free use of it: the man writing is at great pains to show
that he is not influencing the disposition of the property on his behalf.

Even after a marriage had ended, women could still receive property
from it to some degree. Alimony after divorce paid by the man to the
ex-wife is attested in Coptic texts as something that is paid by the year
through negotiation. Some texts use a term (*anhalôma*) from the Greek,
while others use the Coptic *rompe nouôm*, literally "year of sustenance."
The few explicit sources show that this consisted of a combination of
money, food, and clothing.[43] The amounts given in one text show the
alimony to have been more a matter of subsistence than profit; moreover,
as the nature of this text—a complaint over unpaid alimony—indicates,
it was not necessarily a resource upon which the woman could rely,
even if agreed upon previously. Although support was often granted to
an abandoned wife, the mechanics by which this was accomplished are
not always clear. Even when some kind of support was established, it
did not always get paid, as we can see from the petition of a woman to
some unspecified official, probably a local priest or bishop:

[42] From the archaeological context at the Monastery of Epiphanius and wording,
one might assume the man to have been a monk, which would make the wife
problematic, since the monks were supposed to be unmarried. But the woman in
question could be a former wife or even an apparently unwanted follower of the monk
of the sort found frequently in earlier monastic literature and attested for the western
Theban area in the biography of Pisentius.

[43] P.KRU 37 (money and clothing) and the text translated below from Till 1938a
(food and clothing).

May your lordship hear of the injustice against me by Paulos my husband. I bore three children with him before I became weak. God knows (that) since I became weak, I bore another child. When he saw that God had brought sickness upon me, he cast me out. He went with another (woman) and he abandoned the children. After much conflict between me and him and the other woman, he took [on responsibility for me, namely] that he would give maintenance to me every year consisting of four *artabas* of barley and four *xestai*[44] of oil and four [measures] of wine and a dress and a cloak a year. He deprived me of the rest of the maintenance: he has not given (it) to me since last year save merely for an *artaba* of barley. And I do not seek anything except the maintenance that he established for me, for I am weak and that is what I live on. God bless you.[45]

The amounts of food mentioned—four *artabas* of barley and four *xestai* of oil—were not particularly generous for a woman with four children, and the single *artaba* of barley that Paulos actually handed over was completely inadequate. Moreover, barley itself was considered a much poorer grain than wheat for human consumption, more often used as animal fodder. The woman's invocation of her children at the beginning may be to emphasize the severity of her plight, but it may also serve to assert her right to the alimony, just as was done with the bridal gift in the case discussed above.[46] Significantly, the terms for bridal gift and alimony are listed together with the groom's gift (?, using the term *sheleet*) and the "outfit" (see above) in one Jeme text (*P.KRU 37.57–59*) as kinds of divisible property, perhaps indicating similarity of status.

We have already seen, to some extent, how women acquired the property that they owned and also, at least in the case of lenders, how this property could be used and disposed of. A number of sale documents survive from Jeme that are, in some ways, the most

[44] Probably in this period a medium-sized jar; for the *xestes*, see now Kruit and Worp 1999.

[45] Document published Till 1938a; see also Buschhausen, Horak, and Harrauer 1995, 10–11 and Rowlandson 1998, 216.

[46] It may even be the case that the alimony included some element of child support, which would make the mention of the children even more important. (Thanks to Professor Janet Johnson for this suggestion.)

straightforward examples of how Jeme women could dispose of their own property.[47] The most formally documented transactions are the sales of real estate, and the most common documents are those issued by the seller. In a typical example from around 720 or 730, a woman named Koloje sells two plots of land to Solomon, son of Moses, for 3 $^1/_3$ solidi (*P.KRU* 3). As is standard in such contracts, the adjoining properties are noted, from which it is clear that one plot is next to the house of Solomon, while the other plot is nearby. These same pieces of land are resold in 749 by two of Solomon's daughters, acting on behalf of all their sisters, who have inherited the land from their father (*P.KRU* 2). This time, however, the land is cheaper—only 3 solidi. The latter document shows a feature that is relatively common, whereby the sisters authorize the scribe of the document to write on their behalf. Women sell land (*P.KRU* 3 and 4, for example) and parts of houses (*P.CLT* 8, for example) to men in a few texts. More frequently, related men and women (mostly brothers and sisters) buy and sell jointly owned property together, as in *P.KRU* 10 (sale of land by brothers and sisters) and in texts in the "second" Abigaia archive, where such sales sometimes resulted in subsequent disputes between the brothers and sisters (*P.KRU* 28 and 56). Women do not, in general, buy property on their own at Jeme. They either buy property in tandem with male relatives (most often brothers), or they buy property from female relatives and usually only do so to bring together parts of a house of which they already own a portion. Women do rent property from men, as in *BKU* 65 and *O.Crum* Ad 15 (in both cases the women rent houses, and in the latter the term of the lease is explicitly stated as a year) and also rent to men, as in *O.Brit.Mus.Copt.* 73:2. But in general we find more buying than renting in the Jeme texts.

     Other sorts of sales in formal documentation include the sales of livestock and household items; of these women only participate in the latter, as in *P.KRU* 34, in which a woman sells jewelry to a man, and *P.KRU* 32, where a woman sells a man her otherwise unspecified "share" (probably not real estate in this case). On a less formal level of documentation, women are found as sellers or dealers of various items. Thus the woman inquiring about the bronze utensils she has sent

---

[47] The standard work on sale documents in Coptic is still Boulard 1912. For women's ownership and disposition of land in the Greek documentation of the Roman and Late Antique periods, see Hobson 1983 and Rowlandson 1996.

(*O.Medin.HabuCopt.* 183) may be selling the items in question, but the woman sending bronze spears to her "sons" is probably only doing a favor for either secular or spiritual family members (*O.Medin.HabuCopt.* 158). Women frequently appear in texts as dealers in certain items, which makes it more likely that selling and distributing were some sort of regular occupation for them. That women were involved in the production, distribution, and selling of cloth is not surprising, given the longtime association of such crafts with women in Egypt.[48] We have already seen a contract to train a young girl in weaving: *SB Kopt.* I 045, translated above in chapter 4. At Jeme, women make (*P.Pisentius* 28) and sell clothing (*O.Medin.Habu.Copt.* 88),[49] although a certain amount of the region's cloth probably came from the west Theban monastic communities, where weaving was an important craft.[50] Also note the letter in which someone asks a woman to send a dress and a blanket for a solidus (*CPR* XX 33).[51] Women who sell or distribute wine are known at Jeme. *O.Medin.Habu.Copt.* 155 is a complaint to the woman Sabek;[52] she has sent the writer bad wine, and he wants her to send replacements back through the woman who delivers the ostracon. Women are also found dealing in wine in *O.Crum* 167 and *O.Medin.Habu.Copt.* 201, although the context is less clear in these texts.[53] There is little direct evidence for women in agricultural occupations, although we have already mentioned their ownership of land that was presumably for farming. In one case, a woman is seen as an obstacle to agriculture—in *O.Crum* 289 the male correspondent complains that "the wife of Pecosh" is hindering his farming; although this action may be due to the woman's own farming, it is not clear from the text what the situation is.

---

[48] Although Herodotus (II:35) makes the case for weaving as a man's occupation in Egypt, the Pharaonic period evidence contradicts him to some extent (Robins 1993, 103–104). For women as weavers in Graeco-Roman Egypt, see, e.g., Rowlandson 1998, 246–247, 265–270. For the textile industry in general in the Graeco-Roman period, note van Minnen 1986 and Bagnall 1993, 82–83.

[49] Also, the loom a man inherits from his mother in *P.KRU* 27.

[50] See, e.g., Winlock and Crum 1926, 155–158.

[51] The provenance of this text is not certain: probably not from Jeme?

[52] Probably not a letter, as in Stefanski and Lichtheim 1952; see discussion in Wilfong forthcoming. One wonders whether this might be the same Sabek as in the property division above, but the name is not uncommon.

[53] See also the woman as owner of a vineyard in the settlement document *O.Medin.Habu.Copt.* 87 and the non-Jeme document *P.Mon.Apollo* 49, where a woman sells wine to the Monastery of Apollo at Bawit.

In some cases, the Jeme documents record property or money coming to women where the source is ambiguous—sale, inheritance, gift, or repayment of a loan all being possibilities. In one text, one woman acknowledges receipt of goods from another:

> It is I, Sophia, who writes to Korbenesh: three rods came to me, together with two pans. Two vessels came to me, (and) an egg (?), and cup of bronze, a . . . and a mat [. . .] (O.*Medin.* *HabuCopt* 183)[54]

Although this listing contains some obscure vocabulary, the items in question seem to be household goods of some sort, not unexpected in a transaction between women. Even a very terse text can be suggestive:

> +Now, give 20 solidi to her, (namely,) Tsone.+ (O.*Medin.HabuCopt.* 160)

The original editors of this text suggest that it is a scribal exercise,[55] ostensibly because of the casual nature of the text, but they also seem to be implying that it is unlikely to be a "real" document because of the large sum of money that is going to a woman. Yet the format and wording of this ostracon are both entirely acceptable as a record of an actual transaction, a memorandum of a payment to the woman Tsone of the relatively large sum of 20 solidi. The money could be an inheritance, proceeds from a sale (this sum could easily represent money received for sale of a house or a portion thereof), or even repayment of a loan. Assuming that the payment, whatever its ultimate origin, was actually made, it would have left Tsone with a most healthy sum of money at her disposal.

It is difficult to get an estimate of the overall value of women's real and moveable property in Jeme, except in relation to the overall value of what men owned. It seems clear that women controlled somewhat less wealth than men, but their resources were still a significant factor in the economy of Jeme. Their ownership and transfer of property, their activity in moneylending, and, to a lesser extent, their involvement

---

[54] See Wilfong forthcoming for the various items mentioned.
[55] Stefanski and Lichtheim 1952, 24.

in trades and crafts combined to make them a considerable force in the fiscal life of Jeme. Although they were barred from official participation in the town's government, their control of resources gave them at least the potential to exert influence unofficially. In spite of the traditional conceptions of what their roles and behavior should be, the women of Jeme were able to participate in the town's economy. Lacking formal legal barriers to participation in the economy, most women probably were kept or kept themselves out of it on the basis of tradition, perhaps in response to those religious writers like Pisentius who wanted them to stay home. But for those women who did leave the home and transact business, the rewards and risks seem to have been roughly equal to those encountered by men. The women who were active in the economy could become prosperous on many levels, whether in terms of gold coins and agricultural products, like Koloje, or in terms of property like Elizabeth, Abigaia, and their descendants.

The monies and property that women obtained through such activities were often used within the family and community; we have also seen women using their resources to provision and trade with individuals in nearby monasteries. And on occasion, we have seen women put their wealth to a more visible use through donation. As we have already discussed, this aspect of women's involvement in the public life of Jeme can literally be seen in the fragmentary murals of the church in the Ptolemaic temple at Medinet Habu and read about in the many documents of donations of children, land, and other properties to local monasteries.

As these donations to outside monasteries show, the women of Jeme did not limit their sphere of activities to the walls of Jeme itself. Jeme lay at the center of a network of villages and monasteries ranged throughout the western Theban area, extending from the edge of cultivation west into the cliffs and out into the desert. At times, indeed, the whole region could be referred to as Jeme or the Kastron Jeme and the most prominent natural feature—the west Theban "mountain"—was known regularly as the Holy Mountain of Jeme. Between the town of Jeme proper and these outlying communities existed a close relationship, Jeme serving as a financial and administrative center to its neighbors, which in turn provided Jeme with labor, agricultural produce, raw materials, finished goods, and, not insignificantly, centers of spiritual activity and retreat. It was through this west Theban network that women most frequently got beyond the town of Jeme. Most often, such interaction took place with relatives living outside Jeme, particularly male relatives living in monasteries, who often depended on these women for money, food, and clothing. Women also dealt with monks who were not relatives, often in a business capacity: buying and selling from monks, lending them money, carrying out errands for them, and acting as their representatives. Indeed, women formed a vital part of the informal supply networks that kept some monasteries going; this is particularly evident from the Monastery of Epiphanius and may well have been the case for major institutions like the Monastery of Phoibammon (modern Deir el Bahri). As the writings and biography of Pisentius illustrate, the women of Jeme also interacted with the monks on a more spiritual level, seeking and receiving advice and guidance. The women of Jeme had at least the potential to go to and from the communities of the western Theban area.

But women did not even necessarily remain within the natural boundaries of the western Theban area. We have seen how the trade of the moneylenders of Jeme, male and female, went well outside the bounds of the western Theban area; they lent money and engaged in other transactions with individuals in towns like Terkot, Armant, Pashme, and Petemout that involved some travel to and from Jeme. We have also seen, in the child donation documents, how individuals sometimes came from even farther afield to enter into agreements with the Monastery of Phoibammon. Travel could take place on land, but most was probably accomplished using the Nile River as a natural highway, and, indeed, for transacting with people across the river from Jeme, a ferry would have been essential.[56] Traffic went both ways: we find clear cases in the moneylending documents of people coming to Jeme but also agreements sworn in the "Holy Church of Terkot" in that town to the south, implying the presence of the moneylender away from Jeme. The evidence seems to show more people in general to have traveled to western Thebes than from it, although this may be

[56] Curiously, there seems to be relatively little interaction with one of Jeme's closest neighbors just across the Nile—Apê, modern Luxor. But recall the child donation contracts from chapter 4, where both donors and witnesses come from Apê (*P.KRU* 81 and 86). The general impression of the admittedly sketchy documentation is that the residents of Luxor dealt with the inhabitants of western Theban monasteries but possibly avoided interaction with the people of Jeme itself, with the inhabitants of Jeme similarly not interacting with Apê residents. A rivalry between the two larger towns in the area, perhaps?

because travel away from the area would not necessarily have left much evidence in the western Theban area.

Most such travel by both men and women—whether to or from the region and perhaps even within the western Theban area—was subject to some regulations. Restrictions on long-distance travel were in place during much if not all of the lifetime of the western Theban community. Most of the evidence for this is from the early/mid-eighth century, but it is documented both earlier and later. Documentary evidence from elsewhere in Egypt suggests that these restrictions were instituted after the Muslim conquest, if not already in place before. These restrictions were not imposed by the Muslim governors and pagarchs for reasons of security as one might expect; instead, native Egyptian authorities restricted travel in order to prevent people from escaping payment of taxes. In western Thebes, the best evidence for travel restrictions are "protective passes" issued to the traveler by local authorities; these texts usually begin with or contain the words, "Here is the word of God (*eis plogos mpnoute*)," and were apparently called "word of God" for short.[57] These passes are so closely tied to the taxation system that many of them actually appear appended to tax receipts.

More than one hundred of these travel passes survive from the western Theban area. Women appear infrequently in them, in most cases simply described as the named or, more frequently, unnamed wife of the man with whom they would be traveling. Such passes generally note that the husband has paid his tax and is free to travel. Given the fact that women were not subject to the poll tax, the lack of protective passes for women is not surprising. In fact, one of the three passes specifically for a woman is attached to a declaration that she has paid her land tax; this text is unusual in that it gives the woman leave to travel with her daughter:

> [Here is the word] of God for you (fem.), that you may come home, for we will not ask anything (of you) or your daughter, except for her (land) tax (*dêmosion*). [For] your security, I have established [this travel pass] for you and [you assent to it. . . .] (O.*Schutzbriefe* 21)

[57] The corpus is published in Till 1938b, and there has been much discussion of these texts before and since; see Steinwenter 1955, 13, 32, 67, and the references in Schiller 1976, 112–113.

The other two travel passes for women record special cases. One is appended to a letter written by an imprisoned man to his sister; he asks the sister to go to the "great man" and try to get him out, to which he adds a travel pass for another woman, Thabaeis, "to come and greet her father"—presumably the man in prison:

> I am Isak, writing to my sister Tjo[. . .]: Be so good and help me, lest (?) they kill me. Urge Samuel (to help) and go to the place of the Great Man. Perhaps you (can) release me, for I am imprisoned and my camel was impounded. Have mercy and do your . . . [. . .] And here is the word of God for Thabaeis, that she may come forth and greet her father. (O.*Schutzbriefe* 88).

The text is fragmentary, but the situation appears to be that the man sent his daughter Thabaeis to live with his sister when he was imprisoned. The implication is that the daughter is young; perhaps the travel pass is a sort of parental note of permission to travel, since the imprisoned issuer does not seem to be an official. The remaining pass (O.*Schutzbriefe* 65) is obscure; it is issued for a woman named Kyra, allowing her to live (or continue living?) in her son's house, "so that some other wrongdoing not come upon you." It is ambiguous, however, precisely what the situation is here: Is the pass to allow the woman to live with her son as protection against the recurrence of something bad that has happened to her, or is she being forced to live with her son lest she misbehave herself again?

Given all the economic activity on the part of the women of Jeme and surrounding areas, it remains to attempt some sort of estimation of the impact of Jemean women on the economy of seventh- and eighth-century Egypt as a whole. In general, the activities at Jeme and west Thebes seem to have had little effect on the outside world. Such economic isolation would account for the almost total lack of documentation of the town from the outside. Certainly there is no evidence of major trade originating or terminating at Jeme. The religious institutions at Jeme were clearly considered important in southern Egypt, but this interest did not go the other way; west Thebans did not go far out of their area and neither, apparently, did their money or moveable property. The major contribution of Jeme and west Thebes seems to have been tax revenues, and of these the proceeds from the poll tax were certainly the most profitable since it was levied on adult males regardless of land holdings. To money collected for the poll tax women did not contribute directly, so it might seem that the women of Jeme had almost no economic impact outside of west Thebes at all. Bearing in mind the likely use of borrowed money for paying taxes, however, it is probable that the women moneylenders of Jeme contributed indirectly to the outside economy by making ready cash available for the payment of taxes. Beyond this, it is hard to say much more about the impact of the women of Jeme on Egypt as a whole: Jeme inhabitants, in general, do not appear in outside documentation, and it is rare even to find a reference to the town itself in sources from outside the western Theban area. The impression created by the evidence is that the inhabitants of Jeme concentrated their interests and efforts on their own community and region, leaving the outside world of Egypt in the in the seventh and eighth centuries to look after itself as much as possible. Thus turned inward, the women of Jeme focused on their own activities and pursuits, prospering alongside their town for nearly two centuries.

Harriet Martineau at Jeme, 1846

The Coptic town of Jeme seems to have reached its peak by the middle of the eighth century—a time of activity carefully recorded in documents and the archaeological record. As we have seen from the preceding chapters, women played an important part in this town and its prosperity. At first glance, the active and prominent position of women in the evidence may have seemed surprising, given the ideals for women expressed by religious authorities, but once examined as a whole and in context, the roles of the women of Jeme become a logical part of the society and culture of the town. The sources show that many Jemean women took advantage of the relative mobility and independence available to them and acted outside of family and home as well as in it. Women were deeply involved in the economic, social, and religious life of the town, and a certain amount of credit for Jeme's vitality can be ascribed to the activity of the women living there. Yet this very activity and apparent prosperity of Jeme at its height make subsequent events all the more mysterious. Certainly, the documents and material culture of Jeme in the middle of the eight century give no warning that the town would be entirely abandoned by the end of the eighth century.

Over a third of the main corpus of legal documents from Jeme—those texts from the archive stored at the Monastery of Phoibammon—come from the 750s to the 780s, the last major period of activity at Jeme. These three decades seem to have been a time of prosperity for Jeme and the western Theban area; certainly the transactions recorded in the texts show economic activity continuing as usual and no signs of any problems on the horizon. The latest certain date of recorded activity at Jeme was March 781 (*P.KRU* 91), while other documents may date to 782 (*P.KRU* 118) and 785 (*P.KRU* 79, Till 1939).[1] After 785, however,

[1] Dates to the 760s are equally possible for the 782 and 785 texts. *P.KRU* 100 was dated to 813 in its original edition, and this date has been repeated elsewhere (e.g., Steinwenter 1920, 31–32n3); Till 1962, 36–38, however, makes a convincing case for dating this document to the years immediately after 779, which makes greater sense given the otherwise complete lack of Jeme documents after 800.

the documentation breaks off abruptly, and the inhabitants of Jeme disappear—not only are there no records from Jeme itself, but the individuals known from the latest texts do not appear in documents from elsewhere. The archaeological evidence points to a deliberate abandonment of the town by its inhabitants, who possibly intended to return at some point. The excavator noted the removal of wooden doors and the walling up of some doorways as evidence for the intent to return,[2] and the kinds of possessions left behind also suggest that many items were hidden to be retrieved at a later date. This abandonment was not limited to Jeme; documentation for the Monastery of Phoibammon also breaks off in the 780s, and none of the other sites in the western Theban area show significant activity for the period immediately after 785.

Clearly something significant occurred in the early 780s to cause the mass abandonment of such a large area by the many people who lived there. There is, however, no direct evidence for what happened. It is clear that the abandonment of Jeme and the western Theban area was not a gradual migration away from the area due to changes in environmental conditions, as was the case with a number of Graeco-Roman cities and towns in the Fayum in earlier periods.[3] Other possible reasons that might account for the relatively sudden disappearance of the population might include famine or disease, either of which would certainly be possible, but neither archaeological nor textual evidence provides unambiguous support for these reasons. From the vantage point of the twenty-first century, the archaeological record might suggest that overcrowding could have been a factor in the abandonment of Jeme—it is possible that the town simply became too unpleasant to live in—but this judgment may reflect more of modern Western sensibilities about personal space than ancient standards for acceptable living conditions. The textual record does not reflect any discomfort with the condition of Jeme on the part of its inhabitants, and, even if this were a reason for the abandonment of Jeme, it would not necessarily account for the abandonment of other western Theban sites.

More plausible is a connection between the abandonment of Jeme and the contemporary revolt of Dihya ibn Mus'ab. Dihya was an Umayyad pretender who proclaimed himself caliph in Upper Egypt in

---

[2] Hölscher 1954, 47.
[3] See the discussion in van Minnen 1995 relating to Soknopaiou Nesos and Karanis.

782, clearly to the displeasure of the ruling Abbasid officials; this event resulted in considerable fighting, ruinous taxation, and general reprisals after the capture and execution of Dihya in 785.[4] Although we lack certain evidence linking the revolt and the abandonment of Jeme, the coincidence of the two events at least suggests a connection between them. The western Theban population may have supported Dihya, either willingly or unwillingly, and have been subsequently punished for it. Also possible: they simply may have found conditions in the midst of the revolt intolerable and moved with the intention of coming back. Whatever the reason, Jeme and environs were abandoned, and the inhabitants went elsewhere. There are later traditions that the inhabitants of Jeme fled to Esna at the time of the Muslim conquest;[5] these are obviously wrong in terms of timing, but they may well reflect a garbled version of what actually happened around 785. Esna was about 80 kilometers up the river to the south from Jeme—a major Christian center in the early Islamic period, and one that continued in importance for centuries afterward.[6] Although Luxor and Armant were closer to Jeme, they may have also been embroiled in the troubles that led to the abandonment, and the very distance of Esna may have made it more attractive.

The abandonment of Jeme and most of western Thebes by the beginning of the ninth century CE took place at a time of transition in Egyptian society and culture.[7] Although Coptic continued to be written as a language of daily life well into the twelfth century, its use had begun to decline significantly in the ninth century. Arabic, after 705 CE, was the official language of administration for Egypt and quickly came to be used in business and everyday communication as well; the first significant numbers of Arabic papyri come from the eighth century in the form of administrative texts from Aphrodito, and Arabic letters and legal documents appear with increasing frequency in the ninth century and beyond. The shift from Coptic to Arabic in Egypt accompanied significant changes in the religious makeup of the Egyptian population from predominantly Christian to predominantly Muslim.

[4] First suggested in Godlewski 1986, 77–78, where he gives references.
[5] Recorded, e.g., in Wilkinson 1835 and, presumably from such sources, in Martineau 1848, 2:12–13.
[6] Timm 3:1181–1193.
[7] For more detailed treatment of the following with references, see Wilfong 1998b.

Although Christians continued to make up the majority of the population for at least a century beyond the abandonment of Jeme (and continue as a significant minority in Egypt to the present), conversions to Islam began to occur in significant numbers in the ninth century. The ninth century was a time of increasing tension between Christians and Muslims in Egypt; although persecution of Christians was not yet official policy, events such as the violent suppression of Christian-led tax revolts in the north in 832 helped set the tone for the coming centuries and may have served to increase the rates of conversion among the population. The age of relatively uneventful coexistence between Christian population and Muslim rulers seen in the Jeme documents had come to an end not too long after Jeme itself.

During the centuries following the abandonment of Jeme, the western Theban area showed some signs of activity but nothing like the earlier levels of settlement and population. Local monastic activity is attested: a funerary stela dated to 891 CE, which comes from the Quibell excavations at the Ramesseum, records the death of a woman named Maria, who is identified by a monastic administrative title.[8] This stela suggests that the Ramesseum may have been the site of a monastic community surviving well into the ninth century, and a women's monastic community at that. Certainly, monasticism remained one of the major life options for women in an increasingly conservative environment.[9] Although Egypt's Christian communities continued to allow for more autonomous roles for women than found among the contemporary Egyptian Muslim population, possibilities for activity outside the home or the monastery became more and more limited. In general, later Christian authors in Egypt continued, along the lines of earlier authors like Pisentius, to advocate a submissive and secondary role for women,[10] and the monastic life often offered the only possibility for women to get beyond the traditional roles of wife and mother. Monasticism was a popular alternative for Christian women in Egypt, allowing access to education and spiritual development, and continues

[8] OIM 1569, discussed above in chapter 4; see Wilfong forthcoming for notes.

[9] See el-Masri 1958 for a somewhat idealistic picture of women's monasticism in Egypt, especially in the tenth through twelfth centuries, and also Athanasius 1991 in general, even less specific.

[10] See, for instance, the writings of Cyril III Ibn Laqlaq, a prominent Christian author of the thirteenth century: Khs-Burmester 1946–1947, especially the passages on 120–122.

to be valued to the present.[11] Certainly, in the centuries that followed the abandonment of Jeme, women had less and less opportunity to engage in the kinds of activities that they had in Jeme's heyday.

Aside from the probable women's monastic house at the site of the Ramesseum, few Coptic texts survive from the western Theban area that can be securely dated to this period. These few texts consist of Coptic graffiti from the ruins of the Monastery of Phoibammon, which record visitors in the tenth through thirteenth centuries.[12] These graffiti do not seem to indicate rehabitation of the monastery but are rather records of pilgrimages to a venerable, ruined monastery of the past. Although there was certainly never a time when the western Theban area was entirely uninhabited, Christian monasteries and predominantly Christian settlements like Jeme seem not to have been a feature of the area again until relatively recent times. Jeme itself had become a ghost town, an abandoned ruin that was the subject of later legend that may well have scared off any attempts at resettlement of the site.[13] The name Jeme appears in later Christian Arabic sources—mostly individual saints' lives and the Synaxary—as Gabal Shama or Shimi; but because such mentions derive from Coptic sources, they may not represent an independent tradition of knowledge about Jeme.[14] The town otherwise seems to have escaped the notice of both Christian and Muslim historians and geographers writing in Arabic, entirely eclipsed by the earlier ruins of the temple of Ramesses III on which Jeme was built.

The "rediscovery" of Jeme as an archaeological site is perhaps best credited to the inhabitants of the area in the early nineteenth century. It is hard to know what was initially responsible—local farmers carting off the decaying mud brick of the Jeme houses for fertilizer or early guides clearing away the houses to show off the Pharaonic temple reliefs. It was not long before antiquities and texts were discovered during the removal of the houses; these went onto the antiquities market and subsequently to European museums. Once the objects and the texts from Jeme and environs came to be known, scholars became interested in the site. In the meantime, Jeme continued to be destroyed in the interests of agriculture, antiquities dealing, and tourism (the latter even

---

[11] See, e.g., Doorn-Harder 1995.
[12] Godlewski 1986, 141–152.
[13] See Bonomi 1906 (publication of notes made in 1830).
[14] See Timm 1985, 1012–1013.

at the behest of the Egyptian Antiquities Service). Other sites in the region were excavated in the late nineteenth and early twentieth centuries, but it was not until the late 1920s that Jeme itself was properly excavated—by Uvo Hölscher for the University of Chicago's Oriental Institute. This excavation was largely a preliminary to the Oriental Institute's ongoing recording and publication of the Pharaonic temples at Medinet Habu, but Hölscher managed to record much of what he cleared and drew up a detailed plan of the remaining portions of the town. He also found more than two thousand Coptic ostraca and a wide array of the objects of daily life in Jeme; the corpora of ceramic lamps and pottery vessels are among the most extensive known for this period. The excavation suffered from subsequent publication delays: many of the texts are still unpublished, and the excavation report was written up without benefit of Hölscher's field notebooks, which have only relatively recently resurfaced.[15] Very recently, the series of publications of the Medinet Habu excavations has been revived and will include much material from Jeme.[16] Several of the houses on the southwest enclosure wall remain unexcavated and unpublished;[17] there are also extensive traces of unexplored houses outside the wall that were beyond the limit of the Oriental Institute's concession. The majority of the structures that made up the town of Jeme, however, were destroyed in the course of Hölscher's clearance.

Before Hölscher's excavations and the earlier clearances of the site, Jeme's remains figured in the accounts of eighteenth- and nineteenth-century European travelers, who almost unanimously dismissed them as dirty huts covering up the Pharaonic temple—an inconvenience to the tourist and Egyptologist alike. A typical such account can be found in the travel writings of Harriet Martineau, British author, feminist, and social activist who traveled to Egypt in 1846 as part of a larger tour of the Middle East ultimately described in her 1848 book *Eastern Life: Past and Present*. Martineau's trip was partly intended as a rest cure after a breakdown in health, but her passionate interest in the condition of women in Egypt at the time of her travels kept her feminist interests fully engaged and active throughout the trip. Martineau's accounts of

[15] See Teeter 2002, chapter 1.

[16] Wilfong 2002b in Teeter 2002 and Teeter forthcoming.

[17] A cursory examination in 1992 showed these houses to be well preserved, although apparently a favorite playground for children who live nearby.

harem life were much commented on and have often been taken as evidence for her great concern for the conditions of women.[18] Her book, however, is primarily a travel account and, as such, concerned with the sights and circumstances of her trip.[19] Thus we have her account of a visit to Medinet Habu and her reaction to the sight of the town of Jeme:

> When Thebes had so far declined as to become a mere collection of villages in the plain, the Christians took possession of Medeenet Haboo, plastering over the sculptures with mud, putting up an altar at the east end of the temple, introducing their little red columns and low roofs among the massy and gorgeous pillars of the heathen courts; and even defacing the architraves to admit their rafters. Their priests took possession of the small apartments of the temple; and their people built mud houses within the precincts. On the approach of the Arabs, the Christians fled to Isna; and here lie their remains, scattered among the outstanding glories of an older time. (Martineau 1848, 2:12–13)

This account is entirely typical of that of other travelers—deploring the "disfigurement" of the ancient monuments by the Christians with their mud-brick structures—but has a certain vividness thanks to Martineau's talents as writer. One can certainly imagine her striding about the ruins of Jeme in her heavy traveling costume, disdaining a sunshade, her copy of Wilkinson's *Topography of Thebes* in hand as she sets out to capture the scene for her readers.

One wonders if Harriet Martineau would have been so dismissive of the remains of Jeme if she had known of the lives of the women of that town, the evidence for which was buried in those same "mud houses" she wrote about. As an early feminist, Martineau was certainly interested in the stories of women's lives, present and past: her social activism on behalf of women was widely known to her contemporaries. Her successful career as a writer clearly gave her a special insight into

---

[18] But see Melman 1992, who takes a different view. She finds that Martineau's accounts of the harem, particularly her erotically charged descriptions of women bathing, reinforce the traditional Orientalist view of women as exotic props in a narrative.

[19] Her book is also an important early example of a guide directed toward the special needs of women while traveling; see Wheatley 1957, 266–269 for observations on this aspect of the book.

the practicalities and challenges women faced as workers and wage earners. And, closely paralleling the work of the scholar in reconstructing the lives of the women of Jeme, Martineau's own fiction and that of her friends and (now) better-known contemporaries, Charlotte Brontë and Elizabeth Gaskell, often dealt with the revelation of women's lives through their texts, their letters, and their material culture. Thinking about these authors while reading and writing about the documents of the women of Jeme, one cannot help but be reminded of the chapter "Old Letters" in Elizabeth Gaskell's *Cranford*. There, the narrator Mary Smith and her friend Miss Matty use letters, documents, and personal items to reconstruct the story of women of the past. Given these circumstances, it is hard to imagine that Harriet Martineau would have passed such a disdainful verdict over the remains of Jeme had she been aware of the prominence and activities of the women in the town.

ABBREVIATIONS

Editions of Coptic and Greek texts and basic reference works are cited using the standard system of abbreviations in *Checklist of Editions of Greek, Latin, Demotic and Coptic Papyri, Ostraca and Tablets*, 5th edition, by John F. Oates, Roger S. Bagnall, Sarah J. Clackson, Alexandra A. O'Brien, Joshua D. Sosin, Terry G. Wilfong, and Klaas A. Worp, Bulletin of the American Society of Papyrologists Supplements 9 (n.p.: American Society of Papyrologists, 2001). For the convenience of the reader, I reproduce the most common of these abbreviations (in which "P." = "papyrus/ parchment" and "O." = "ostracon") used in the present book below:

BKU = *Aegyptische Urkunden aus den Koeniglichen Museen zu Berlin: Koptische Urkunden* (Berlin: Wiedmannsche Buchhandlung, 1904)

CPR IV = W. C. Till, *Die Koptischen Rechtsurkunden der Papyrussammlung der Osterreichischen Nationalbibliothek*, Corpus Papyrorum Raineri 4. (Vienna: Adolf Holzhausens, 1958)

CPR XII = M. R. M. Hasitzka, *Koptische Texte*, Corpus Papyrorum Raineri 12 (Vienna: Verlag Brüder Hollinek, 1987)

O.Brit.Mus.Copt. I = H. R. Hall, *Coptic and Greek Texts of the Christian Period from Ostraka, Stelae, etc. in the British Museum* (London: British Museum, 1905) [cited by plate number]

O.Crum = W. E. Crum, *Coptic Ostraca from the Collections of the Egypt Exploration Fund, the Cairo Museum and Others* (London: Egypt Exploration Fund, 1902)

O.CrumST = W. E. Crum, *Short Texts from Coptic Ostraca and Papyri* (London: Oxford University Press, 1921)

O.CrumVC = W. E. Crum, *Varia Coptica* (Aberdeen: The University Press, 1939)

O.Medin.HabuCopt. = E. M. Stefanski and M. Lichtheim, *Coptic Ostraca from Medinet Habu*, Oriental Institute Publications 71 (Chicago: University of Chicago Press, 1952)

O.*Mon.Epiph.* = W. E. Crum and H. G. Evelyn White, *The Monastery of Epiphanius at Thebes: Part II: Coptic Ostraca and Papyri; Greek Ostraca and Papyri* (New York: Metropolitan Museum of Art, 1926)

O.*Schutzbriefe* = W. C. Till, "Koptische Schützbriefe," *Mitteilungen des Deutschen Archäologischen Instituts Abteilung Kairo* 8 (1938) 71–127

O.*Theb.* = *Theban Ostraca*, University of Toronto Studies, Philological Series 1 (London: Oxford University Press, 1913)

P.*CLT* = A. A. Schiller, *Ten Coptic Legal Texts* (New York: Metropolitan Museum of Art, 1932)

P.*KRU* = W. E. Crum and G. Steindorff, *Koptische Rechtsurkunden des achten Jahrhunderts aus Djême (Theben)* (Leipzig: J. C. Hinrichs, 1912; reprinted 1971, with a new introduction by A. Arthur Schiller)

P.*Lond.* IV = H. I. Bell and W. E. Crum, *Greek Papyri in the British Museum: Catalogue, with Texts. Vol. IV: The Aphrodito Papyri* (London: British Museum, 1914)

P.*Lond.Copt.* I = W. E. Crum, *Catalogue of the Coptic Manuscripts in the British Museum* (London: British Museum, 1905)

P.*Mon.Apollo* = S. J. Clackson, *Coptic and Greek Texts Relating to the Hermopolite Monastery of Apa Apollo*, Griffith Institute Monographs (Oxford: Griffith Institute, 2000)

P.*Mon.Epiph.* = W. E. Crum and H. G. Evelyn White, *The Monastery of Epiphanius at Thebes: Part II: Coptic Ostraca and Papyri; Greek Ostraca and Papyri* (New York: Metropolitan Museum of Art, 1926)

P.*Pisentius* = E. Revillout, "Textes coptes: Extraits de la correspondance de St. Pésunthius, évêque de Coptos, et de plusiers documents analogues (juridiques ou économiques)," *Revue Égyptologique* 9 (1900) 133–177; 10 (1902) 34–47; 14 (1914) 22–32

P.*Ryl.Copt.* = W. E. Crum, *Catalogue of the Coptic Manuscripts in the Collection of the John Rylands Library Manchester* (Manchester: University Press, 1909)

Pap.Eleph.Eng. = B. Porten, ed., *The Elephantine Papyri in English: Three Millennia of Cross-Cultural Continuity and Change* (Leiden: E. J. Brill, 1996)

SB XX = H.-A. Rupprecht, *Sammelbuch Griechischer Urkunden aus Ägypten*
XX (Wiesbaden: Harrassowitz, 1997)

SB XXII = H.-A. Rupprecht, *Sammelbuch Griechischer Urkunden aus*
Ägypten XXII (Wiesbaden: Harrassowitz, 2001)

SB Kopt. I = M. R. M. Hasitzka, *Kopstisches Sammelbuch I* <*KSB*>,
Mitteilungen aus der Papyrussammlung der österreichischen
Nationalbibliothek (Papyrus Erzherzog Rainer), Neue Serie, 23
(Vienna: Verlag Brüder Hollinek, 1993)

The following standard reference works are also cited by *Checklist*
abbreviations:

Crum, *Dict.* = W. E. Crum, *A Coptic Dictionary* (Oxford: Clarendon
Press, 1939), cited by page and column

Timm = S. Timm, *Das christlich-koptische Ägypten in arabischer Zeit*, Beiheft
zum Tubinger Atlas des Vorderen Orients, Reihe B
(Geisteswissenschaften) 41/1-6 (Wiesbaden: Dr. Ludwig
Reichert Verlag, 1984-1992), 6 volumes, cited by volume and
page

On the model of the *Checklist* cited above, I have created the following
abbreviations for citations of texts from two important collections of
ancient graffiti:

Gr.Mon.Epiph. For the graffiti in W. E. Crum and H. G. Evelyn White,
The Monastery of Epiphanius at Thebes: Part II: Coptic
Ostraca and Papyri; Greek Ostraca and Papyri (New York:
Metropolitan Museum of Art, 1926)

Gr.Mont.Theb. For the graffiti in *Graffiti de la Montagne Thébaine*,
Collection Scientifique (Cairo: Centre de
Documentation et d'Études sur l'ancienne Égypte,
1969-1974), cited by graffito number

GLOSSARY

Ama, amma: women's monastic superior.

Amir: Arabic title for the pagarch.

Apa: common men's monastic title.

Apolashane: former occupant of office of *lashane.*

Artaba: standard unit of dry measure: in the Jeme texts an *artaba* was probably somewhat more than an American or British bushel.

Carat: denomination of coin (usually bronze) in use at Jeme: 24 carats equal 1 solidus.

Cor: smallest denomination of bronze coin in common use at Jeme: 960 *cor* = 1 solidus.

Dinar: see solidus.

Dioiketes: in the Jeme documents, administrative district official directly under the pagarch.

Ho: dry measure roughly equal to the *artaba.*

Holokottinos (plural holokottinoi): see solidus.

Indiction: fifteen-year administrative cycle for taxation purposes; Jeme documents are often dated by their indiction year.

Kerat, Keration: see carat.

Lashane: town magistrate/administrator; at Jeme there were usually two at any given time.

Maje: dry measure; 12 *maje* = 1 *artaba.*

Ment: dry measure; possibly 24 *ment* = 1 *artaba.*

Mosne: dry measure; probably 3 *mosne* = 1 *artaba.*

Nomisma (plural nomismata): see solidus.

Oipe: dry measure; 6 *oipe* = 1 *artaba.*

Ostracon (plural ostraca): broken piece of pottery or chip of stone used as a writing surface.

Pagarch: major district administrator, frequently known in the Jeme documents under the Arabic title amir.

She: small denomination bronze coin in common use at Jeme: the value of the *she* seems to have varied over time, from 240 to 288 *she* = 1 solidus.

Shokas: dry measure, probably equal to 2 *artabas*.

Solidus (plural solidi): largest denomination of gold coin commonly in use at Jeme: often known in Jeme documents as the holokottinos or nomisma, roughly equivalent to the Arab dinar.

Tremis: gold coin equal to one-third of the solidus.

Abbott, N. 1941. "Arabic Marriage Contracts among Copts." *Zeitschrift der Deutschen Morgenländishen Gesellschaft* 95:59-81.

Albrecht, R. 1986. *Das Leben der heiligen Makrina auf dem Hintergrund der Thekla-Traditionen. Studien zu den Ursprüngen des weiblichen Mönchtums im 4. Jahrhundert in Kleinasien.* Forschungen zur Kirchen- und Dogmengeschichte 38. Göttingen: Vandenhoeck & Ruprecht.

Alexandre, M. 1992. "Early Christian Women." In *A History of Women in the West: I. From Ancient Goddesses to Christian Saints*, ed. P. Schmitt Pantel, 409-444. Cambridge MA: Harvard University Press.

Allen, E. B. 1947. "A Coptic Solar Eclipse Record." *Journal of the American Oriental Society* 67:267-269.

Allen, M. L. 1985. "The Terracotta Figurines from Karanis: A Study of Technique, Style and Chronology in Fayoumic Coroplastics." 3 volumes. Ph.D. dissertation, University of Michigan.

Amélineau, E. 1888. *Monuments pour servir à l'histoire de l'Égypte chrétienne aux IVe, Ve, VIe et VIIe siècles.* Paris: E. Leroux.

———. 1889. "Un évêque de Keft au VIIe siècle." *Mémoires de l'Institut d'Égypte* 2:261-424.

Arjava, A. 1996. *Women and Law in Late Antiquity.* Oxford: Clarendon Press.

Athanasius, Bishop. 1991. "Women's Religious Communities." In *The Coptic Encyclopedia*, ed. A. S. Atiya, 7:2324-2325. New York: Macmillan.

Atiya, A. S. 1991. "Martyrs, Coptic." In *The Coptic Encyclopedia*, ed. A. S. Atiya, 5:1550-1559. New York: Macmillan.

Bachatly, C. 1961. *Le Monastère de Phoebammon dans la Thébaïde, Tome III: Identifications botaniques, zoologiques et chimiques.* Rapports de Fouilles. Cairo: Société d'Archéologie Copte.

———. 1965. *Le Monastère de Phoebammon dans la Thébaïde, Tome II: Graffiti, inscriptions et ostraca.* Rapports de Fouilles. Cairo: Société d'Archéologie Copte.

Bachatly, C. 1981. *Le Monastère de Phoebammon dans la Thébaïde, Tome I: L'archéologie du site*. Rapports de Fouilles. Cairo: Société d'Archéologie Copte.

Bacot, S. 1999. "Avons-nous retrouvé la grand-mère de Koloje?" In *Ägypten und Nubien in spätanitker und christlicher Zeit: Akten des 6. Internationalen Koptologenkongresses*, ed. S. Emmel [and others], 2:241–247. Wiesbaden: Reichert.

Bács, T. 2000. "The So-called 'Monastery of Syriacus' at Thebes." *Egyptian Archaeology* 17:34–36.

Badawy, A. 1978. *Coptic Art and Archaeology: The Art of the Christian Egyptians from the Late Antique to the Middle Ages*. Cambridge MA: MIT Press.

Baek Simonsen, J. 1988. *Studies in the Genesis and Early Development of the Caliphal Taxation System, with Special Reference to Circumstances in the Arab Peninsula, Egypt and Palestine*. Copenhagen: Akademisk Forlag.

Bagnall, R. S. 1987. "Church, State and Divorce in Late Roman Egypt." In *Florilegium Columbianum: Essays in Honor of Paul Oskar Kristeller*, ed. K.-L. Selig and R. Somerville, 41–61. New York: Italica Press.

——. 1991. "A Trick a Day to Keep the Tax Man at Bay: The Prostitute Tax in Roman Egypt." *Bulletin of the American Society of Papyrologists* 28:5–12.

——. 1993. *Egypt in Late Antiquity*. Princeton: Princeton University Press.

——. 1995a. *Reading Papyri, Writing Ancient History*. Approaching the Ancient World. London: Routledge.

——. 1995b "Women, Law and Social Realities in Late Antiquity: A Review Article." *Bulletin of the American Society of Papyrologists* 32:65–86.

Bagnall, R. S. and B. W. Frier. 1994. *The Demography of Roman Egypt*. Cambridge Studies in Population, Economy and Society in Past Time 23. Cambridge: Cambridge University Press.

Ballet, P. 1991. "Ceramics, Coptic: Figurines." In *The Coptic Encyclopedia*, ed. A. S. Atiya, 3:500–504. New York: Macmillan.

Bard, K. A. 1999. *Encyclopedia of the Archaeology of Ancient Egypt*. New York: Routledge.

Bataille, A. 1952. *Les Memnonia*. Recherches d'Archéologie, de Philologie et d'Histoire 23. Cairo: Institut Français d'Archéologie Orientale.

Beaucamp, J. 1990. *Le statut de la femme à Byzance (4e–7e siècles) I: Le droit impérial*. Travaux et Mémoires du Centre de Recherche d'Histoire et Civilisation de Byzance, Collège de France: Monographies 5. Paris: De Boccard.

———. 1992. *Le statut de la femme à Byzance (4e–7e siècles) II: Les pratiques sociales*. Travaux et Mémoires du Centre de Recherche d'Histoire et Civilisation de Byzance, Collège de France: Monographies 6. Paris: De Boccard.

Behlmer, H. 2000. "Koptische Quellen zu (männlicher) 'Homosexualität.'" *Studien zur altägyptischen Kultur* 28:27–53.

Bell, H. I. 1925. "Two Official Letters of the Arab Period." *Journal of Egyptian Archaeology* 11:265–281.

Bell, H. I., and W. E. Crum. 1910. *Greek Papyri in the British Museum: Catalogue, with Texts. Vol. IV: The Aphrodito Papyri*. London: British Museum.

Bénazeth, D. 1992. *L'art du métal au début de l'ère chrétienne*. Catalogue du Département des Antiquités Égyptiennes, Musée du Louvre. Paris: Réunion des Musées Nationaux.

Biedenkopf-Ziehner, A. 1983. *Untersuchungen zum koptischen Briefformular unter berücksichtig ägyptischer und greichischer Parallelen*. Koptische Studien 1. Würzburg: Gisela Zauzich Verlag.

———. 2000. *Koptische Ostraka*. 2 volumes. Wiesbaden: Harrassowitz Verlag.

———. 2001. *Koptische Schenkungsurkunden aus der Thebais: Formeln und Topoi der Urkunden, Aussagen der Urkunden, Indices*. Göttinger Orientforschungen, 4. Reihe: Ägypten, 41. Wiesbaden: Harrassowitz Verlag.

Bolman, E. S. 1997. "The Coptic *Galaktrophousa* as the Medicine of Immortality." Ph.D. dissertation, Bryn Mawr College.

Bonomi, J. 1906. "Topographical Notes on Western Thebes Collected in 1830." *Annales du Service des Antiquités* 7:78–86.

Boswell, J. 1988. *The Kindness of Strangers: The Abandonment of Children in Western Europe from Late Antiquity to the Renaissance*. New York: Pantheon Books.

Boud'Hors, A. 1996. "Reçus d'impôt coptes de Djémé." *Cahier de Recherches de l'Institut de Papyrologie et d'Égyptologie de Lille* 18:161–175.

Boulard, L. 1912. "La vente dans les actes coptes." In *Études d'histoire juridique offertes à Paul Frédéric Girard*, 1–94. Paris: Librairie Paul Geuthner.

Boutros Ghali, M. 1991. "Dayr Apa Phoibammon: History." In *The Coptic Encyclopedia*, ed. A. S. Atiya, 3:779–780. New York: Macmillan.

Bowman, A. K. 1996. *Egypt after the Pharaohs, 332 BC–AD642.* 2nd paperback edition. Berkeley: University of California Press.

Brashear, W. M. 1983. "The Coptic Three Wise Men." *Chronique d'Égypte* 58:297–310.

Brooten, B. 1996. *Love between Women: Early Christian Responses to Female Homoeroticism.* Chicago Series on Sexuality, History and Society. Chicago: University of Chicago Press.

Brown, P. 1971. *The World of Late Antiquity, AD 150–750.* History of European Civilization Library. London: Thames and Hudson.

——. 1988. *The Body and Society: Men, Women and Sexual Renunciation in Early Christianity.* New York: Columbia University Press.

Brown, S. K. 1991 "Ostracon." In *The Coptic Encyclopedia*, ed. A. S. Atiya, 6: 1856. New York: Macmillan.

Brunsch, W. 1979. "Drei koptische Ostrakonbriefe aus der Sammlung des Ägyptologischen Instituts in Heidelberg." *Zeitschrift für Ägyptische Sprache und Altertumskunde* 106:25–36.

——. 1983. "Griechische und koptische Graffiti aus Medinet Habu." *Wiener Zeitschrift für die Kunde des Morgenlandes* 75:19–34.

——. 1984. "Index zu Heusers *Personennamen der Kopten.*" *Enchoria* 12:119–153.

Budge, E. A. W. 1913. *Coptic Apocrypha in the Dialect of Upper Egypt.* London: British Museum.

Buschhausen, H., U. Horak, and H. Harrauer. 1995. *Der Lebenskreis der Kopten. Dokumente, Textilien, Funde, Ausgrabungen.* Vienna: Hollinek.

Castel, G. 1979. "Étude d'une momie copte." In *Hommages à la mémoire de Serge Sauneron 1927–1976, II: Égypte post-pharaonique*, 122–143. Bibliothèque d'Étude 82. Cairo: Institut Français d'Archéologie Orientale.

Castelli, E. 1991. "'I Will Make Mary Male': Pieties of Body and Gender Transformation of Christian Women in Late Antiquity." In *Body Guards: The Cultural Politics of Gender Ambiguity*, ed. J. Epstein and K. Straub, 29–49. New York: Routledge.

Clackson, S. J. 2000. *Coptic and Greek Texts Relating to the Hermopolite Monastery of Apa Apollo.* Griffith Institute Monographs. Oxford: Griffith Institute.

Clark, G. 1993. *Women in Late Antiquity: Pagan and Christian Lifestyles.* Oxford: Clarendon Press.

Coquin, R.-G. 1975. "Le catalogue de la Bibliothèque du Couvent de Saint Élie du Rocher (Ostracon IFAO 13315)." *Bulletin de l'Institut Français d'Archéologie Orientale* 75:207–239.

——. 1991a. "Moses of Abydos." In *The Coptic Encyclopedia*, ed. A. S. Atiya, 5:1679–1681. New York: Macmillan.

——. 1991b. "Pisentius, Saint." In *The Coptic Encyclopedia*, ed. A. S. Atiya, 6:1978. New York: Macmillan.

Coquin, R.-G., and M. Martin. 1991. "Dayr Anba Pisentius." In *The Coptic Encyclopedia*, ed. A. S. Atiya, 3:757. New York: Macmillan.

Coquin, R.-G., M. Martin, and P. Grossman. 1991. "Dayr al-Bakhit." In *The Coptic Encyclopedia*, ed. A. S. Atiya, 3:785–787. New York: Macmillan.

Cribiore, R. 1996. *Writing, Teachers, and Students in Graeco-Roman Egypt.* American Studies in Papyrology 36. Atlanta: Scholars Press.

——. 1999. "Greek and Coptic Education in Late Antique Egypt." In *Ägypten und Nubien in spätanitker und christlicher Zeit: Akten des 6. Internationalen Koptologenkongresses*, ed. S. Emmel [and others], 2:279–286. Wiesbaden: Reichert.

Crum, W. E. 1902. *Coptic Ostraca from the Collections of the Egypt Exploration Fund, the Cairo Museum and Others.* London: Egypt Exploration Fund.

——. 1904. "Coptic Graffiti &c." In *The Osireion at Abydos*, ed. M. A. Murray, 38–44. Egyptian Research Account Publications 9. London: Egyptian Research Account.

——. 1905. *Catalogue of the Coptic Manuscripts in the British Museum.* London: British Museum.

——. 1909. *Catalogue of the Coptic Manuscripts in the Collection of the John Rylands Library Manchester.* Manchester: University Press.

——. 1914. Book Review of E. A. Wallis Budge, *Coptic Apocrypha in the Dialect of Upper Egypt. Zeitschrift der Deutschen Morgenländischen Gesellschaft* 68:176–184.

——. 1915–1917. "Discours de Pisenthius sur Saint Onnophrius." *Revue de l'Orient Chrétien* 20:38–67.

——. 1921. *Short Texts from Coptic Ostraca and Papyri.* London: Oxford University Press.

——. 1939. *Varia Coptica.* Aberdeen: The University Press.

Crum, W. E., and G. Steindorff. 1912. *Koptische Rechtsurkunden des achten Jahrhunderts aus Djême (Theben).* Leipzig: J. C. Hinrichs. Reprinted 1971, with a new introduction by A. Arthur Schiller.

Crum, W. E., and H. G. Evelyn White. 1926. *The Monastery of Epiphanius at Thebes: Part II: Coptic Ostraca and Papyri; Greek Ostraca and Papyri.* New York: Metropolitan Museum of Art.

Delattre, A. 2001. "Une femme scribe de village à l'époque copte?" *Acta Orientalia Belgica* 15:119–122.

Depauw, M. 1997. *A Companion to Demotic Studies.* Papyrologica Bruxellensia 28. Brussels: Fondation Égyptologique Reine Élisabeth.

Derda, T., and E. Wipszycka. 1994. "L'emploi des titres *abba, apa* et *papas* dans l'Égypte byzantine." *Journal of Juristic Papyrology* 24:23–56.

Doorn-Harder, P. van. 1995. *Contemporary Coptic Nuns.* Columbia SC: University of South Carolina Press.

Doresse, J. 1949. "Monastères coptes aux environs d'Armant en Thébaide." *Analecta Bollandiana* 67:327–349.

Drescher, J. 1944. "A Widow's Petition." *Bulletin de la Société d'Archéologie Copte* 10:91–96.

———. 1946. *Apa Mena: A Selection of Coptic Texts Relating to St. Menas.* Textes et Documents. Cairo: Société d'Archéologie Copte.

———. 1947. *Three Coptic Legends: Hilaria, Archellites, The Seven Sleepers.* Supplément aux Annales du Service des Antiquités de l'Égypte 4. Cairo: Imprimerie de l'Institut Français d'Archéologie Orientale.

Edgerton, W. F. 1937. *Medinet Habu Graffiti: Facsimiles.* Oriental Institute Publications 36. Chicago: University of Chicago Press.

El-Masri, I. H. 1958. "A Historical Survey of the Convents for Women in Egypt up to the Present Day." *Bulletin de la Société d'Archéologie Copte* 14:63–111.

El-Saghir, M. [and others]. 1986. *Le camp romain de Louqsor.* Mémoires 83. Cairo: Institute Français d'Archéologie Orientale.

Elm, S. 1994. *"Virgins of God": The Making of Asceticism in Late Antiquity.* Oxford Classical Monographs. Oxford: Clarendon Press.

———. 1996. "'Pierced by Bronze Needles': Anti-Montanist Charges of Ritual Stigmatization in Their Fourth-Century Context." *Journal of Early Christian Studies* 4:409–439.

Foucault, M. 1971. *The Archaeology of Knowledge and the Discourse on Language.* New York: Pantheon.

Foucault, M. 1989. *Foucault Live (Interviews 1966–1984)*. Foreign Agents Series. New York: Semiotext(e).

Fournet, J.-L. 2000. "Coptos dans l'antiquité tardive (fin IIIe–VIIe siècle)." In *Coptos: L'Égypte antique aux portes du désert*, 196–215. Lyon: Musée des Beaux Arts.

Frankfurter, D. T. 1998a. *Religion in Roman Egypt: Assimilation and Resistance*. Princeton: Princeton University Press.

——. 1998b. *Pilgrimage and Holy Space in Late Antique Egypt*. Religions in the Graeco-Roman World 134. Leiden: Brill.

Frederick, V. 1991. "Pseudo-Pisentius of Qift." In *The Coptic Encyclopedia*, ed. A. S. Atiya, 6:2028. New York: Macmillan.

Friedman, F. D. 1989. *Beyond the Pharaohs: Egypt and the Copts in the 2nd to 7th Centuries A.D.* Providence: Museum of Art, Rhode Island School of Design.

Gabra, G. A. S. 1984. *Untersuchungen zu den Texten über Pesyntheus, Bischof von Coptos (569–632)*. Habelts Dissertationdrücke, Reihe Ägyptologie 4. Bonn: Dr. Rudolph Habelt.

——. 1991. "Pisentius, Saint." In *The Coptic Encyclopedia*, ed. A. S. Atiya, 6:1978. New York: Macmillan.

Gagos, T., L. Koenen, and B. E. McNellen. 1992. "A First Century Archive from Oxyrhynchos: Oxyrhynchite Loan Contracts and Egyptian Marriage." In *Life in a Multi-Cultural Society: Egypt from Cambyses to Constantine and Beyond*, ed. J. H. Johnson, 181–205. Studies in Ancient Oriental Civilization 51. Chicago: Oriental Institute Press.

Gagos, T., and P. van Minnen. 1994. *Settling a Dispute: Toward a Legal Anthropology of Late Antique Egypt*. New Texts from Ancient Cultures 1. Ann Arbor: University of Michigan Press.

Gascou, J. 1979. "Ostraca de Djémé." *Bulletin de l'Institut Français d'Archéologie Orientale* 79:77–86.

Giamberardini, G. 1974–1978. *Il culto mariano in Egitto*. 3 volumes. Jerusalem: Studium Biblicum Franciscanum.

Gilchrist, R. 1994. *Gender and Material Culture: The Archaeology of Religious Women*. London: Routledge.

Godlewski, W. 1986. *Le monastère de St Phoibammon*. Deir el-Bahari 5. Warsaw: PWN-Éditions scientifiques de Pologne.

——. 1991. "Dayr Apa Phoibammon: Buildings." In *The Coptic Encyclopedia*, ed. A. S. Atiya, 3:780–781. New York: Macmillan.

Goodwin, C. W. 1863. "Account of Three Coptic Papyri, and Other Manuscripts, Brought from the East by J. S. Stuart Glennie, Esq." *Archaeologia* 39:447–456.

Green, A. H. 1993. "A Late 19th-Century Coptic Marriage Contract and the Coptic Documentary Tradition." *Le Muséon* 106:361–371.

Grubbs, J. E. 1995. *Law and Family in Late Antiquity: The Emperor Constantine's Marriage Legislation.* Oxford: Clarendon Press.

Hall, H. R. 1905. *Coptic and Greek Texts of the Christian Period from Ostraka, Stelae, etc. in the British Museum.* London: British Museum.

———. 1911. "Two Coptic Acknowledgments of Loans." *Proceedings of the Society for Biblical Archaeology* 33:254–258.

Hanson, A. E. 1987. "The Eight Months' Child and the Etiquette of Birth." *Bulletin of the History of Medicine* 61:589–602.

———. 1990. "The Medical Writers' Woman." In *Before Sexuality: The Construction of Erotic Experience in the Ancient Greek World*, ed. D. M. Halperin, J. J. Winkler, and F. I. Zeitlin, 309–338. Princeton: Princeton University Press.

———. 2000. "Widows Too Young in Their Widowhood." In *I, Claudia II*, ed. D. Kleiner and S. B. Matheson, 149–165. Austin: University of Texas Press.

Hasitzka, M. R. M., ed. 1987. *Koptische Texte.* Corpus Papyrorum Raineri 12. Vienna: Verlag Brüder Hollinek.

———. 1990. *Neue Texte und Dokumentation zur Koptisch-Unterricht.* Mitteilungen aus der Papyrussammlung der österreichischen Nationalbibliothek (Papyrus Erzherzog Rainer), Neue Serie 18. Vienna: Verlag Brüder Hollinek.

———. 1993. *Kopstisches Sammelbuch I <KSB>.* Mitteilungen aus der Papyrussammlung der österreichischen Nationalbibliothek (Papyrus Erzherzog Rainer), Neue Serie 23. Vienna: Verlag Brüder Hollinek.

———. 1995. *Ein neues Arciv koptischer Ostraka.* Corpus Papyrorum Raineri 22. Vienna: Verlag Brüder Hollinek.

Hayes, J. W. 1972. *Late Roman Pottery.* London: British School at Rome.

Herdt, G. 1994. "Introduction: Third Sexes and Third Genders." In *Third Sex, Third Gender: Beyond Sexual Dimorphism in Culture and History*, ed. G. Herdt, 21–81. New York: Zone.

Heuser, G. 1929. *Die Personennamen der Kopten.* Studien zur Epigraphik und Papyruskunde 1.2. Leipzig: J. C. Hinrichs.

Hobson, D. W. 1983. "Women as Property Owners in Roman Egypt." *Transactions of the American Philological Association* 113:311–321.

———. 1989. "Naming Practices in Roman Egypt." *Bulletin of the American Society of Papyrologists* 26:157–174.

Hölscher, U. 1934. *The Excavation of Medinet Habu, I: General Plans and Views.* Oriental Institute Publications 21. Chicago: University of Chicago Press.

———. 1954. *The Excavation of Medinet Habu, V: Post-Ramessid Remains.* Oriental Institute Publications 66. Chicago: University of Chicago Press.

Hotchkiss, V. R. 1996. *Clothes Make the Man: Female Cross-Dressing in Medieval Europe.* The New Middle Ages. New York: Garland.

Husselman, E. M. 1952. "The Granaries of Karanis." *Transactions of the American Philological Association* 83:56–73.

———. 1979. *Karanis Excavations of the University of Michigan in Egypt 1928–1935: Topography and Architecture.* Kelsey Museum of Archaeology Studies 5. Ann Arbor: University of Michigan Press.

Husson, G. 1983. *OIKIA: Le vocabulaire de la maison privée de Égypte d'après les papyrus grecs.* Publications de la Sorbonne: Serie "Papyrologie" 2. Paris: Sorbonne.

Junker, H. 1908–1911. *Koptische Poesie des 10. Jahrhunderts.* 2 volumes. Berlin: K. Curtius.

Kaegi, W. E. 1998. "Egypt on the Eve of the Muslim Conquest." In *The Cambridge History of Egypt I: Islamic Egypt: From the Arab Invasion to the Ottoman Conquest (641–1517),* ed. C. F. Petry, 34–61. Cambridge: Cambridge University Press.

Kahle, P. E. 1954. *Bala'izah: Coptic Texts from Deir el-Bala'izah in Upper Egypt.* London: Oxford University Press.

———. 1974. "Zu den koptischen Steuerquittungen." In *Festschrift zum 150 jährigen Bestehen des Berliner Ägyptischen Museums,* 283–285. Mitteilungen aus der ägyptischen Sammlung, Staatliche Museen zu Berlin 8. Berlin: Akademie-Verlag.

Keenan, J. G. 1985. "Village Shepherds and Social Tension in Byzantine Egypt." *Yale Classical Studies* 28:245–259.

———. 2001. "Egypt." *Cambridge Ancient History, Volume 14: Late Antiquity (425–600 CE),* 612–637. Cambridge: Cambridge University Press.

Khs-Burmester, O. H. E. 1946–1947. "The Canons of Cyril III Ibn Laklak." *Bulletin de la Société d'Archéologie Copte* 12:81–144.

Khs-Burmester, O. H. E. 1967. *The Egyptian or Coptic Church: A Detailed Description of Her Liturgical Services and the Rites and Ceremonies Observed in the Administration of Her Sacraments.* Cairo: Société d'Archéologie Copte.

Krause, J.-U. 1994–1995. *Witwen und Waisen im römischen Reich.* 4 volumes. Stuttgart: Steiner.

Krause, M. 1956. "Apa Abraham von Hermonthis: Ein oberägyptischer Bischof um 600." Ph.D. dissertation, Humboldt-Universität, Berlin.

———. 1981. "Zwei Phoibammon-Klöster in Theben-West." *Mitteilungen des Deutschen Archäologischen Instituts, Abteilung Kairo* 37:261–266.

———. 1982. "Das christlichen Theben: Neuere Arbeiten und Funde." *Bulletin de la Société d'Archéologie Copte* 24:21–33.

———. 1985. "Die Beziehungen zwischen den beiden Phoibammon-Klöstern auf dem thebanischen Westufer." *Bulletin de la Société d'Archéologie Copte* 27:31–44.

———. 1991. "Menas the Miracle Maker, Saint." In *The Coptic Encyclopedia*, ed. A. S. Atiya, 5:1589–1590. New York: Macmillan.

———. 1993. "Recent Research in Coptic Papyrology and Epigraphy." In *Acts of the Fifth International Congress of Coptic Studies*, ed. T. Orlandi, 1:77–95. Rome: C.I.M.

Krawiec, R. 2002. *Shenoute and the Women of the White Monastery: Egyptian Monasticism in Late Antiquity.* New York: Oxford University Press.

Kruit, N., and K. A. Worp. 1999. "Metrological Notes and Containers of Liquids in Graeco-Roman and Byzantine Egypt." *Archiv für Papyrusforschung und verwandte Gebiete* 45:96–128.

Kuhn, K. H. 1960. *Pseudo-Shenoute on Christian Behavior.* 2 volumes. Corpus Scriptorum Christianorum Orientalium 205–206. Leuven: Peeters.

Kutzner, E. 1989. *Untersuchungen zur Stellung der Frau im römischen Oxyrhynchos.* Europäische Hochschulschriften, Reihe III: Geschichte und ihre Hilfswissenschaften 392. Frankfurt am Main: Peter Lang.

Layton, B. 1987. *Catalogue of Coptic Literary Manuscripts in the British Library Acquired since the Year 1906.* London: The British Library.

———. 2000. *A Coptic Grammar, with Chrestomathy and Glossary: Sahidic Dialect.* Porta Linguarum Orientalium 20. Wiesbaden: Harrassowitz Verlag.

Leclercq, H. 1912. "Prière à la Vierge Marie sur un ostracon de Louqsor." *Bulletin d'ancienne littérature et d'archéologie chrétiennes* 2:3–32.

Lefort, L. T. 1956. *Œuvres de S. Pachôme et ses disciples.* Leuven: Imprimerie Orientaliste.

Legrain, G. 1914. *Louqsor sans les pharaons: Légendes et chansons populaires de la Haute Égypte.* Brussels: Vromant & Co.

Lent, A. M. J. M. van, and J. van der Vliet. 1996. "De vele levens van Pisentius van Koptos: Een Egyptische heilige aan de vooravond van de Arabische veroevering." *Het Christelijk Oosten* 48:195-213.

Lewis, B., and S. Burstein. 2001. *Land of Enchanters: Egyptian Short Stories from the Earliest Times to the Present Day.* Princeton: Markus Wiener.

Lichtheim, M. 1957. *Demotic Ostraca from Medinet Habu.* Oriental Institute Publications 71. Chicago: University of Chicago Press.

Lüddeckens, E. 1960. *Ägyptische Eheverträge.* Ägyptologische Abhandlungen 1. Wiesbaden: Otto Harrassowitz.

MacCoull, L. S. B. 1979. "Child Donations and Child Saints in Coptic Egypt." *East European Quarterly* 13:409-415.

———. 1988. *Dioscorus of Aphrodito: His Work and His World.* Transformation of the Classical Heritage 16. Berkeley: University of California Press.

———. 1991. "Law, Coptic." In *The Coptic Encyclopedia*, ed. A. S. Atiya, 5:1428-1432. New York: Macmillan.

———. 2000. "Apa Abraham: Testament of Apa Abraham." In *Byzantine Monastic Foundation Documents* I, ed. J. Thomas and A. C. Hero, 51-58. Washington DC: Dumbarton Oaks.

Maresch, K. 1994. *Nomisma und Nomismatia: Beiträge zum Geldgeschichte Ägyptens im 6. Jahrhundert n.Chr.* Papyrologica Coloniensia 21. Opladen: Westdeutscher Verlag.

Martin, M., R.-G. Coquin, and G. Castel. 1991. "Qurnat Mar'i." In *The Coptic Encyclopedia*, ed. A. S. Atiya, 7:2040-2043. New York: Macmillan.

Martineau, H. 1848. *Eastern Life: Past and Present.* 3 volumes. London: E. Moxon.

Melman, B. 1992. *Women's Orients, English Women and the Middle East, 1718-1918: Sexuality, Religion, and Work.* Ann Arbor: University of Michigan Press.

Meskell, L. 1999. *Archaeologies of Social Life: Age, Sex, Class, et cetera in Ancient Egypt.* Oxford: Blackwell.

Meyer, C. 2001. "Ancient Population of Bir Umm Fawakhir." In *Bir Umm Fawakhir Survey Project 1993: A Byzantine Gold-Mining Town in Egypt*, ed. C. Meyer [and others], 15-17. Oriental Institute Communications 28. Chicago: Oriental Institute Press.

Meyer, M., and R. Smith. 1994. *Ancient Christian Magic: Coptic Texts of Ritual Power.* San Francisco: Harper San Francisco.

Minnen, P. van. 1986. "The Volume of the Oxyrhynchite Textile Trade." *Münstersche Beiträge zum anitken Handelsgeschichte* 5:88–95.

———. 1995. "Deserted Villages: Two Late Antique Town Sites in Egypt." *Bulletin of the American Society of Papyrologists* 32:41–56.

Montserrat, D. 1991. "Mallocouria and Therapeuteria: Rituals of Transition in a Mixed Society?" *Bulletin of the American Society of Papyrologists* 28:43–49.

———. 1995. "Early Byzantine Church Lighting: A New Text." *Orientalia* 64:430–444.

———. 1996a. "Coptic Art, 5: Personal." In *The Macmillan Dictionary of Art*, ed. J. S. Turner, 7:829–830. London: Macmillan.

———. 1996b. *Sex and Society in Graeco-Roman Egypt.* London: Routledge.

Moorsel, P. van. 1990. "Forerunners of the Lord: The Meaning of Old Testament Saints in the Daily Office and Liturgy Reflected in Medieval Church Decorations." In *Coptic Art and Culture*, ed. H. Hondelink, 19–42. Cairo: Netherlands Institute for Archaeology and Arabic Studies in Cairo.

Müller, C. D. G., and G. Gabra. 1991. "Pisentius, Saint." In *The Coptic Encyclopedia*, ed. A. S. Atiya, 6:1978–1980. New York: Macmillan.

Mysliwiec, K. 1987. *Keramik und Kleinfunde aus den Grabung im Tempel Sethos' I. im Gurna.* Archäologische Veröffentlichungen 57. Mainz am Rhein: Philipp von Zabern.

O'Brien, A. A. 1999. "Private Tradition, Public State: Women in Demotic Business and Administrative Texts from Ptolemaic and Roman Thebes." Ph.D. dissertation, University of Chicago.

O'Leary, D. L. 1930. *The Arabic Life of St. Pisentius according to the Text of the Two Manuscripts Paris Bib. Nat. Arabe 4785, and Arabe 4794.* Patrologia Orientalia 22. Turnhout: Brepols.

Otto, E. 1975. "Djeme." In *Lexikon der Ägyptologie I*, ed. W. Helck and E. Otto, 1108–1109. Wiesbaden: Harrassowitz Verlag.

Parker, R. A. 1940. "A Late Demotic Gardening Agreement: Medinet Habu 4038." *Journal of Egyptian Archaeology* 26:84–113.

Peel, M. L. 1991. "Dayr Epiphanius." In *The Coptic Encyclopedia*, ed. A. S. Atiya, 3:800–802. New York: Macmillan.

Pestman, P. W. 1961. *Marriage and Matrimonial Property in Ancient Egypt: A Contribution to Establishing the Legal Position of the Woman.* Papyrological Lugduno-Batava 9. Leiden: E. J. Brill.

Piankoff, A. 1958-1960. "The Osireion of Seti I at Abydos during the Graeco-Roman Period and the Christian Occupation." *Bulletin de la Société d'Archéologie Copte* 15:125-149.

Poll. I. 1999. "Die diagraphon-Steuer im spätbyzantinischen und früharabischen Ägypten." *Tyche* 14:237-274.

Pomeroy, S. 1984. *Women in Hellenistic Egypt: From Alexander to Cleopatra.* Detroit: Wayne State University Press.

———. 1988. "Women in Roman Egypt: A Preliminary Study Based on Papyri." In *Aufstieg und Niedergang der Römischen Welt*, II:10:1, ed. H. Temporini, 709-723. Berlin: Walter de Gruyter.

Reeves, C. N., and R. Wilkinson. 1996. *The Complete Valley of the Kings: Tombs and Treasures of Egypt's Greatest Pharaohs.* New York: Thames and Hudson.

Revillout, E. 1900-1914. "Textes coptes: Extraits de la correspondance de St. Pésunthius, évêque de Coptos, et de plusiers documents analogues (juridiques ou économiques)." *Revue Égyptologique* 9:133-177; 10:34-47; 14:22-32.

Richter, S. 1998. "Zwei Urkunden des koptischen Notars Daniel, des Sohnes des Psate." *Archiv für Papyrusforschung und verwandte Gebiete* 44:69-85.

Ringrose, K. M. 1994. "Living in the Shadows: Eunuchs and Gender in Byzantium." In *Third Sex, Third Gender: Beyond Sexual Dimorphism in Culture and History*, ed. G. Herdt, 85-109. New York: Zone.

Ritner, R. K. 1998. "Egypt under Roman Rule: The Legacy of Ancient Egypt." In *The Cambridge History of Egypt I: Islamic Egypt: From the Arab Invasion to the Ottoman Conquest (641-1517)*, ed. C. F. Petry, 1-33. Cambridge: Cambridge University Press.

Robins, G. 1993. *Women in Ancient Egypt.* London: British Museum Press.

Rowlandson, J. 1996. *Landowners and Tenants in Roman Egypt: The Social Relations of Agriculture in the Oxyrhynchite Nome.* Oxford Classical Monographs. Oxford: Clarendon Press.

———. 1998. *Women and Society in Greek and Roman Egypt: A Sourcebook.* Cambridge: Cambridge University Press.

Rutschowskaya, M.-H. 1990. *Coptic Fabrics.* Paris: A. Biro.

Satzinger, H. 1986. "Zwei koptische Brief-Ostraka in Krakau." *Enchoria* 14:107–110.

Schaten, S. 1996. "Koptische Kinderschenkungsurkunden." *Bulletin de la Société d'Archéologie Copte* 35:129–142.

Scheidel, W. 2001. *Death on the Nile: Disease and the Demography of Roman Egypt.* Mnemosyne Supplements 228. Leiden: Brill.

Schiller, A. A. 1932. *Ten Coptic Legal Texts.* New York: Metropolitan Museum of Art.

———. 1952. "A Family Archive from Jeme." In *Studi in onore di Vincenzo Arangio-Ruiz*, 325–375. Naples: Casa Editrice Dott. Eugenio Jovene.

———. 1976. "A Checklist of Coptic Documents and Letters." *Bulletin of the American Society of Papyrologists* 13:99–123.

Schmidt, C., and V. MacDermot. 1978. *The Books of Jeu and the Untitled Text in the Bruce Codex.* Nag Hammadi Studies 9. Leiden: E. J. Brill.

Scott, J. W. 1986. "Gender: A Useful Category of Historical Analysis." *American Historical Review* 91:1053–1075.

———. 1991. "The Evidence of Experience." *Critical Inquiry* 17:773–797.

———. 1992. "Women's History." In *New Perspectives on Historical Writing*, ed. P. Burke, 42–66. University Park PA: Pennsylvania State University Press.

Setälä, P. 1989. "Brick Stamps and Women's Economic Opportunities in Imperial Rome." In *Current Issues in Women's History*, ed. A. Angerman [and others], 61–73. London: Routledge.

Sheridan, J. 1998. "Not at a Loss for Words: The Economic Power of Literate Women in Late Antique Egypt." *Transactions of the American Philological Association* 128:189–203.

Shisha-Halevy, A. 1989. *The Proper Name: Structural Prolegomena to Its Syntax. A Case Study in Coptic.* Beihefte zur Wiener Zeitschrift für die Kunde des Morgenlandes 15. Vienna: VWGÖ.

Sottas, H. 1922. "Une nouvelle pièce de la correspondance de Saint Pesunthios." In *Recueil d'études égyptologiques dediées à la mémoire de Jean-François Champollion*, 494–502. Bibliothèque de l'École des Hautes Études 234. Paris: Ernst Leroux.

Stefanski, E., and M. Lichtheim. 1952. *Coptic Ostraca from Medinet Habu.* Oriental Institute Publications 71. Chicago: University of Chicago Press.

Steinwenter, A. 1920. *Studien zu den koptischen Rechtsurkunden aus Oberägypten.* Studien zur Palaeographie und Papyruskunde 19. Leipzig: Verlag H. Haessel.

Steinwenter, A. 1955. *Das Recht der Koptischen Urkunden*. Handbuch der Altertumswissenschaften 10:4:2. Munich: C. H. Beck.

Steinmann, F. 1974. "Die Schreiberkenntnise der Kopten nach der Aussagen der Djeme-Urkunden." In *Studia Coptica*, ed. P. Nagel, 101–110. Berliner Byzantinistische Arbeiten 45. Berlin: Akademie-Verlag.

Stern, L. 1878. "Sahidische Inschriften." *Zeitschrift für Aegyptische Sprache und Altertumskunde* 18:9–28.

Strudwick, N., and H. Strudwick. 1999. *Thebes in Egypt: A Guide to the Temples and Tombs of Ancient Luxor*. London: British Museum Press.

Teeter, E. 2002. *Scarabs, Scaraboids, Seals and Seal Impressions from Medinet Habu, Based on Notes of Uvo Hölscher and Rudolf Anthes: Excavations at Medinet Habu VI*. Oriental Institute Publications 118. Chicago: Oriental Institute Press.

———. Forthcoming. *Baked Clay Figurines from Medinet Habu: Excavations at Medinet Habu VII*. Oriental Institute Publications. Chicago: Oriental Institute Press.

Thissen, H. 1984. "Koptische und Griechische Graffiti aus Medinet Habu." *Göttinger Miszellen* 75:53–55.

———. 1986. "Koptische Kinderschenkungsurkunden. Zur Hierodulie im christlichen Ägypten." *Enchoria* 14:117–128.

Thomas, T. K. 2001. *Artifacts of Everyday Life: Textiles from Karanis, Egypt, in the Kelsey Museum of Archaeology*. Ann Arbor: Kelsey Museum of Archaeology.

Till, W. C. 1938a. "Eine koptische Alimentforderung." *Bulletin de la Société d'Archéologie Copte* 4:71–78.

———. 1938b. "Koptische Schützbriefe." *Mitteilungen des Deutschen Archäologischen Instituts Abteilung Kairo* 8:71–127.

———. 1939. "Eine Verkaufsurkunden aus Dschême." *Bulletin de la Société d'Archéologie Copte* 5:43–59.

———. 1948. "Die koptischen Eheverträge." In *Die Österreichische National-bibliothek: Festschrift Herausgegeben zum 25jährigen Dienstjubiläum des Generaldirektors Univ.-Prof. Dr. Josef Bick*, ed. J. Stummvoll, 627–638. Vienna: H. Bauer-Verlag.

———. 1951. *Die Arzneikunde der Kopten*. Berlin: Akademie-Verlag.

———. 1954. *Erbrechtliche Untersuchungen auf Grund der koptischen Urkunden*. Sitzungsberichte, Philosophisch-Historische Klasse Österreichische Akademie der Wissenschaften 229, 2. Vienna: Rudolf M. Rohrer.

Till, W. C. 1955. "Zu den Coptic Ostraca from Medinet Habu." *Orientalia* 24:145–155.

———. 1958. "Die koptischen Bürgschaftsurkunden." *Bulletin de la Société d'Archéologie Copte* 14:165–226.

———. 1960. *Koptische Grammatik (Saïdischer Dialekt).* Leipzig: VEB Verlag.

———. 1962. *Datierung und Prosopographie der Koptischen Urkunden aus Theben.* Sitzungsberichte, Philosophisch-Historische Klasse Österreichische Akademie der Wissenschaften 240, 1. Vienna: Hermann Böhlaus Nachf.

———. 1964. *Die Koptischen Rechtsurkunden aus Theben.* Sitzungsberichte, Philosophisch-Historische Klasse Österreichische Akademie der Wissenschaften 244, 3. Vienna: Hermann Böhlaus Nachf.

Timm, S. 1984–1992. *Das christlich-koptische Ägypten in arabischer Zeit.* 6 volumes. Beiheft zum Tübinger Atlas des Vorderen Orients, Reihe B (Geisteswissenschaften) 41/1–6. Wiesbaden: Dr. Ludwig Reichert Verlag.

Tougher, S. F. 1997. "Byzantine Eunuchs: An Overview, with Special Reference to Their Creation and Origin." In *Women, Men and Eunuchs: Gender in Byzantium,* ed. L. James, 168–184. London: Routledge.

Urbaniak-Walczak, K. 1992. *Die "conceptio per aurem": Untersuchungen zum Marienbild in Ägypten unter besonderer Berücksichtigung der Malereien in El-Bagawat.* Arbeiten zum spätantiken und koptischen Ägypten 2. Altenberge: Oros Verlag.

Vandorpe, K. 1995. "City of Many a Gate, Harbour for Many a Rebel: Historical and Topographical Outline of Graeco-Roman Thebes." In *Hundred-Gated Thebes: Acts of a Colloquium on Thebes and the Theban Area in the Graeco-Roman Period,* ed. S. Vleeming, 203–239. Papyrological Lugduno-Batava 27. Leiden: Brill.

Vleeming, S. 1995. *Hundred-Gated Thebes: Acts of a Colloquium on Thebes and the Theban Area in the Graeco-Roman Period.* Papyrological Lugduno-Batava 27. Leiden: Brill.

Ward, B. 1987. *Harlots of the Desert: A Study of Repentance in Early Monastic Sources.* Kalamazoo MI: Cistercian Publications.

Wheatley, V. 1957. *The Life and Work of Harriet Martineau.* London: Secker & Warburg.

Wikgren, A. 1946. "Two Ostraca Fragments of the Septuagint Psalter." *Journal of Near Eastern Studies* 5:181–185.

Wilber, D. M. 1940. "The Coptic Frescoes of Saint Menas at Medinet Habu." *The Art Bulletin* 22:86–103.

Wilfong, T. G. 1989. "The Western Theban Area in the Seventh and Eighth Centuries." *Bulletin of the American Society of Papyrologists* 26:89–147.

———. 1990. "The Archive of a Family of Moneylenders from Jême." *Bulletin of the American Society of Papyrologists* 27:169–181.

———. 1992. "Greek and Coptic Texts from The Oriental Institute Museum Exhibition 'Another Egypt.'" *Bulletin of the American Society of Papyrologists* 29:85–95.

———. 1993. Review of Monika Hasitzka, *Neue Dokumentation zur Koptisch-Unterricht*. *Bulletin of the American Society of Papyrologists* 30:76–78.

———. 1995. "Mummy-Labels from the Oriental Institute Museum Excavation of Medinet Habu." *Bulletin of the American Society of Papyrologists* 32:157–181.

———. 1997. *Women and Gender in Ancient Egypt–From Prehistory to Late Antiquity: An Exhibition at the Kelsey Museum of Archaeology*. Ann Arbor: Kelsey Museum of Archaeology, University of Michigan.

———. 1998a. "Reading the Disjointed Body in Coptic: From Physical Modification to Textual Fragmentation." In *Changing Bodies, Changing Meanings: Studies on the Human Body in Antiquity*, ed. D. Montserrat, 116–136. London: Routledge.

———. 1998b. "The Non-Muslim Communities: The Christians." In *The Cambridge History of Egypt I: Islamic Egypt: From the Arab Invasion to the Ottoman Conquest (641–1517)*, ed. C. F. Petry, 175–197. Cambridge: Cambridge University Press.

———. 1998c. "Constantine in Coptic: Coptic Constructions of Constantine the Great and His Family." In *Constantine: History, Historiography and Legend*, ed. D. Montserrat and S. Lieu, 177–188. London: Routledge.

———. 2000. "Synchronous Menstruation and the 'Place of Women' in Ancient Egypt (Hieratic Ostracon Oriental Institute Museum 13512)." In *Gold of Praise: Studies on Ancient Egypt in Honor of Edward F. Wente*, ed. E. Teeter and J. Larson, 419–434. Studies in Ancient Oriental Civilization 58. Chicago: Oriental Institute Press.

Wilfong, T. G. 2002a. "'Friendship and Physical Desire': The Discourse of Female Homoeroticism in Fifth Century CE Egypt." In *Among Women: From the Homosocial to the Homoerotic in the Ancient World*, ed. N. Sorkin Rabinowitz and L. Auanger, 304–329. Austin TX: University of Texas Press.

———. 2002b. "The Post-Pharaonic Seals and Seal Impressions from Medinet Habu." In *Scarabs, Scaraboids, Seals and Seal Impressions from Medinet Habu, Based on Notes of Uvo Hölscher and Rudolf Anthes: Excavations at Medinet Habu VI*, by E. Teeter, 273–309. Oriental Institute Publications 118. Chicago: Oriental Institute Press.

———. Forthcoming. "'Women's Things' and 'Men's Things': Gendered Property in the Jeme Texts and Related Matters." *Bulletin of the American Society of Papyrologists*.

Wilkinson, J. G. 1835. *Topography of Thebes and General View of Egypt*. London: John Murray.

Winlock, H. E., and W. E. Crum. 1926. *The Monastery of Epiphanius at Thebes: Part I: The Archaeological Material; The Literary Material*. New York: Metropolitan Museum of Art.

Wipszycka, E. 1972. *Les ressources et les activités économiques des églises en Égypte du IVe au VIIIe siècle*. Papyrologica Bruxellensia 10. Brussels: Fondation Égyptologique Reine Élisabeth.

———. 1992. "Fonctionnement de l'église égyptienne aux IVe–VIIIe siècles (sur quelques aspects)." In *Itinéraires d'Égypte: Mélanges offerts au père Maurice Martin*, 115–145. Bibliothèque d'Étude 107. Cairo: Institut Français d'Archéologie Orientale.

———. 1994. "Le monachisme égyptien et les villes." *Travaux et Mémoires* 12:1–44.

Worp, K. A. 1990. "A Forgotten Coptic Inscription from the Monastery of Epiphanius: Some Remarks on Dated Coptic Documents from the Pre-Conquest Period." *Analecta Papyrologica* 2:139–143.

———. 1999. "Coptic Tax Receipts: An Inventory." *Tyche* 14:309–324.

Young, D. W. 1971. "The Distribution of *shime* and *hime* in Literary Sahidic." *Journal of the American Oriental Society* 91:507–509.

INDEX OF TEXTS CITED

Translations of individual texts (or substantial portions thereof) noted with italics

Other Texts (cited by name or bibliographical reference):

Biography of Pisentius 36–37, *38–39*
Epiphanius "discard" VI.14A.153 111
Hall 1911 *130–131*
Lecerq 1912 32
MH [Medinet Habu] 2404 121
MH [Medinet Habu] 2417 126
Meyer and Smith 1994 73
Papyrus Carnarvon 5, 114
Pisentius, Homily on Onnophrios 24,
    25–27, 34

Sottas 1922 40
Stern 1878 1
Till 1938a *140–141*
Till 1939 151
Till 1951 73
Till 1960 *76*
Wikgren 1946 114

Biblical Citations:

Genesis 1:26–27 29, 31
Numbers 5:12 39
Deuteronomy 22:29 39

1 Samuel 1:27–28 104
Psalm 38:5 86
Matthew 19:12 36

Plates

Plate 1. General view of the ruins of Jeme in 1927
(Courtesy of the Oriental Institute of the University of Chicago,
Oriental Institute Museum Negative 29481)

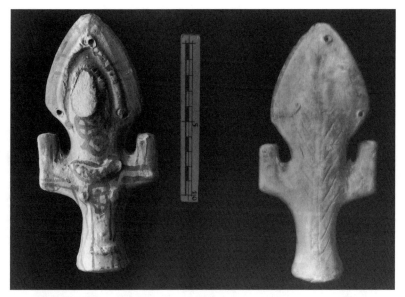

Plate 2a. Complete female orant figure from the Jeme excavation
(Courtesy of the Oriental Institute of the University of Chicago,
Oriental Institute Museum Negative 29422)

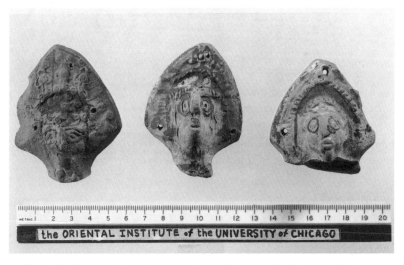

Plate 2b. Heads of female orant figures (left to right Oriental Institute
Museum numbers 14641, 14642, and 15539) from the Jeme excavation
(Courtesy of the Oriental Institute of the University of Chicago,
Oriental Institute Museum Negative 30235)

*Plate 3. Group of Jeme houses, including House 34, during the course of excavation
(Courtesy of the Oriental Institute of the University of Chicago,
Oriental Institute Museum Negative 29483)*

Plate 4a–b. Two documents from the Koloje archive:
O.Medin.HabuCopt. *151 (a) and 93 (b)*
(Courtesy of the Oriental Institute of the University of Chicago,
Oriental Institute Museum Negative Lichtheim 117)